Cooper,
from Don
Prov. 3:5 & 6

Radical Heart/Radical Marriage

By Dr. Dow Pursley
and
Gordon Puls

Copyright 05/2011

Revised 02/22/2017

ISBN: 978-1-5448-9471-3

This book is not for sale.

This book along with *Finances: Biblical Wisdom/Radical Action* are both available for download on kindle. To receive a kindle reader copy it can be found under free books on Amazon.com, however there is a modest processing fee. For a hard copy it can also be purchased on createspace.com.

Sincerely,

Dr. Dow Pursley and Gordon Puls

Radical Heart/Radical Marriage
Copyright © 2011 by Dr. Dow Pursley
Revised 2017
ISBN: 978-1-5448-9471-3

This book is now available in Spanish.
Requests for information should be addressed to:

Alethia Publishing House	Editorial Vida & Esperanza
15358 Twin Pines Rd.	CC La Rotonda II – 2052
Lowell, Ar. 72745	Av. La Fontana 440 La Molina
	Lima 12, Peru

Library of Congress Cataloging-in-Publication Data
Pursley, Dow
      Radical Heart/Radical Marriage, Dow Pursley and Gordon
Puls

Unless otherwise noted, all quotes from the Bible are from the
thought for thought translation of The Living Bible, Copyright
©1971 by Tyndale House Publishers, Inc. Wheaton, Illinois

Cover Design by Dawn Jacobs

Contents

Preface

Radical Heart/Radical Marriage is my manifesto and
legacy after years of marriage and ministry. Drawing from
my own education, professional training, practice and over
five decades of marriage, I open my office door, my mind and
my heart. I invite you to take what profit you can from the
understanding and insight I have accumulated. My academic
credentials and clinical experience have given me numerous
opportunities to serve as a conference speaker and seminar
leader among fellow professionals as well as to wider audiences.
This interaction with colleagues and the public has exposed
my ideas to critical and practical feedback, as have discussions
with my students. My early association with Ed Wheat, M.D. has
given me unparalleled mentoring in all aspects of counseling,
particularly concerning the sexual dimension of marriage.
Friendship with Ed and Gaye Wheat gave me insight into
their exemplary marriage and ministry. It has established my
commitment to thoroughly biblical counseling. Personally,
Joanne and I found our first years of marriage so challenging
that more than one conservative Christian counselor advised us
to get a divorce. Our struggles showed me my own weakness,
which made me less prone to be judgmental. Principles and
actions, which have corrected and healed us have shown me
God's power, and make me eager to share the remedies He
provides for distressed marriages. I am neither a disinterested
scholar nor a self-righteous moralist. I am simply a man who has
learned to listen and advise without unnecessary discomfort
to those who call on me. The necessary discomfort of facing
responsibility is alleviated by the hope that hard work will bring
positive change. I want to be known for pointing the people I
meet to positive biblical change in their lives.

At the beginning of my academic career and of my walk with God, I met an English professor whom I credit with life-changing influence on my own thinking. Joanne and I lived with Gordon Puls for a time, sharing our zeal for ministry and seeing each other's imperfections. Among our friends, Joanne and I might have seemed least likely to stay married and Gordon, least likely ever to get married. Now, more than three decades later, Joanne and I along with Gordon and Joyce Puls, celebrate the mighty works of God that brought us together and kept our marriages intact. Gordon and Joyce have not struggled in the ways Joanne and I have, but they have endured the "in sickness," "for poorer" and "or worse" side of marriage, including the very worst: the accidental death of their first-born daughter. The faith which holds people close to God, to each other, and the faith which builds and heals marriages, is expressed in the principles outlined in *Radical Heart/Radical Marriage*.

This faith is rational but not rationalistic, simple but not simplistic. The truth of God's Word and the facts of human existence are the same for everyone and must be considered reasonably. A blind faith, which ignores unpleasant facts about humanity, is no more tenable than an arrogant humanism that ignores discomforting truth about God. Assuming that knowledge of God leaves us nothing to learn from or about our fellow human beings is heartless and contrary to Scripture. Assuming that knowledge of humanity leaves us nothing to learn from or about God is mindless and contrary to reason. I take a pre-suppositional stance, believing that assumptions people do not question determine how they frame and answer the questions they do ask. My early conversations with Gordon were flavored heavily by Francis Schaeffer's writings, which is still the most accessible presentation of this position.[1] With our equally zealous friends, we rented a storefront and greeted everyone who entered with the question, "What do you believe?" We questioned the assumptions they lived by and presented the Gospel as simply as we could. When asked for opinions, one of us might say, "I don't want to trade opinions, let's see what God says." If the inquirer was an unbeliever, the reply might be, "I know God and you don't, so you might not like my answer, but I'll tell you what God says about this." This approach is apparent in my life and ministry to this day.

Years of schooling have not interfered with my education. I still know whom I have believed and I am unashamed of the transforming power of God's Word. In both professional and personal life I follow the example of my mentor, colleague, and friend Ed Wheat. After his conversion at age thirty-eight, Dr. Wheat applied his intellect to the study of the Scriptures and became a Bible scholar. He went on to use his medical knowledge as a platform to share the Gospel with all of his patients. Working with him at The Wheat Medical Clinic, teaching Love-Life Marriage Seminars, writing a chapter of Dr. Wheat's book, *Secret Choices*, expanding his book *Intended for Pleasure*, and completing a Study guide for the *Love-Life* book, I admired and absorbed Dr. Wheat's professional methods. I experienced one of the warmest and most significant friendships a person can have in this life. When God was pleased to take his servant Ed Wheat home in September of 2001 I felt great personal loss, yet was honored to have known and learned from this man of God. I am committed to building upon Dr. Wheat's foundational principles and multiplying their use in

---

[1] Crossway Books publishes a set of Schaeffer's works. For further study, I also recommend the writings of Cornelius Van Til. Presuppositionalism does not put up a wall against any source of information, but provides a filter through which information can be separated from interpretations and applications drawn from wrong assumptions. The apologist Ravi Zacharias is enriching new generations of Christians in their thinking.

ministry. My counseling techniques, my devotion to God and my marriage took shape through the efforts and example of Ed Wheat.

When I called Gordon Puls alongside to help communicate the heart of my message and ministry, he warmed to the spirit and urgency of the work. He contributed insights from his own study and life experience to reinforce what I wanted to say. I have called Gordon the smartest man I know: he suggests that I get out and meet people and get better acquainted with my colleagues, clients and students. Without Gordon's gift for arranging and focusing my thoughts, *Radical Heart/Radical Marriage* might have remained in my heart as a dream of the book I would write if I could. Our collaboration has created a book born in friendship, proven in experience and expressing the single vision of two very different believers whose lives of faith bring them together as witnesses to the truth and the glory of God's plan for marriage.

Special thanks go to Debbie Nichols and Dawn Jacobs who always find time to help me with their expertise. Their attention to detail and the good spirit that permeates their work is greatly appreciated. Dawn Jacobs also designed the book cover.

Many others at Baptist Bible College and at the Love-Life Marriage and Family Center have had their parts in this project. Colleagues, staff, clients and students have been among the friends whose input helped shape this book. T.J. Puls understands computers better than his dad does, and created the diagrams illustrating the circles of love.

My good friend and colleague went to be with the Lord on August 30, 2011. Heaven is richer, but we here are certainly missing his presence!
Since Gordon Puls' death the world has changed a lot. We have seen the generation of the "Closing of the American Mind" replaced by the generation of 'The Exploding of the American

Mind' the sodomite and friends with an incredibly minute percent of the U.S. Population have managed with the help of the Executive branch and the Judicial branch of our "progressive" government to undo over two hundred years of the founding fathers ideas and morals, literally giving away our true birthright for a mess of anti-Christian governmental porridge. The stench and chaos these four forces, sodomites, Satan, and the two branches of government have imposed on an already confused and morally compromised generation is non-parallel in history. Has any other generation learned such moral degradation, parasitical behavior, out of control debt from their government? Our government would make Rome blush!

Many in the generations of X, Y, and Z had self centered, sexually perverse commitment-phobic parents and grandparents who lied to themselves as well as their parents about the virtues of pot smoking, and Free "love", which was neither love or free. Many of the hippies of my generation, now geriatric hippies, have produced non-launching children who never leave the nest, or return to it repeatedly. Sinful experimentation with drugs and sex accentuated the selfishness and unreliability of people whose children now lack direction and purpose. Ironically, some of these young people find help in the legacy of their hardworking great grandparents – the very "establishment" against which the hippies rebelled. Healthy parents of the same generation do help their children, but most of the late bloomers are out of the home by the mid-twenties, rarely staying through the early thirties. The high cost of free "love" ran into the trillions treating their deceased bodies full of Hepatitis C, Aids, Aids related diseases, multiple STD's, Abortions, and Personal debt. Their legacy is a drug induced, entitled, non-launching generation that has given birth to generations that are confused, abandoned and angry with little since of purpose or trust that is not self serving.

Is there any hope for these generations? Fortunately yes! I have met many in these current generations who aspire to more than their parents and grandparents, tons of young people both talented and virtuous, real world changers and people shakers. These generations, born out of the ruins of two past murderous generations without moral, financial, or spiritual character. They have survived, now thrive, not fearing to confront their generation with the real gospel, which is the only good news. They are learning what the U.S. Constitution means, and will not compromise its values, principles, or original purposes.

Many in these generations love God, His Church and contend for its purity and peace.
I'm proud to say that. My children and grandchildren are some of the best of these generations. It takes collective as well as individual repentance and a lot of courage to attempt to help save a fast falling country, but if God would have saved Sodom and Gomorrah for the sake of ten righteous people (Genesis 18:32), He may save these generations futures as well, pray for the remnant of these generations, pray for their friendships, their marriages, their commitments to each other and their commitment to the only wise God our savior Jesus Christ. Fast for them, encourage them, and help them. This Book revision is dedicated to the generations of X, Y, and Z. I have done what God has put in my hands to do for them.

Foreword

Dow Pursley and Gordon Puls have made significant contributions to pastors, Christian counselors, and couples in their counseling book *Radical Heart/Radical Marriage*. Dr. Pursley is a lifetime student of Scripture and Christian literature, a seasoned veteran in biblical counseling, marriage of over forty years, professor and the director of the Baptist Bible Graduate school counseling center where people receive biblical help and Christ-centered hope while future counselors are being equipped, Dow is qualified to put all he has learned in print. There is strong emphasis on seeing marriage as a covenant relationship between a man and woman over a lifetime together with excellent biblical and theological foundations for counseling theory and practice and practical helps for understanding marriage and dealing with the issues that can undermine marital foundations. This resource is a tool to help anyone who wants to help build strong Christian homes.

Dr. James. E. Jeffery, President
Baptist Bible College, Graduate School & Seminary

Introduction

Attempting to communicate and uphold a biblical view of marriage is a formidable challenge. Uncertainties about values and morals have eroded any remnants of whatever ethical consensus may have existed in some golden era of the past. This is no cause for alarm or for jeremiads, which bewail the hopeless sinfulness of our culture. Outside of a covenant relationship with God, all humanity has always been hopelessly sinful. There may be some advantages in speaking into a culture which openly admits and exults in its separation from God. Losing the gray areas of unthinking consensus frees people to make more conscious choices and makes them more responsible for the choices they make. An unquestioning acceptance of traditional morality is an inadequate foundation for marriage or for counseling. Tradition is simply what has been handed from one generation to another, and what does not slip through our fingers is often rendered inconsequential by its lack of an authoritative source. Morality is the sum effect of human mores, the customs and taboos which have more or less successfully kept humankind from self-annihilation, with no more solid foundation than the will to survive and flourish. Where the will to survive and flourish is lacking, human morality is helpless. A psychologist lecturing on the psycho-social aspects of drug abuse was asked, "Given a consensus which favors being alive and sane, by what authority do you impose those values on someone who prefers insanity or death?" The lecturer made a perfunctory evasion about needing at least twelve hours to answer fully, and later confided to a colleague, "I've never been crucified like that!"

In a world separated from God the sources of guidance through life are reduced to tradition, morality and personal choice. As Bonhoeffer has pointed out, separation from God distorts human perception of good and evil by "a falling away from the origin. Man at his origin knows only one thing: God."[2] Making a choice which opposed God separated Adam from God as an autonomous judge of good and evil. Satan's "I will" broke his union with God (Isaiah 14:12-15): Adam's assertion of his own will against God's will brought disunion into all human relationships. As Bonhoeffer says, "Man's life is now disunion with God, with man, with things, and with himself."[3] Disunion, disconnectedness in all areas of life is the consequence of original separation from God. Human perceptions of good and evil are expressed in traditions and morals which attempt to guide personal choices towards restoration of unity on the human level: unity with God is relegated to an irrational religious dimension, Schaeffer has called this "upper storey." If hope for correction of human disunion excludes God, there are no absolute criteria of good and evil and no ultimate foundation for relationships. "The world giveth and the world taketh away." Where positive influences support the survival of society and individuals, life can go along fairly smoothly until negative influences (read: hopeless sinfulness) cause division and dysfunction. As we shall see, marriages based on the positive influences of society and the good intentions of individuals can fall easily into dysfunctionality, divisiveness and destructiveness. In a society without ethical absolutes, unrestrained individualism makes every individual a victim or perpetrator of one or more forms of abuse.

At a discussion of a deeply-ingrained social problem, three questions led to an impasse. "Who is guilty?" That was easy enough to answer: we all are. "How did I get this way?" Again the answer seemed simple: the negative influences of

---

[2] Dietrich Bonhoeffer, *Ethics*, Macmillan, 1975, p.17.

[3] Op. cit, p. 20. The late Francis Schaeffer used the term "discontinuity," which indicates that the separation is also an incompleteness. Man is not now what he intrinsically was, but stands in discontinuity because of the Fall.

society have corrupted us all. "Why are we scapegoating?" That was the snag. Without ultimate authority there can be no ultimate responsibility. A young Communist eventually shouted, "Well, we can't take it back to Adam!"

Why not? A biblical view of marriage goes directly back to Adam and Eve, and finds its ultimate authority at the feet of the One who really was crucified to rescue us from our hopeless sinfulness. There is a traditionalistic Christian way of looking at the division of humankind as a division between those who live righteously and those who do not, yielding what purports to be a sanctified list of customs and taboos. In contrast, the biblical Christian view sees the division as being between those who believe and those who do not believe God's revelation of Himself in Jesus Christ, His living Word, and the Bible, His written Word. Those who place their faith in God seek His guidance. Those who place their faith in themselves look elsewhere.

A young woman came to faith in Christ through a street ministry. She was surprised when she was told that the church she attended did not proclaim the Gospel she had just received. Two of her new friends in Christ went with her to talk with her pastor. They asked the man about his beliefs and he spoke warmly about love and tolerance. One of the Christians asked: "But what if there really is a God and His character determines what's right and wrong?" The man rose, leaned across his desk and pointed a trembling finger. "I don't even like to think of that concept! You're not sharing, you're preaching!"

Questioning the psychologist, the discussion group and the atheistic pastor were typical events in the confrontational evangelism, which began my lifelong conversation with Gordon Puls. I still believe that the Gospel is to be proclaimed as God's absolute truth, not shared as one faith among many. Believing

15

that all truth is God's truth,[4] I have gleaned lessons from years of education and experience, seeking rational faith which is not rationalistic. Believing that no lie is God's truth, I challenge and reject unbiblical assumptions, seeking simple faith which is not simplistic.

A biblical world-view sees God as the only perfectly reliable object of faith. Those who do not place their faith in God cannot find anything or anyone worthy of ultimate trust and can only fear that the negative influences (hopeless sinfulness) of society will devour them when their fragile objects of faith fail. The choice, then, is not between faith in God and faith in something else, but between faith in God and fear of catastrophe. Popular culture's emphasis on self-love, self-fulfillment and self-protection indicates fear that if we do not look out for ourselves, everybody and everything will eat us up. This position of fear is the source of many marriage problems which only a position of faith can fully address.

Counseling from a position of faith assumes the existence, presence and active assistance of a faithful God. A position of faith assumes that God has revealed what marriage is and how it works and that to the degree that couples understand and live by what He says, their marriages will thrive.

Counseling from a position of fear assumes that each human being is an autonomous individual who is at the mercy of a merciless world. A position of fear assumes that what marriage is and how it works depends on cultural and personal interests and that to the degree that couples can avoid interfering with each other's interests, their marriages will survive.

---

[4] Not in the dualistic sense of accepting other sources as equal to the Bible in authority, but in recognizing that biblical truth is consistent with valid inferences from experience and study. When Frank Gaebelein introduced the expression "all truth is God's truth," he was speaking as a Christian educator seeking to bring all fields of study into captivity to Christ, not as a dualistic or syncretistic scholar elevating his area of specialization into equality with Scripture.

Radical Heart/Radical Marriage is a book for counselors, pastors, couples and other concerned persons who are willing to consider looking at marriage from a position of faith. Christians who consider the Bible the only authoritative foundation for living life as God planned it will welcome the biblical perspective which permeates this book as it does my ministry. Those who do not share this perspective will find practical tools for building or repairing marriages and may feel refreshed by the rationality of a unified approach to the subject, as contrasted with eclectic advice from the three hundred plus distinct humanly-generated perspectives.

Those who believe that God instituted marriage as the most vital link of human society must be diligent in seeking to know what He has said about it and in seeking to apply God's truth about marriage to complex issues of the real world. *Radical Heart/Radical Marriage* attempts to do that, bringing into focus the lessons of decades of study, counseling experience and marriage. More ambitious than preventive or corrective approaches, this book proclaims the purpose of God as the presupposition and goal of counseling. Too much counseling concentrates on how to make individuals or couples more comfortable or functional in an admittedly dysfunctional society. A Christian approach must be biblical, concentrating on why individuals should accept responsibility to rethink their lives, their marriages and even their society in the light of what pleases God: obedient faith.

Obedient faith in God is both rational and simple. God's people must be thinking people. The challenges of marriage require deliberate consideration and reasonable communication. For biblical Christians, unexamined lives are not worthy of our calling (Ephesians 4:13). God's people must be simple, without guile. The intimacy of marriage requires unconditional love,[5] full disclosure and full trust. For biblical Christians, defensiveness and manipulation are not guided by the simplicity which is in Christ (II Corinthians 11:3).

Radical Heart/Radical Marriage approaches the "how" of marriage from the foundation of the "why" of marriage. Scholars with impeccable credentials have expounded on psycho-social aspects of marriage. Medical experts have analyzed sexual adjustment in marriage. Experienced marriage counselors have popularized theories and methods which they say have worked for them. Christian writers have presented biblical and theological studies of God's standard for marriage. Couples who have survived extraordinary challenges have written and spoken about the lessons they have learned. Each of these approaches is usually presented by itself, although there have been attempts to integrate several of them. The result is that most books about marriage have been written and read by people with specific areas of interest and levels of expertise and are of limited usefulness to others. *Radical Heart/Radical Marriage* bridges some of the gaps as it proclaims God's plan for marriage and proposes principles for bringing marriages into conformity with that plan.

What God says about marriage is true for everyone, in every cultural context; the Bible's teachings transcend all human traditions. Biblical principles will work not only for a faithful few but for anyone who will apply them consistently

---

[5] The unconditional love of God for His people and of His people for one another is a mark of His presence in the world. When humans speak of loving unconditionally, they are always aware of the conditions, the deficiencies which they are conscious of overlooking. God's unconditional love does not overlook any of our deficiencies, but God takes it upon Himself to correct the deficiencies which make us unlovable, Himself meeting all the conditions for our reconciliation. Believers live in this love, and are expected to demonstrate it in their marriages. Unbelievers are more limited, yet their marital love should bring them into a degree of empathy which makes them sensitive to each other's needs and mitigates their respective demands.

to the challenges of life.[6] *Radical Heart/Radical Marriage* is not just another how-to book listing tips for handling perceived problems. To a degree, relieving discomfort and restoring function can be done without addressing core issues. *Radical Heart/Radical Marriage* is more than a survival handbook for flawed marriages. It is a call to consider and apply the highest view of what marriage should (and can) be.

Starting with the "why" of marriage, Section I of *Radical Heart/Radical Marriage* makes the foundations of marriage explicit. Instead of assuming a consensus regarding the meaning and value of marriage, a *Marriage Manifesto* exposes and explains the presuppositions underlying everything said in the rest of the book. Marriage as God planned it is not only the primary link of human society but also a primary place of God's presence and blessing. Beginning from a view of marriage as related to God's covenant and dwelling place, a challenge is given to enter into and establish marriage according to biblical principles. The key concepts are wise choices and careful planning.

Section II presents a *Blueprint for Blessing*, to help couples plan with God for a successful marriage. A spiritual plan for developing their relationship to God, plans for building their relationship with each other and for relating as a couple to other people in their lives can build a couple's marriage from the inside out. Financial, educational and recreational planning can secure the couple's place and progress in the world.

The *Catalogue of Catastrophe* in Section III points out typical hazards which threaten marriages and the disastrous consequences of abandoning God's plan. Facing problems in

---

[6] Where biblical principles are not applied, the depth and richness of marriage are diminished. Where couples do not decisively leave their parents and cleave to each other, the life-defining oneness of marriage is compromised. Educators can verify that where parents do not discipline children consistently, lawlessness reigns. When cultural norms violate biblical principles, marriage and child-rearing quickly disintegrate: things fall apart. It takes courage to go against the cultural tide, but it is better to obey God than to follow every politically correct whim of popular opinion.

fear rather than in faith and faithfulness detours couples from the open road of blessing into the blind alleys of destruction and divorce. Asking for directions before marriage or at any difficult point of the journey can turn couples towards a contented rather than contentious home.

There are *Resources for Reconciliation* as couples return to God's plan. Section IV presents what counselors need to know and what couples need to do to bring about rethinking and recovery. Assessing the couple's spiritual and personal resources, the counselor can help them make the best use of tools which are already in their hands. Assignments tailored to their needs and abilities further equip them to deal with current and future issues. If the course of counseling proposed in *Radical Heart/Radical Marriage* is followed productively, these resources will be valuable for further research and growth.

Hope for Healing, Section V, extends the reach of counselors and couples, expanding on key principles and concerns, providing proven counseling tools and recommending procedures for conflict resolution. Emphasis is on productive communication patterns which can be practiced during counseling sessions and implemented in a couple's conversations at home.

Radical Heart/Radical Marriage is not meant to be "all things to all men and women." It is an attempt to consolidate and clarify a biblical Christian view of marriage and marriage counseling. I appreciate the rich ministry of others in this field, but I have not found a text which I could recommend to colleagues or students as a comprehensive overview of principles and issues that I consider vital. This book is my attempt to fill that gap. I have done what I have found in my hand to do, and pray that God will multiply seeds planted here into more fruitful marriages and ministries.

A Marriage Manifesto

Marriage as God planned it is a covenant relationship entered by vow, modeled after and illustrating God's covenant relationship with His people. Instituted by God as the basic unit of human society, marriage connects one woman and one man in a one-flesh union in which sustained self-disclosure and trust make them of one mind. The bonds of Christian marriage presuppose covenant bonds between husband and wife and God. This three-fold cord makes a marriage a dwelling place of God and a place of blessing as the couple's obedient faith demonstrates God's presence and activity among His people on earth. Covenant marriage is also a basic unit of Christian fellowship. As husband and wife accept, and supplement each other's weakness (and just as freely celebrate and encourage each other's strength), they illustrate and enact the spirit of mutual ministry which should characterize the Body of Christ, the Church.

Marriage

Christian marriage counseling is a special form of discipling, a way of equipping and encouraging people to live according to God's plan. Discipling is necessary because knowing the truth does not set people free until they entrust themselves to the truth and act it out in their lives. Marriage counseling is necessary because false concepts of marriage bind people in distrust and fear, leaving them unable to enjoy life freely and abundantly. If a marriage is built on a foundation of truth and truthfulness, counseling can help tone up an already basically healthy relationship. If such a foundation is lacking or has been destroyed, counseling must help to eliminate the negative as well as to accentuate the positive. Most couples who admit their need for counseling have a heavy load of the negative. Those who seek professional help come with problems to solve. They need tools and skills to clean up their acts and get on with their lives.

In an increasingly pluralistic culture, we cannot assume that solving marriage problems means the same thing to every person who comes through our doors. To some, the problem is marriage itself. They disparage binding commitment to any relationship.[7] Some spouses think their problems are personal issues: they seek answers individually rather than together. Marriage is not the problem, but a marriage may have problems. Not his problems or her problems, but the marriage's problems. Perceived problems must be identified and addressed. The core problem of many couples is the mistake of viewing and attacking perceived problems as separate competing individuals rather than as a one-flesh unit attempting to be of one mind. The real issue is how to bring the marriage into closer conformity to God's standard. Personal issues of concern to either spouse are at best secondary. Discomfort or difficulty need not destroy a marriage. Firm commitment to endure discomfort and to grow through difficulty builds a marriage. If a couple's commitment to each other is weak, any distraction can bring destruction. In some cases even a commitment to endure and grow through the counseling process seems too much to ask.

Building a marriage requires a foundation which can stand firm in the storms of life. Lacking such a foundation, many marriages are tossed about with every wind of temptation.[8] In a culture which questions whether a firm foundation is either necessary or possible the prospects for any marriage are clouded with uncertainty. Even the word "marriage" is up for grabs,

---

[7] Our culture of self-gratification encourages people to be commitment-phobic in all areas of life. Marriage, parenting, employment, friendship and community involvement all require sustained attention and effort. An attention-deficit autonomous individual prefers quick fixes which give the illusion of connection to other human beings without the effort to make the connection real and lasting.

being applied to homosexual monogamy or being avoided by those who prefer to be known as "partners" or "long-time companions."[8] Speaking into a culture which has redefined, compromised or abandoned former views of marriage we cannot, like Tevye, simply cry, "Tradition!" and expect to be heard.[9]

Nostalgia may blur perception of this cultural shift. A rural pastor mowing his expansive lawn (a field of weeds) was suddenly interrupted. A car swerved off the road and drove right up to him. A middle-aged woman jumped out of the driver's seat, shouting, "I want you to do a wedding for my son and his girlfriend!" She said they had been living together for some time and "a church wedding would be nice. You know, with flowers and a pretty dress." After a brief exchange about spiritual matters, church policy and premarital counseling requirements, she got back into her car, yelling, "Well, then they'll just go on living in sin." We can assume they did just that.

If tradition is insufficient grounds for marriage, we must dig deeper. The world-view shift in Western culture is not merely a shift away from marriage, morality or generic Judeo-Christian values. The meaning and value of marriage can be shifted with shifting morals. If human beings are autonomous, meanings and values are determined by personal choice and

---

[8] Sadly, when a poorly founded marriage fails, the temptation is to try to construct a new marriage on a destructive foundation. The rubble heap of bitterness and broken dreams does not provide a suitable basis for a lifetime of happiness and fulfillment. Marriages built on the garbage dumps of divorce are doubly doomed. They have no real foundation, and the corrosive materials on which they are built eventually seep to the surface. The only hope for such marriages is to discard the refuse of the past and dig deep to lay a new foundation of trusting love grounded in God's truth.

[9] Ironically, this term is close to the true significance of marriage. Recent legal debate over whether a civil union can be called a marriage indicates a recognition that the word "marriage" still carries the weight of its historical usage, if not the weight of its biblical significance. Sadly many states are now accepting it's false idea of marriage between Sodomites with the help of our legislative and judicial branches of government.

23

popular consensus. Redefining marriage, morals and values to describe the current human condition is more than a shift away from traditions and laws which have prescribed what the human condition should be. It is a shift away from God. Whether in ignorance, delusion or defiance, people are trying to get on with their lives without a clear consciousness of the existence and activity of God. In my counseling, I have seen practical results from applying biblical principles to the lives of non-believing clients, but the full presence and power of God come only to those who know Him.

If God rewards those who acknowledge His existence and seek His intervention, couples with even this mustard-seed faith can invite Him into the counseling process. The world has fuzzy ideas about prayer as a mystical, magical or occult practice.[10] The Bible demystifies prayer. Genesis 4:26 notes that people began to "call upon the name of the Lord." Romans 10:13 identifies believers as those who "call upon the name of the Lord." Jim Cymbala relates how the Brooklyn Tabernacle was transformed by the discovery that calling upon the Lord is not only the essence of prayer but also the biblical definition of a life in relationship with God. So let them call. Let counselees know they can talk to God as a living, caring friend.

The prayers of many counselees will be problem-centered. The prayers of Christian counselors must be God-centered. Clients sense their needs of the moment and want God to intervene in their perceived problems. They want Him to enter their lives at the point of most intense pain. From God's side, a proper relationship with Him is the only secure foundation for a relationship with anyone else. He wants us to

---

[10] Recently, studies in the fields of psychology and medicine have taken an increased interest in the benefits of prayer and spirituality in the healing process. These studies imply that the mental state of generic religiosity can have therapeutic value, regardless of the content or truthfulness of the beliefs involved. The weakness of this non-committal nod to "people of faith" disregards the fact that nobody seriously addresses prayer "to whom it may concern." A mental attitude cannot move a mountain or make a mustard seed grow, nor can it mend a broken arm — or marriage.

enter His life at the point of most intense grace: Jesus Christ. Counselors would do well to study and pray the prayers recorded in the New Testament epistles. We can follow Paul's example in calling upon the Lord for the spiritual enlightenment and growth of those within the range of our ministries.

Paul speaks to God about people in much the same terms Jesus uses in speaking to the churches in chapters two and three of the book of Revelation. There is a review of the current situation, an assessment of resources and a challenge for the future. This pattern has parallels in our ministry: defining problems, gathering needed tools and working out solutions. At all stages of the counseling process we can pray that God will bring His wisdom, love and power into our work.

If we can tell the living God what is on our minds and hearts, how can we know what is on His? The only God who is really there is not silent. If God does not exist, everything is permissible. If He is really there but silent, we can only guess at how to reach Him, know Him or please Him. If He is there and has spoken, we must respond in faith and obedience to what He has said. God is really there and He has spoken in many ways to many people and has chosen to record His essential message in a book we call the Bible. Beyond that, He has appeared in human flesh to authenticate that message and accomplish its purpose (Hebrews 1:1-4).[11]

Those who know God in Jesus Christ accept the Bible as sufficient foundation for a life of faith and obedience. The Bible's words are meaningful, its pronouncements purposeful. It reveals the mind and heart of God. Hearing what God says, we understand; understanding what God says, we respond. At least we are made responsible. God has told us what we need to know (Deuteronomy 29:29). Just as the Bible demystifies calling

---

[11] This is the liberating message of Francis Schaeffer's key books. *The God Who is There, He Is There* and *He is Not Silent*, and *Escape from Reason*, now included in *The Complete Works of Francis Schaeffer*, Crossway Books,

upon the Lord, calling upon the Lord demystifies the Bible. God speaks and we must respond (Deuteronomy 30:11-14, 16, 19; Joshua 1:7-8; 24:14-25; Romans 10:5-10).

What has God said about marriage? The Bible supports a view of marriage as a covenant relationship entered by vow.[12] The marriage relationship is the fundamental human relationship. God created us for relationship, primarily with Himself and also among ourselves. God's observation that it was not good for Adam to be alone (Genesis 2:18) is the bedrock upon which marriage, family and all levels of social interaction are built. Marriage is the fundamental institution established by God to relieve human aloneness; it is the primary unit of human connectedness. This connectedness was not meant to be just among human beings; God included Himself in the relationship. Excluding God from marriage and society leaves lifeless structures which can hold people together tentatively but lack God's presence, power and blessing.

Looking closely at the marriage of Adam and Eve, we see God active in all the details. According to Genesis 2, God formed Adam (verse 7), put him where he was meant to be (verse 8) and told him what he was meant to do (verse 16). Then God made Eve and brought her to Adam (verse 18). Genesis 1:28 says God blessed Adam and Eve. They were where they were meant to be doing what they were meant to do and they were brought together by direct action of God. They were in the place of blessing, the place of obedient faith. God's plan for marriage still follows this pattern.

---

[12] Jay Adams calls it the covenant of companionship, citing Proverbs 2:17 and Malachi 2:14. He points to the fact that in biblical times betrothal was a binding contract of companionship entered long before sexual union, in contrast to the current perception of engagement as a trial companionship, often including sexual union, before taking the covenant vows of marriage. In either case, marriage is a covenant relationship entered by vow (see Jay Adams, *Marriage, Divorce and Remarriage*, Presbyterian and Reformed, 1980, pp. 11-15).

For Adam and Eve the place of blessing was also the place of God's presence on earth, the place where His people met with Him. Out of all the places in Creation where the omnipresent God might show Himself locally, He came to where Adam and Eve were to talk with them and to enjoy their company. They heard the sound of His voice and were aware of His presence even after they had sinned against His command (Genesis 3:8). Departure from obedient faith meant departure from God's blessing but not departure from God's presence. The response of those who disobey God must always echo Adam's confession: "I heard your voice, and I was afraid (Genesis 3:10)." The place of disobedience is the place of fear.[13] Adam had set himself up as a judge of God's Word, and moved from a position of faith to a position of fear. The basic structure of the relationship did not change. What changed was the capacity of Adam and Eve to enjoy the full blessing of relating to God and to each other in the full freedom of obedient faith.[14] The pattern of disobedient fear is still at the root of the dysfunction, division and destruction seen in many marriages.

Marriage is still the foundation upon which the structures of society must be built. If this foundation is threatened with destruction through redefinition, compromise and abandonment, Christians must act in the power God gives us to rebuild and preserve it. This is the mandate of Christian marriage counseling.

---

[13] Christians operate well under faith and poorly under fear in every realm, not just in marriage. The just are to live by faith in victory over the world (Romans 1:17; Habakkuk 2:4; I John 5:4). The perfect love of God displaces fear of death, fear of human opposition and fear of judgment (I John 4:18; Hebrews 2:15; 13:6; 10:27). Fear brings torment (I John 4:18). Those who do not place themselves in God's hands in faith will ultimately fall into God's hands in fear (Hebrews 10:31).

[14] Imagine the original innocence of Adam and Eve, naked and not ashamed. A virgin male and a virgin female, never having seen the nakedness of any other human being, walking together with God in the place He prepared for them. Their joy in each other and in God was unlimited. Impossible as it may seem in a sinful world, this remains God's ideal for a couple entering marriage. Preaching and teaching this ideal is crucial in a culture which has chosen a

position of disobedience.

As marriage is the foundation of society, the one-flesh concept of Genesis 2:23-24 is the foundation of marriage. "Bone of my bones and flesh of my flesh:" husband and wife are unified in their common humanity. In the Genesis account Adam and Eve are literally of the same substance. Genesis 1:27 says God created humanity as male and female. The generic name Adam (Man) is related to the Hebrew word for earth, out of which God formed the male (Genesis 2:7). As God called all things into being we are told repeatedly, "God saw that it was good," but of Adam's solitary existence God said, "It is not good (Genesis 2:18)." God used some of the man's very substance to form the woman. The great theologian Matthew Henry wrote, "Eve was made by God, not out of Adam's head to rule over him, or out of his feet to be trampled over by him, but out of his side to be equal, and under his arm to be protected by him, and near his heart to be loved by him."[15]

It is vitally significant that the biblical institution of marriage is heterosexual. The woman is "of" the man through creation, men are subsequently "by" the woman through reproduction (I Corinthians 11:12). The man was incomplete without a suitable counterpart. God's answer was to create a woman and bring her to the man (Genesis 2:22). The companionship and potentially reproductive sexual union of a man and a woman create the one-flesh bond which the marriage covenant honors. Both for enjoyment (Proverbs 5:18-19) and for reproduction (Psalm 128:3), heterosexual monogamy is God's provision for human completeness.

In Mark 10:6-9 Jesus cites the one-flesh reference as defining God's view of marriage. "God made them male and female:" marriage is heterosexual. "Leave father and mother:" marriage is life-defining. "Joined, one flesh:" marriage is monogamous. "God hath joined:" marriage is sacred. "Let not man separate:" marriage is permanent. God's ideal from the beginning of the creation is that marriage is a permanent,

---

[15] Matthew Henry, *Commentary*, 1706, in loc. Genesis 2:18-22.

sacred, monogamous, life-defining heterosexual union of one man and one woman.

The union of a man and a woman in marriage is so highly regarded in the Bible that it is often used to illustrate the bond between God and His people. From the Hebrew prophets to the marriage supper of the Lamb in the book of Revelation, bride/bridegroom and husband/wife imagery depicts God's love, faithfulness and desire to possess and to protect His own. Hosea 1-3 is an extended example of this marriage metaphor, including what may be a parallel to Hebrew betrothal vows: "I will betroth you to me forever, yes, I will betroth you to me in righteousness and justice, in loving-kindness and mercy; I will betroth you to me in faithfulness (Hosea 2:19-20a)." God binds Himself to His people by a covenant of betrothal. The one-flesh union of a man and a woman is acknowledged in a covenant entered by vow in the presence of God and other witnesses.

The concept of covenant is unknown in most marriages. In Western culture marriage is considered a contract, and like other contracts, may be modified or broken. A traditional church wedding may be a nice feature of a day of celebration, but the marriage is thought of as a legal bond rather than a lifelong covenant entered by vows in the presence of the living God. The bond of marriage reaches no higher than the authority which legitimates it. What human law has joined together human law may put asunder. Couples joined to each other and to God through covenant vows are bound together for life, and can live in the place of God's blessing through continued obedient faith.

Marriage is not a casual relationship or a merely legal partnership. It is meant to be a covenant relationship. In Malachi

2:14 God speaks against dealing treacherously against "the wife of your youth, your companion, your wife by covenant." Similarly, Proverbs 2:17 warns against the adulterous woman who abandons "the companion of her youth" and "the covenant of her God." A covenant relationship from youth until death is God's standard for marriage. God's plan is to join together. He severely warns those who think lightly of a covenant relationship and seek to dissolve it.

Biblical covenants were binding agreements which were sealed by ceremony. Typically, an animal would be cut in half and the parties to the covenant would walk between the halves. This part of the ceremony implied that each party would deserve the fate of the animal if responsible for violation of the covenant. In Jeremiah 34:18-20 God describes making such a covenant with people whose violation of it would make them "meat for the birds."[16] God is a covenant God who guarantees the fulfillment of what He covenants to do.

Our covenant-keeping God expects us to be covenant-keeping people. He calls those who violate vows fools (Ecclesiastes 5:4). A covenant relationship entered by vow is God's plan for marriage, the foundation of God's plan for society. God considers it foolish to rebel against His plan by diminishing, distorting or destroying marriages.

If marriage is a covenant relationship entered by vow, then counselors must deal with the foolishness and rebellion which threaten marriages. The cultural shift away from a high view of marriage is, at bottom, a shift away from God. If creatures value the opinions of fellow creatures more than the revealed will of the Creator, they are left to their own futile thoughts and foolish hearts (Romans 1:21). Attempting to banish God from their thoughts and feelings about marriage leaves emptiness and loneliness. True fulfillment in marriage is

---

[16] Perhaps there is some propriety in saying that views of marriage which disregard its covenantal dimension are "for the birds" in this biblical sense.

founded on a covenant relationship subject to God's plan, not on a mere contractual agreement subject to misguided human reason and emotion.

Western culture has elevated the thoughts and feelings of the human individual into the place of authority previously reserved for deity. Even without speaking of a god within you as some neo-pagans do, emphasis has shifted to whatever seems right or whatever feels good. Disappointed with imperfect marriages, men and women think they need time and space to "find themselves." How many people in search of themselves have lost sight of God, spouse, family and friends? People have become narcissistic, preoccupied with personal success and comfort, looking for happiness everywhere but where God put it.[17] The grass may look greener on the other side of the fence, but the fence God has built around marriage is there to keep the happiness inside and to prevent spouses from straying into disaster.

Psalm 1 says we are happy in proportion to our commitment to hear and obey God.[18] Paying attention to what God says and disregarding the competing voices of human opinion establishes secure lives and marriages. What God says about marriage must not be diluted or distorted to suit the whims of sinful humanity. As a covenant relationship entered by vow, Christian marriage is a commitment to God to accept His plan for our connectedness. Marriage is not a tentative

---

[17] Russell Conwell became famous for his story of a man who sold his farm to seek his fortune. The farmer had grown bored with his home, and looked for prosperity elsewhere. Meanwhile, back at the farm, the purchaser began plowing a barren field and discovered that there were millions of diamonds just beneath the surface. (R.H. Conwell, *Acres of Diamonds*, Harper and Brothers, 1915). Cultivating the home ground is always wiser than sowing wild oats and praying for a crop failure.

[18] What God says about how to be happy will not be found in the self-help books of pop psychology. In Proverbs, He says that happiness comes through knowing the difference between right and wrong, being generous to the poor and earnestly seeking friendship with God.

agreement between self-centered persons, each maintaining the aloneness of an individualistic world-view. It is a covenant of companionship for life in a growing one-flesh, one-mind union. If we want the happiness of a marriage that works, we have to see it God's way and work at it according to God's plan.

One Flesh

"They shall be one flesh (Genesis 2:24)." What does this mean? How does it happen? In what sense and to what degree are they united? How do varieties of sexual identity and activity affect the physical significance of marriage? To appreciate the uniquely comprehensive nature of the one-flesh union of marriage it is necessary to clear away misconceptions. Jay Adams dismisses several erroneously inadequate views of marriage before expounding his concept of the covenant of companionship.[19] He points out that marriage is not a human invention devised according to social needs and desires.

Marriage was designed by God, and human deviations from His design carry the germs of personal and social destruction. Marriage is not an addendum to tribal or cultural bonds, but is itself the foundational institution of God's order in the world. Marriage is not a mere legalization of mating for the propagation of the race, but a context for intimate lifelong companionship. Adams gets to the crux of the one-flesh issue when he says "A sexual union is not (as some who study the Bible carelessly think) to be equated with the marriage union... Marriage is different from, bigger than, and inclusive of sexual union, but the two are not the same."[20]

If a one-night stand is not a one-flesh union, then what is? Adams reasons that if a single act of copulation constituted

---

[19] Jay Adams, *Marriage, Divorce and Remarriage in the Bible*, Presbyterian and Reformed, 1980, pp. 3-6.

[20] Ibid. p. 5.

marriage in the sight of God, the Bible would not use the term fornication for an act which would establish an informal marriage. For the married, a single act of adultery does not automatically dissolve an existing one-flesh union and create a new one. While this distinguishing of differences could be misconstrued to excuse promiscuity, its real import is to elevate the one-flesh union of marriage to its rightful status.[21] Both Jay Adams and my mentor, Ed Wheat, presented a highly biblical view of marriage which did not shy away from the difficulty of explaining and advocating a one-flesh union in the midst of what was termed a sexual revolution. Dr. Wheat's book, *Intended for Pleasure*, retains its value as perhaps the most detailed and comprehensive resource for sexual adjustment in marriage.[22]

The sexual revolution of the mid-twentieth century left many casualties, including a vocabulary for discussing the differences between human opinion and biblical truth. The words "fornication" and "promiscuity" remain in the dictionary, but have been displaced from use in private conversation or public discourse. It is no longer deplored that a few teens are promiscuous: it is accepted as a matter of course that all but a few teens are "sexually active." The moral force of the word fornication has been discarded in favor of the demeaning amoral connotations of the crudest scatological slang for copulation.[23] Bible-believers do not speak the same language as those whose

---

[21] A few months after a sermon which emphasized that forgiveness is preferable to divorce and that a single act of adultery does not dissolve a marriage, a man had a brief affair with one of his female employees. He later explained, "My pastor said it was all right." Neither the pastor nor Jay Adams endorsed adultery in moderation. The point is that marriage is bigger and stronger than any other relationship.

[22] Ed Wheat M.D. and Gaye Wheat, *Intended for Pleasure*, fourth edition, Revell, 2010. Revised and updated by Dr. Dow Pursley 2010.

[23] English teachers sometimes point out the meaningless of such language by noting that one of the most popular of these slang words is used indiscriminately as a verb, a noun, an adjective, an adverb, an exclamation and an expletive—almost always with no connection to its original literal definition.

views of sex and marriage are dictated by a culture which calls evil good, and good evil (Isaiah 5:20).

Christians have erred in two directions when confronting the world's view of sex: acceptance of popular opinions without asking questions or denial of popular opinions without providing answers. Acceptance of the world's values may not be a conscious choice. The presuppositions of a society are absorbed to some degree by all of its members. American society almost unanimously giggled at President Carter's admission that he had lusted after women in his heart. The President's terminology was biblical, echoing the words of Jesus in Matthew 5:28: "I say unto you that whosoever looketh on a woman to lust after her hath committed adultery with her already in his heart."[24] Christians who say, "It's okay to look, but don't touch," are directly contradicting Jesus. Many professing Christians go much further in accepting the sexual morality of society rather than the biblical truth about sex. At the opposite extreme are Christians who reject the world's immorality so severely that they virtually deny their own sexuality. Sexual identity and activity are among the highest blessings of physical life on earth, but without conscious commitment to God's clearly revealed standards, people merely pick and choose from options suggested by the culture around them.

---

[24] The fact that Mr. Carter made his comment in the context of a *Playboy* interview trivialized its impact as a confession and legitimized a basically pornographic magazine. Men do not buy *Playboy* to gain insight into the views of Presidential candidates, but to lust after women in their hearts.

In a culture which appears to be headed for Hell in a self-help handbook, calling for adherence to biblical standards is perceived as rebellious. So be it. It is not reactionary to proclaim what God said "at the beginning (Matthew 19:4-6)." It is not anachronistic to obey the One who is "the same yesterday, today and forever" rather than those whose "strange doctrines" (Hebrews 13:9) reflect the errors of their times. The heart of marriage comes from the loving heart of God, not from the darkened mind of the latest sex guru. A one-flesh union is formed in the context of a covenant relationship entered by vow, a covenant of companionship which satisfies all dimensions of the human need for connectedness. Any view of sex and marriage which does not adhere to biblical standards falls short of the glory of God's purpose.

Now with the so-called marriages of sodomites and lesbians being promoted by the executive branch and the department of justice of our government and approved by all fifty states the definition of marriage has indeed changed. By eliminating the Defense of Marriage Act by an act of judicial fiat we as a nation have determined that that which was once a crime against nature is now the new "normal". The most vile time in a countries downward spiral is when it's leadership promotes sin and calls healthy that which is historically been considered abhorrent and sinful. Proverbs 14:34 "Righteousness exalts a nation, But sin is a disgrace to any people."

The government now sponsors domestic terrorism by attempting to prosecute Christian's; their businesses, and other moral citizens for their opposition to these newly accepted Satan inspired behaviors. Satan inspired because he hates all creation, especially the procreation of people. In the same way he inspired Roe vs. Wade in 1973, for only Satan could think up sodomite behavior and only Satan could convince a mother to have her baby killed, and then convince her to believe that killing her baby is a compassionate act. Proverbs 14:28 A growing population is a king's glory; a dwindling nation is his doom.
We have only begun to see the camel's nose enter the tent. What is

the new normal today, will in short order create chaos and immorality unprecedented in history. Isaiah 5:20 Woe to those who call evil good, and good evil...;

Who would have thought that within a few short years America could degrade to the point of moral suicide. We are quickly becoming our worst nightmare, the new Babylon.

"Babylon the great is fallen, is fallen, and has become a dwelling place of demons, a prison for every foul spirit, and a cage for every unclean and hated bird! [3] For all the nations have drunk of the wine of the wrath of her fornication, the kings of the earth have committed fornication with her, and the merchants of the earth have become rich through the abundance of her luxury." [4] And I heard another voice from heaven saying, "Come out of her, my people, lest you share in her sins, and lest you receive of her plagues. [5] For her sins have reached[b] to heaven, and God has remembered her iniquities. [6] Render to her just as she rendered to you,[c] and repay her double according to her works; in the cup which she has mixed, mix double for her. [7] In the measure that she glorified herself and lived luxuriously, in the same measure give her torment and sorrow; for she says in her heart, 'I sit *as* queen, and am no widow, and will not see sorrow.'[8] Therefore her plagues will come in one day — death and mourning and famine. And she will be utterly burned with fire, for strong *is* the Lord God who judges[d]her.

[9] "The kings of the earth who committed fornication and lived luxuriously with her will weep and lament for her, when they see the smoke of her burning, [10] standing at a distance for fear of her torment, saying, 'Alas, alas, that great city Babylon, that mighty city! For in one hour your judgment has come.'

[11] "And the merchants of the earth will weep and mourn over her, for no one buys their merchandise anymore: [12] merchandise of gold and silver, precious stones and pearls, fine linen and purple, silk and scarlet, every kind of citron wood, every kind of object of ivory, every kind of object of most precious wood, bronze, iron, and marble; [13] and cinnamon and incense, fragrant oil and frankincense, wine and oil, fine flour and wheat, cattle and sheep,

horses and chariots, and bodies and souls of men. [14] The fruit that your soul longed for has gone from you, and all the things which are rich and splendid have gone from you,[c] and you shall find them no more at all. [15] The merchants of these things, who became rich by her, will stand at a distance for fear of her torment, weeping and wailing, [16] and saying, 'Alas, alas, that great city that was clothed in fine linen, purple, and scarlet, and adorned with gold and precious stones and pearls! [17] For in one hour such great riches came to nothing.' Every shipmaster, all who travel by ship, sailors, and as many as trade on the sea, stood at a distance [18] and cried out when they saw the smoke of her burning, saying, 'What *is* like this great city?'

[19] "They threw dust on their heads and cried out, weeping and wailing, and saying, 'Alas, alas, that great city, in which all who had ships on the sea became rich by her wealth! For in one hour she is made desolate.'

[20] "Rejoice over her, O heaven, and *you* holy apostles[d] and prophets, for God has avenged you on her!"

The world's view of sex takes a dive into inglorious purposelessness. Blocking God out of their thoughts and turning to idols of their own making, people enslave themselves to perverted lust. "So God let them go ahead into every sort of sex sin, and do whatever they wanted to — yes, vile and sinful things with each other's bodies (Romans 1:24, Living Bible)." Romans 1:26-27 gives homosexuality as an example of departure from God's purpose. God tells His people they should not "act like heathen" in indulging in incest, adultery, bestiality, child abuse and human sacrifice, saying, "Yes, all these abominations have been done continually by the people of the land... and the land is defiled (Leviticus 18:3, 27)." The undefiled marriage bed provides the only divinely blessed context for sexual pleasure. Physical, visual and psychological stimuli can arouse sexual responses outside this context, and the adrenaline rush of risk, anger, intense activity or even pain can be wrongly associated with sexual ecstasy. If the only sex sin a culture recognizes is lack of consent, there is no restraint of sexual experimentation. Masturbation, sexploitation, sado-masochism and murder may excite passion, but cannot satisfy the God-given need to experience sex as a full person fully related to an equally complex person in lifetime companionship.[25]

God designed male and female bodies to bring sensual delight to each other. Human genitals and sensitive erogenous zones are intended for sexual ecstasy. The woman's clitoris seems to have no other purpose.[26] God gave Adam and Eve sexual identities which complemented each other, most obviously in their physical compatibility. The sight of each other's bodies, the sound of each other's voices, taste, smell and most ecstatically touch — all the senses would be aroused and satisfied in their one-flesh union. Their differences would fulfill their desires. God's direct command to multiply would lead to their discovery of the heights of physical pleasure as well as to the increase of the human race.[27] Bearing the image of God as personalities in relationship, the man and the woman were physiologically designed to form a one-flesh union as husband and wife.

Those who depart from God and do what is right in their own eyes do not appreciate the glory of God's design for sexual joy. Rejecting a relationship with God brings disorder and pollution to all other relationships. Whether male or female, the human self becomes the judge of purpose and pleasure in sexual

---

[25] Even Christian counselors have treated masturbation lightly, as if its narcissistic obsession with self-gratification were not a serious threat to the purity of a one-flesh union with a spouse. The evolution of sexual mores and sex education can be traced in the changing dictionary definitions of masturbation. In the mid-twentieth century it was "sexual self-abuse;" a few decades later it was "sexual self-stimulation." Current dictionary entries include descriptions of technique. The Bible calls some acts sin, moralists call them abuses, rationalists call them statistically normal and pragmatists say, "If you're going to do it anyway, you might as well do it well."

[26] Some patriarchal tribal cultures have practiced "female circumcision," the removal of the clitoris, to keep women under male control. As women from these tribes have been enlightened through broader cultural contacts, their

protests and court cases have become newsworthy.

27 Exaggerating the threat of overpopulation is a convenient tool for controlling prolific peoples and justifying abortion and other forms of genocide.

experience. Mixed signals from family and society obscure the glories of male and female sexuality, leading to a plethora of sexual disorientations. Cultural idolization of the autonomous individual glorifies self-satisfaction over commitment to another person. God's design for human bodies is distorted into what the Bible calls abominations — indiscriminate experiments in physical ecstasy.[28] "If it feels good, do it," is a fitting motto for those obsessed with the pursuit of pleasure. Their pursuit is doomed. By God's design, sexuality and the capacity for sexual satisfaction bloom gloriously only when planted securely in a covenant of companionship which assures a man and a woman a lifetime to explore and enjoy each other. When uprooted from this home ground, sexuality loses its strength and the capacity for sexual satisfaction is diverted into a never-ending search for new thrills. The braggadocio of sexual excess can never match the contentment of sexual success in a lifetime of being ravished with a faithful spouse (Proverbs 5:18-19).

"The two shall become one flesh (Matthew 19:5, NKJV)." Human sexuality and sexual satisfaction find their rightful context in the permanent, sacred, monogamous, life-defining heterosexual union of one man and one woman. "The two" cannot be any other combination than God's original intention: "he which made them at the beginning made them male and female (Matthew 19:4)." Two, no more than two, one male and one female. A one-flesh union cannot be a so-called open marriage which tolerates adultery. A one-flesh union cannot be a revolving-door marriage which makes a pretense of serial monogamy, changing partners when "things don't work out." The "shall become" of marriage is based on the premise that things will have to work out, because the commitment is for

---

[28] The abominations of the homosexual culture and the pornography industry demonstrate the depths of the continually evil imaginations of sinful humanity (Genesis 6:5; Romans 1:21; Proverbs 6:18, etc.). Christian propriety as prescribed in Ephesians 5:3-4 precludes detailed discussion of these degrading "depths of Satan (Revelation 2:24)."

life. When husband and wife say, "I do," the fences go up, and they are committed to a one-flesh union exclusive of all others. They continue to become one flesh more intimately and emphatically throughout their life together. Discovering and rediscovering each other's desires and delights, they grow together through anticipating each other's physical needs and surprising each other with a growing repertoire of expressions of affection. Sexual identity is built on shared experience and sexual experience is rooted in the secure sexual identity of their covenant union. The couple becomes "one flesh" as they focus all of their sexual identity and experience in their shared intimacy.

Adam and Eve had the advantage of being the only people on earth when they were married. They could not compare each other to anybody else, and they had no magazine surveys or romance novels to tell them their sex life could be better. They only had each other. Theirs was an ideal honeymoon, with prospects for continuing as a perfect marriage. We all know what happened to them. What chance does a couple have now, surrounded by seduction in a society obsessed with sex and self? Does everyone who is not a movie star need a makeover? Is there really such a thing as a sexy car? Can a rich chocolate cake be "better than sex?" How can a couple of modest means and physiques measure up to the steamy sex in the movies and novels, let alone the exotic gymnastics of hard-core pornography? Freud thought infants were "polymorphous perverse," finding the equivalent of sexual pleasure in almost any stimulation. The term may well apply to the infantile sexual obsession which permeates modern society. When almost any commodity or activity is perceived as sexually charged, people understandably feel too sexy for their shirts. In the midst of this orgy, both the sanctity and the sexuality of an undefiled marriage bed are disparaged. Even some Christian books and seminars emphasize spicing up sexual relations with various tricks of the trade, novelty products or techniques to make the best of an essentially humdrum physical relationship. God's plan from the beginning was for a man and a woman to become one without comparison with others, to come together in a one-flesh union untainted by sexual experience in any other context. Rather than advice about spicing up the marriage bed,[29] couples need counsel to defend their marriage from being peppered to death by constant sexual distractions.

Concentrating on bringing sexual satisfaction to each other in a lifetime of love-building, a faithful husband and wife find the secret everybody else is seeking. They become sex friends, giving themselves to each other freely within the full acceptance and security of a covenant marriage. The Song of Solomon celebrates the joyous freedom of a secure one-flesh union.[30] The Song is not erotic literature intended to arouse passionate fantasies, but a love poem celebrating actual experience. In a true one-flesh union, sex is not a bodily function with no context other than its own momentary pleasure. It is the physical part of the couple's lifelong conversation. God intends that couples should have a history of love-building, an ongoing exchange of words and actions which are self-revealing and mutually satisfying. A loving chat between husband and wife may adjourn to the bedroom, and the afterglow of sexual intercourse may include expressions of joy such as those found in the Song of Solomon. It is all the same conversation, the same process of becoming one flesh and one mind.

In the Song of Solomon, there is no denial of the role of the flesh in becoming one. An anatomist could assemble both

---

[29] According to Song of Solomon 4:10-16; 5:13; 6:2; and 8:14, a healthy sexual relationship between husband and wife has its own spices, and needs no help from imported imitations.

[30] Despite Solomon's harem-building, the Song depicts monogamous love. The book of Proverbs includes many references to the risks and responsibilities of relationships between men and women. Ecclesiastes 7:27-29 may be an admission of failure to find happiness in marriage. Regardless of Solomon's polygamy and its sad consequences, his Song suggests that at least once he understood what it meant to be happily married.

male and female bodies from the parts mentioned by name or by metaphor in this poem. The husband and wife know each other's bodies as familiarly as a sculptor's hand knows every millimeter of a meticulously crafted statue. A one-flesh union builds on shared full-body experience of each other. Even without the narrative of their love recorded in the song, simply reviewing their descriptions of each other gives a clear picture of what they are doing. They are naked and unashamed, reveling in the glories of each other's bodies as they offer themselves to each other.

The lovers face each other, and each admires the other's head, hair, temples, eyes, nose and cheeks—the features which distinguish the beloved from all others and express the unique personality which joins in this loving relationship. The mouth gets detailed attention from lovers who are delightedly attentive to each other's lips, teeth and tongues. Comparing the roof of the mouth to fine wine indicates that they know each other by intimate experience, and are passionate in their mutual appreciation. The Hebrew word for neck may refer to the back of the neck, which may well have felt the kisses of the lover's mouth (1:2). The breasts of the wife are obviously ravishing (Proverbs 5:19), and are the objects of the husband's grasping and caressing. The navel is compared to a glass of liquor, and the word for belly may refer to the womb as well as to the external abdomen. The "bowels" of 5:4 could include the organs of procreation as well as the seat of the emotions. The thighs, legs and feet of each spouse are fully involved. Hands and fingers are remarkably active. Characteristically, the husband has one hand under his wife's head bringing her physical comfort and the assurance that he is attentive to her full personality. The other hand embraces her with wandering caresses which stimulate her sexual response (8:3). Whatever their physiques or techniques, husband and wife enter a comprehensive erogenous zone where the look in her eyes, the tone of his voice and everything else about each other evokes passionate response.

Physiques and techniques vary, and couples may need expert information and advice to enjoy each other as fully as possible. Dr. Wheat's *Intended for Pleasure* provides detailed medically accurate counsel for building a one-flesh union according to God's design. I was privileged to participate in preparing the third and fourth edition of this book, updating medical information and helping write the new chapter on sexually transmitted diseases. *Intended for Pleasure* stands almost alone in its lasting value as a reference book for sexual adjustment in marriage.[31] It is unparalleled in providing clear, accurate and practical guidance through potential problem areas. While there is no need for couples to compare their bodies with anybody else's or to gauge their sexual performance against statistical averages, it is helpful to clear away obstacles to building their own history of satisfying each other.[32]

An Arranged Marriage

People who want to build a marriage according to God's standards will make plans which follow His plan. At its most basic level, planning is simply a choice to do what works and to avoid doing what does not work. A couple in financial troubles takes stock of their resources and makes choices about what they can afford. Any marriage problem can be ameliorated by making wiser choices, which is the essence of planning.

---

[31] *The Act of Marriage*, by Tim and Beverly LaHaye (Zondervan, 1976) has also outlasted a spate of how-to books because of its solid biblical and medical base. Dr. Wheat's *Love Life*, (Zondervan, 1980) is also a standard, more directly addressed to couples as an aid in building one-flesh one-mind marriages.

[32] In his thirties, Gordon Puls fought ulcerative colitis for five years. Before surgery to remove his colon, doctors informed him of risks which could affect sexual function, and counselors took a personality profile to prepare for body image trauma. Through God's grace, the surgeon's skill and Joyce's love there was no physical or psychological crisis. Gordon and Joyce were one flesh and one mind in facing the challenge.

Bringing order out of chaos, and cleaning up the messes in our lives, requires difficult choices and sustained effort to live more effectively.

"Cleaning up messes" is an apt description of a counselor's ministry. We may wax nostalgic about an imagined golden age in the past when everybody lived by higher standards, every marriage was made in heaven and all the children were above average. From the beginning it was not so. God's standard for marriage has not changed; neither has sinful humanity's refusal to accept it. Adam and Eve valued self-interest over God's command, and set a pattern of blame-shifting which is still familiar to marriage counselors. Abraham and Isaac were willing to risk losing their wives to pagans to save their own skins. Rebekah schemed against her husband to benefit her favorite son. Judah, Samson and David compromised their callings through sexual indulgence. Solomon multiplied wives for political advantage and turned away from God.

We are still cleaning up messes caused by rejecting God's standard and falling short of the glory He intends for humanity. We can be discouraged if we forget that this ministry of reconciliation was given to us by Jesus Christ, who came to earth to save the sinful, not to congratulate the self-righteous. Although even the people of the Bible were finite and sinful, God's truth is infinitely and eternally righteous. Ideally, all people would be saved, come to full knowledge of the truth, and live abundantly in a close walk with God and with each other. There would be no need for marriage counselors. The second best of all possible worlds would be a world in which all marriages were perfectly established in God's truth. There would be no messes to clean up, and marriage counselors could delight in helping engaged couples prepare for wedded bliss. Back on this planet, marriage counselors can still find great satisfaction in disarming marital time bombs through effective premarital counseling.

The arranged marriage of Isaac and Rebekah, described in Genesis 24, suggests some principles for premarital counseling. As distant as this incident may seem, it has timeless cross-cultural implications. Isaac, the child of the promise, personified the foundation of a nation chosen to represent God on earth, a line of descent which would culminate in the coming of the Messiah, the incarnate Son of God. Throughout the history of this chosen people, their pagan neighbors would seek marriage alliances which would bring them a share of God's blessing. But the promise was to Abraham and his seed, a pure line of descent to the perfect heir of all things, Jesus Christ. There could be no intermingling with followers of false gods if the blessing of the one true God were to remain upon His people.

How much freedom did Isaac have in the choice of a mate? He could have chosen to marry anyone who was willing among neighbors who envied God's blessing upon his family. Exercising this apparently total freedom of choice would have been disastrous. Trusting God to indicate and confirm His own choice may have seemed like retaining no personal freedom, but it meant deliverance from the potential bondage of a marriage made somewhere other than in heaven. Similarly, marriageable individuals in our culture have at least theoretical freedom to accept any willing mate, risking disastrous consequences. True freedom comes through waiting for God's choice, and remaining in the place of God's blessing.

A girl, who I will call "Wendy" committed herself to the Lord and served Him in an organization known to insiders as "the never-daters," which effectively kept romance out of her life. She also worked for a campus ministry which did not allow staff members to date each other or students at the institutions they served. This kept Wendy "off the market" through what might have been considered her marriageable years. When she was thirty-seven her parents introduced her to a fine Marine lieutenant colonel. He and Wendy eventually married and had a child. Both had waited for God's best in a mate, and together they found the blessing of patiently following God's will.

The marriage of Isaac and Rebekah followed the customs of their cultural context, with variations affected by their faith in God. Abraham had learned that God's ways are infinitely higher than man's ways. In the humanly devised religions of his era, sacrificing children was not uncommon; Abraham's God provided a substitute, delivering Isaac from death (Genesis 22:1-19). Marrying within one's tribe or extended family was customary, but Abraham's faith made that difficult. He had already moved from his original homeland in Ur, leaving all his friends and relatives except his father and his nephew. When his father died, Abraham followed God's call to move again into a land where God promised to bless his descendants. When the time came to choose a wife for Isaac, the nearest eligible female relative lived almost five hundred miles away.

Abraham faced a dilemma. His family was in the place of God's blessing, quite literally. They were in the land God promised to Abraham and his descendants. If Isaac returned to the family's original homeland to seek a wife, he would be tempted to stay there. That would put him outside the place of blessing, and leave him in the place where his ancestors had worshipped idols (Joshua 24:2). The simplest alternative was equally unacceptable. If Isaac remained in the Promised Land and took a Canaanite wife, he and his descendants would be tempted to identify with the pagan culture of his in-laws, a departure from God which would forfeit enjoyment of God's blessing. Isaac needed to stay in the land to be in the place of God's blessing, but he could not take a wife from a culture whose iniquity was ripening toward God's judgment (Genesis 15:16). How could Isaac stay where God wanted him to be and still find the woman God wanted him to marry?

48

For believers today, the way to find the right mate when the surrounding culture is so wrong is to do what Isaac did: wait. As Isaac's father arranged to bring Rebekah from a far country, our heavenly Father works things together for the good of His children, sometimes bringing couples to each other in unexpected ways. Christian parents who know their children well may pray for years that the Lord will send the unique partner for a remarkable son or daughter. When both the bride's parents and the groom's parents have seen such prayers answered, great is the rejoicing on earth.

A woman, who I will call "Katy" was a thirty-eight-year-old teacher at a small Bible college. The desire of her heart was to marry and have children. A talented girl from a faithful Christian family, she was always active in church ministries. Persistently praying for a husband, she was equally persistent in pursuing the academic career which seemed to be God's will for her. She continued in the place of blessing, earning her doctorate and entering her teaching ministry. Then she met Brian, a successful contractor who had also been praying for a spouse while doing what God had equipped him to do. They married and were blessed with two lovely children. Both waited for God's best, not passively bemoaning their singleness but taking advantage of it to develop and use the gifts God had given them. The blessing of God was their great reward, and their parents rejoiced to see their son and daughter walking in the truth.[33]

Meanwhile, back in the Promised Land, Abraham sees the solution to the dilemma. Isaac will stay where he belongs. A servant will go to the far country to bring back a suitable wife. Does this mean their marriage will begin as a blind date? Not

---

[33] When Amy Puls decided to marry, she and Kevin were working on advanced degrees in psychology and medicine, respectively. When Kevin asked for her father's blessing, Gordon said something like, "This is the next step in life you are sure is right. Take it, and the steps after it will become clearer as you take them together."

exactly. As we follow the story we see elements of any strong marriage: planning, hard work and God's blessing.

The plan involved packing a caravan of ten camels with customary gifts for the potential bride's family, as well as provisions for the trip. The servant would seek out the appropriate young woman, negotiate with her and her family, and return as soon as possible. Carrying out this plan would be hard work, particularly as it was entrusted to Abraham's oldest servant, who may have been well into his eighties. What if after traveling for some five hundred miles he found no suitable girl? What if she refused to come? What if her family refused to let her go? What response might be expected when he suggested that the daughter of a comfortably established household should drop everything, hop onto a camel and ride five hundred dusty, bumpy miles to spend the rest of her life in a place she had never seen, married to a man she had not yet met? Clearly, God's blessing would be a major factor in the success of the mission.

We cannot speculate about the background of Abraham's servant, but the narrative gives evidence of his character. If we identify him as Eliezer, he was Abraham's business manager and would have inherited the entire estate if Isaac had not been born. Abraham displayed his faith in God and his trust in Eliezer by sending this man to seek a wife for his son. Eliezer had seen Abraham's faith at work, and his own actions show that he shared this faith. This wise servant included God in his plan, praying very specifically for clear confirmation of his choice. God sent an answer even before Eliezer finished his prayer. A humble, obedient walk with God makes confident, effective prayer as natural as conversation with a friend. Being honest with God is more productive than losing patience and striking out on our own.

Eliezer's walk with God carried God's blessing from Abraham's encampment to Rebekah's home. He went where he was sent, and God went with him. "As for me, being on the way, the Lord led me (Genesis 24:27, NKJV)." He was where he was supposed to be, doing what his master had sent him to do, and God blessed him with further guidance. Following God today puts you where you can expect His guidance for tomorrow. Eliezer was in the right place because he followed instructions. Therefore, he was in the place where he could expect further direction. God introduced him to Rebekah as a direct answer to a specific prayer.

What about Rebekah's character? Again, speculation about her background is unnecessary. Her decision demonstrated her suitability. God's call to Abraham had involved a dramatic uprooting for the sake of great blessing (Genesis 12:1-3). Abraham believed God and acted on what God said. Paul and James agree that this is the prototype for response to the Gospel (Romans 4; James 2:21-24). What did God ask of Abraham in that original call? "Get out of your country, from your family and your father's house to a land that I will show you (Genesis 12:1)." This is precisely what Rebekah was asked to do. The call of Abraham was a call to total dependence upon God, demonstrated by literally stepping out in faith into an unknown future where the only certainty was God's continuing presence. Rebekah took this step of faith. Her agreement to leave her home to marry Isaac was a declaration of her willingness to be identified as a daughter of Abraham, joining his household of faith.

The confirmation of Eliezer's choice also confirmed Rebekah's character. Although Rebekah's beauty was remarkable (Genesis 24:16; 26:7), that was not what Eliezer was seeking. He had asked God for a more practical sign. If he asked her for a drink, would she offer to water the camels? Asking for a drink for himself would be a request that common courtesy might grant to any weary traveler. It would be highly presumptuous to ask a stranger to draw water for ten camels. Even a relatively dehydrated man would have to catch his breath after drinking a quart of water. A thirsty camel could take in about twenty-five gallons. Eliezer was not looking for a girl who would give him a cup of water in Abraham's name. He was looking for one who would volunteer to keep drawing water until ten camels sighed in satisfaction. A girl drawing a jug of water for her family would not casually accept the task of drawing two hundred fifty extra gallons for somebody else's camels. Eliezer did not even ask her to do that. She saw a need and was quick to respond. Eliezer earned her trust by treating her respectfully. He asked for a little water from a pitcher she had already filled. Then, with apparent eagerness, she went on to water all ten camels. If she would do this for a stranger in need, how eagerly would she serve her own household? Rebekah would certainly be a suitable helper for Isaac.

After Rebekah watered the camels, Eliezer gave her jewelry he had brought as gifts for Isaac's prospective bride. He then inquired about her family. Were they indeed Abraham's close relatives? Would they welcome him? How would they respond when they learned of his mission? Rebekah assured him that he would be received and cared for, and ran ahead of him to announce his arrival. Again, Eliezer's success was confirmed.

Laban, Rebekah's brother, came out to welcome Eliezer. Before he would partake of the family's hospitality, Eliezer presented the details of his commission from Abraham and his conversation with Rebekah, not failing to mention the direct answer to his very specific prayer.

Laban and Bethuel, Rebekah's father, acknowledged that the matter was in God's hands, and gave assent to Rebekah's departure to be Isaac's wife. When God brings a man and a woman together, their marriage is doubly blessed by the approval of both sets of parents. As they leave their childhood homes to establish an independent household, the love and prayers of their parents go with them.

In Rebekah's case, it is interesting to note that her father is mentioned as approving her departure (Genesis 24:50-51), while her mother is on record as wanting to delay it (verse 55). Even in families which respond quickly to God's will, there will be reluctance to disturb well-formed bonds of affection. Rebekah's evident closeness to her parents, especially to her mother, is exemplary. When a young man and a young woman marry, it is a good sign when their parents are willing to let them go but reluctant to see them leave.

Somewhat remarkably for that time and culture, Rebekah's parents left the final decision up to her. "Will you go with this man?" She responded, "I will go (Genesis 24:58)." And she went. The pattern of this arranged marriage can be expanded from other Scripture and updated to accommodate cultural differences, but there is timeless wisdom in the simple narrative of Genesis 24: Look in the right place, the place of God's blessing. Do not compromise fellowship with God and His people in a desperate search for a mate.

Ask for and expect God's help. Pray specifically for a mate whose gifts and limitations will complement yours as you pursue God's purposes for your life together.

Be patient, and let God bring you together. True love grows through observation and reflection. If there is such a thing as love at first sight, it will be confirmed as you learn more about each other's character and commitment.

Get acquainted with the family. Unanimous enthusiastic support of all relatives is not necessary for a couple's survival, but severe opposition from a few can eat away at their relationship. Seek advice. Family, friends, pastors and others close to you may know you better than you know yourself. Their counsel can keep you from rushing ahead blindly and help you make a well-informed choice. Act decisively. Hurrying can be disastrous; unnecessary waiting can be frustrating. When you know that you are going to end up together, it is time to begin together.

When the search is over, God will be glorified. Isaac was meditating in a field at sunset when Rebekah arrived (Genesis 24:63).[34] This is reminiscent of the communion of Adam and Eve with God in the garden in the cool of the day. Isaac seems to have been contentedly awaiting God's will concerning his marriage. Abraham's arrangement, the agreement with Rebekah's family and the consent of Rebekah and Isaac confirmed a marriage planned by God. Rebekah was brought to Isaac, and he took her home as his wife. It would be disingenuous to imply that once God brings a woman and a man together in marriage they will live happily ever after. Rebekah and Isaac had their problems, which are duly noted in Scripture. The Bible tells the truth about people, and the truth about marriage is that choosing well improves the prospects for living well as husband and wife. The spiritual and personal resources each spouse brings to marriage will affect the couple's ability to fulfill God's plan.

Choose You This Day

People are often surprised to hear how extensive my premarital counseling is. My program consists of seventeen sessions, complete with homework assignments each week. This intense pre-marriage package grew from my observation of thousands of couples over the years at the Wheat Clinic. Many of these couples found themselves in trouble because of poor planning. Nobody arranged their marriages for them: they chose each other and gave little thought to choices they made after that. When consequences of unwise choices created a crisis, the familiar question was, "What were you thinking?" The answer, of course, was that choices were made without thinking.

---

[34] Every single person should long for someone like Isaac: praying, meditating and waiting for God's best.

I reasoned that if couples could be trained to think through their choices they would choose more wisely and have more successful marriages. It seemed that the sooner they learned to choose wisely, the better. Premarital counseling which emphasizes making wise choices has a predictable side effect: a high drop-out rate. Many couples who begin my premarital program decide that marrying each other would not be a wise choice. I consider counseling successful if it makes people more aware of what they are thinking and helps them think more clearly about their choices.

Clear thinking is needed even before couples come for premarital counseling. A high view of marriage includes a high view of dating and courtship. Young men who wanted to date my daughters may have considered the questionnaire and the interview at least a bit unconventional, but I considered them necessary. Personal identity and goals, basic assumptions about life and core beliefs and values may be far from a couple's thoughts when they exchange glances across a crowded room and feel strong mutual attraction. For Christians, spiritual issues must be considered thoroughly. Pastors and counselors should be particularly concerned when a believer considers marriage to an unbeliever. When popular culture tolerates behavior reminiscent of ancient paganism, knowing God and following His plan contrasts sharply with not knowing God and following the crowd.

God's plan for marriage as a one-flesh one-mind union sets a very high standard. The communion between husband and wife should be patterned after the communion between Christ and His Church (Ephesians 5:22-32). When partaking of the Lord's Supper, believers remember and celebrate their union with Christ and with each other. I Corinthians 11:17-32 describes the seriousness of participating in the external portrayal of union while neglecting the internal reality. Divisions, factions and selfish indulgence make light of the bread and cup which picture Christ's body and blood. Partaking unworthily, without self-examination and without conscious identification with Christ and His Church, brings God's judgment. The spiritual oneness between Christ and His Church, between Christ and individual believers and between a Christian husband and wife cannot be understood or attained outside a covenant relationship with God. Church attendance or a church wedding may be socially commendable, but without the inner reality of union with God through obedient faith, all outward religious acts are spiritually empty. A marriage built on God's plan is built by God's power: the external form needs the internal power to attain its full purpose.

There are commendable marriage covenants between unbelieving husbands and wives who are sincerely devoted to each other, but these do not include God as the guarantor of the vows. He may be invoked generically, but if He is not in their lives individually, He is not a full partner in their marriage, and does not guarantee its permanence. Marriage covenants between believers are grounded in a covenant relationship with God and make oneness in Christ the basis of oneness in marriage. God is a full partner in the marriage covenant because each spouse is in a covenant relationship with Him: God guarantees the permanence (not the uninterrupted happiness) of the marriage, and provides remedies for its difficulties. A marriage between a believer and an unbeliever is reduced to a human covenant, at best. The believer's covenant relationship with God is secure, but the marriage covenant is not, because the unbeliever does not recognize God as a full partner in either life or marriage; God guarantees nothing but judgment to those who do not trust Him. A marriage is only as secure as the guarantor of its covenant.

The admonition of II Corinthians 6:14 against being unequally yoked suggests the depth of the differences between believers and unbelievers. The most important differences are not external, but concern the internal realities of covenant relationship with God. The immediate context speaks of believers as temples of God through the indwelling Holy Spirit. Unbelievers are alienated from God and associated with idols of their own making. Their world-views and values come from human culture, if not from direct communion with demons. Such communion is mentioned explicitly in I Corinthians 10:14-22 where the bread and cup of Christian communion are contrasted with sacrificial meals which represent union with demons: "You cannot partake of the Lord's Table and the table of demons (I Corinthians 10:21)." In a pluralistic society the precise limits of a believer's involvement with unbelievers are a matter of conscience before God (I Corinthians 8:1-13), but it seems clear that a one-flesh physical bond should not be joined between two people who are not of one mind spiritually.

Joshua 24:14-15 succinctly presents the challenge believers face: "Choose ye this day whom ye will serve." For the Israelites at that time turning from the God who had delivered them would leave two basic options. They could worship the idols of their ancestors or adopt the religions of the people around them. The options are the same today. People who are not biblical Christians can choose between their nostalgic ties with religious traditions (including external Christian practices) and their fascination with the popular world-views and values of the day. Like Joshua, true people of God are neither enslaved to tradition nor enamored with innovation: "As for me and my house, we will serve the Lord." Joshua 23:6-13 reinforces the division this choice makes. Belief in God cannot be intermingled with belief in idols; believers in God must not intermarry with believers in idols. A "me and my house" commitment means that devotion to the one true God will establish a believer's marriage and household.

God's plan for marriage is valid wherever it is applied. Unbelievers can be warned to turn from attitudes and activities which threaten their marriages. They can be encouraged to develop habits of thought and action which can strengthen their marriages. In marriages between believers and unbelievers, especially, emphasis should not be on wrong decisions of the past but on choosing to do what can be done right in the present and future. The sad realities of human experience must be met with the hopeful truth of God's Word.

The truth of God's Word tells us that a covenant relationship with God is the only secure foundation for a covenant relationship in marriage. "Unless the Lord builds the house, they labor in vain who build it (Psalm 127:1)." God's faithfulness provides the standard and empowerment for faithfulness in marriage. To establish a covenant with His people, God revealed Himself to them, spoke to them and acted on their behalf. He initiated two-way communication, inviting His people to speak to Him in prayer as He speaks to them in revelation. The Song of Solomon illustrates the effect of being related to the only God who is really there to interact with His own. The wisest man in the world composed a love poem in which a woman and a man speak with equal freedom and passion about their relationship. This two-way communication in marriage was revolutionary in the only one of Solomon's songs to be recorded as divinely inspired. In covenant relationship with God both man and woman have full partnership in establishing and enjoying a lifelong conversation in which sexuality is expressed freely in one-flesh physical union and full personhood is shared in a one-mind view of God and the world.[35]

---

[35] Ed Wheat described the Song of Solomon as "a pattern for lovers," and wrote eloquently of the unique value of this poem in developing exquisite sexual companionship as an expression of total freedom and trust within marriage. (Ed Wheat, M.D., *Love-Life for Every Married Couple*, Zondervan, 1980 pp.151-176. Dr. Wheat's comments are followed by S. Craig Glickman's paraphrase of the poem (from S. Craig Glickman, *A Song for Lovers*, Intervarsity, 1976). *Love-Life* has been reprinted and retains its value.

Outside of a covenant relationship with God, all humans have sinned and fall short of His glorious purposes for humankind. Without a secure relationship with God, people invent their own religious and social authorities. Uncertainty in relationships with the alleged gods of paganism leaves uncertainty in marriage relationships. The inherent instability of creature-centered religion leads to instability in creature-centered marriages. Where there is no clear, accurate and dependable message from God, humanly-manufactured religion is a jumble of speculation and trial-and-error attempts to contact and control the supernatural. Approach to the supernatural is a one-way attempt at communication with no assurance of any kind of response. A one-sided approach to religion fosters a one-sided approach to sex. Without a faithful God, sexual partners are faithless to each other. They do not relate to each other as full persons because they do not perceive themselves as the full persons God created them to be. In post-modern culture as in ancient fertility cults, God's glorious ideal of marriage is violated by an approach to sexual intimacy that is nothing more than reproductive necessity and recreational ecstasy. In ancient paganism as in post-modern culture, the human person is perceived as a creator of gods, relating to gods and other persons as a competitor for personal achievement, recognition and satisfaction. Sexuality is seen as a dimension of an individual's lifelong search for self-gratification.

"Unless the Lord builds the house, they labor in vain that build it (Psalm 127:1)." It is easier to trust God than to be God and more satisfying to obey God than to invent gods. All of God's purposes are accomplished with decency and order. The beauty of His arrangement for marriage includes whole-person whole-life one-flesh one-mind union. Proverbs 5:18-19 speaks frankly of the security and joy of monogamous sex: "let your fountain be blessed, and rejoice in the wife of thy youth. As a loving deer and a graceful doe, let her breasts satisfy thee at all times, and always be enraptured with her love." The implication is that a true one-flesh union deepens throughout life as the husband and wife learn to appreciate and enjoy each other through total openness and trust. The intimate conversation recorded in the Song of Solomon expresses the excitement and freedom of an exclusive one-man one-woman relationship. All the senses are aroused and satisfied in their one-flesh physical union, and their whole persons are fulfilled in the one-mind union which defines and protects their relationship.

The Bible does not hide the fact that even the man who wrote this song of marital bliss fell from the high standard of love he so beautifully expressed. Nobody has immunity from temptation. It may be significant that three of the most remarkable characters in the Bible fell through lust: Solomon, the wisest man; Samson, the strongest man: even David, the godliest man. Biblical faith leaves no room for smug self-righteousness or pompous legalism. We are all sinful and it is only by the grace of God that we have not all expressed our sinfulness more openly. Maintaining God's ideal of marriage requires the constant vigilance of faithful obedience.

The place of blessing in marriage, as in all of life, is in the place of obedient faith. Believers enter the marriage covenant in the context of an already established covenant relationship with God. Exchanging vows in the wedding ceremony seals their commitment in the presence of God and other witnesses. The faithfulness of the covenant-keeping God is invoked to preserve the faithfulness of a covenant-keeping couple. A shared relationship with God is the foundation of the relationship between wife and husband.

Where there is no shared relationship with God there is no ultimate foundation for a marriage covenant. In one-sided approaches to the supernatural there is no assurance of reliable supernatural assistance in any endeavor. If there is no divine revelation there is no guarantee of divine response to prayer.

The priests of Baal on Mount Carmel prepared their sacrifice, called out to Baal for hours, leaped around their altar in a frenzied dance and slashed themselves until blood gushed out, but "there was no voice; no one answered; no one paid attention (I Kings 18:26-29)." When no god speaks or answers, pagans lose restraint and go out of control. If there is no one to answer, there is no one to answer to. Anything is permissible in a world which rejects God, and humans feel responsible to nobody but themselves. In such a world marriage is reduced to a contract between consenting partners rather than a covenant under God's authority and blessing. Obedient faith is replaced by "vain imaginations (Romans 1:21)."

Exodus 19:3-9 introduces God's covenant offer to the ancient Israelites. Verses three and four speak of the deliverance God has accomplished as the basis for a response of obedient faith. The covenant relationship would establish Israel as God's special treasure, a kingdom of priests; a holy nation (verses 5-6). The response of the people was a commitment to obedient faith (verses 7-9). God invited them into the place of blessing and they responded willingly. I Peter 2:9 indicates that faith in Jesus Christ brings believers under a new covenant relationship with God which includes similar blessings. They are a chosen generation, a royal priesthood, a holy nation and God's own special people. For God's special people the context for choosing a mate and establishing a marriage must be within the place of blessing, the place of shared faith and obedience.

When faith and obedience are challenged, God's people are tempted to depart from the place of blessing. Unbelief draws attention away from God to some object which seems more attractive and less demanding. Having once turned to God from idols (I Thessalonians 1:9), God's people may be tempted to turn from God to idols. While Moses was on the mountain in the presence of God, the impatience of the Israelites turned into unbelief, and unbelief led to disobedience (Exodus 32:1-6).

They formed an image, a more tangible and controllable object of worship.[36] They chose that day to serve an idol of their own making rather than the God who made them. Significantly, turning to an idol not only violated their covenant relationship with God but also dissolved the moral bonds of obedient faith. Various translations of the condition described in Exodus 32:25 tell us that the people were unrestrained, out of control or naked when Moses returned from the mountain. They sacrificed to an idol, ate and drank excessively, and engaged in riotous dancing, perhaps in imitation of the orgiastic revelry of fertility cults.[37] Their departure from obedient faith left them outside the place of blessing. Their religious practices and their values sank to the level of the pagans around them.

Departure from covenant responsibility to God brings departure from covenant responsibility in marriage. In Leviticus worship sacrifices to God would be accompanied by fellowship meals which bonded families together. The feasts of Israel were family celebrations, times when children learned the blessings of obedient faith (Deuteronomy 6). Pagan worship was more often associated with loss of restraint in abandonment to the gods, whether in drunken orgies or even in offering children as sacrifices to idols.[38] Exodus 34:10-16 warns that a covenant relationship with God precludes any covenant relationship with followers of idols. The specific dangers mentioned are sharing in sacrifices, feasts or sexual unions. Unbelievers no

[36] Besides the idols of materialism and individualism, people today invent tame gods such as "the man upstairs" who has no recognizable attributes other than remoteness, or a doting grandfatherly god created in the image of the security blanket carried by the *Peanuts* character, Linus.

[37] It certainly was not a square dance. The ritual dancing of pagan religion was often sexually-charged if not openly orgiastic.

[38] As a vocal pro-life advocate, I must note that in our allegedly enlightened culture, many children have been sacrificed to the idols of comfort and convenience. Ancient pagans, in fact, may have taken their sacrifices more seriously, surrounding them with public ritual and ceremony, rather than considering them matters of privacy and personal choice.

longer pretend to dedicate themselves to supernatural beings, but they still tend to think that having a good time includes abandoning restraints and going out of control in indulging their appetites.[39] In I Corinthians 8 Christians are told that liberty in Christ does not mean that there is no harm in enjoying something which is identified with idolatry. Limited association with the customs and practices of paganism may lead some to compromise their identification with Christ. "Whatever is not of faith is sin (Romans 13:23)." Being sensitive to God's work in our consciences, we must avoid any appearance of evil, any act or association which may lead us or fellow Christians out of the place of blessing.

God delivers His people from the disobedience which incurred His wrath as they pursued unrestrained indulgence of their sinful desires (Ephesians 2:1-3). Turning to God involves turning away from the corruption which is in the world. In Deuteronomy 7:1-9 Moses reminds the Israelites of their covenant privileges and responsibilities. God's deliverance separates His people from the evil around them and they are to maintain the separation (verses 1-2). Intermarriage with unbelievers is forbidden because it implies acceptance of idolatry: the marriage contract would acknowledge an authority other than God (verses 3-5). Solomon's case is instructive here. Solomon was warned that if he or any king of Israel would "go and serve other gods, and worship them" Israel would be exiled from the land of blessing. In later life Solomon "loved many foreign women," and "his wives turned his heart after other gods (I Kings 9:6-7; 11:14)." God's people must not depart from their place of blessing as a treasured holy people belonging to

---

[39] The dehumanizing effects of abandoning restraints are apparent not only in the proliferation of violence and pornography in the media but also in so-called reality shows which televise the self-dehumanization of contestants. The fact that all this is considered entertainment indicates the direction the culture is taking.

God Himself. God's loving deliverance calls for a response of loving obedience (Deuteronomy 7:6-11).

The warning against an unequal yoke does not impugn the character of individuals. People without God may be admirable human beings in many respects. Even Shechem, who raped Jacob's daughter, was "more honorable than all the household of his father (Genesis 34:19)." He wanted to marry Dinah because he loved her. His father's clan had a more mercenary motive. Seeing Jacob's prosperity, they reasoned that marriage alliances would bring them a share in these riches, and would (in a pagan sense) put them in a place of blessing.

An unequal yoke creates a double-minded marriage in which one partner is loyal to God and the other is guided by other motives. A believer considers marriage a sacred union founded on a covenant relationship with God. Marriage vows, for believers, are solemnized in the presence of the God to whom they must give account, the God whose blessing is invoked upon the marriage. Unbelievers have only traditional moral notions about marriage. Their sense of responsibility to God is mere cultural religion, and no sound basis for expecting or experiencing His presence or assistance in their marriages. If they call on God, He may answer in ways which increase their "faith", but they have no covenant relationship with Him. This is the root problem of the unequal yoke. One partner is enlightened by the Holy Spirit and partakes of the hope of God's calling, God's riches and God's power (Ephesians 1:15-21). The other partner is without Christ, alienated from God's household, without hope and without God in the world (Ephesians 2:12). Rather than sharing the fullness of God's blessing in the place of obedient faith, the couple will have divided loyalties and their marriage, their possessions and their children are likely to be diverted to worldly interests rather than fully devoted to God.

The sobering truth about the dangers of an unequal yoke must be included in preaching, teaching and counseling directed towards unmarried believers. Where an unequal yoke already exists, there is still hope. Whatever remains of mutual love and respect can be channeled into problem-solving and planning. The believer's quiet witness and Christ-like character may help bring the unbelieving spouse to true faith. I always try to present God's standard as the ideal, while recognizing that the complexities of real marital situations are often far from that ideal. I strive to bring substantial healing to imperfect marriages with all the compassion and wisdom God gives me. It is impossible to bring true healing without a clear vision of what a perfectly healthy marriage would be. God's Word provides that vision. While trying to view marriage through God's eyes, it is important to remember that He looks on sinful humanity with love and grace. He knows that all of us fall far short of His glorious purposes, and He provides the only way of deliverance and growth. People who suffer the consequences of wrong choices can learn to make right choices. The best marriages are those in which right choices are made from the very beginning.

Seek Ye First

Beginning together in marriage is affected by how a couple begins together in courtship. Many couples do not start from deeply rooted connections to family, local church and community. Their courtship and marriage is not arranged (and sometimes not approved) by anyone other than themselves. They just fall in love and things progress from there. The concept of falling in love is too often almost literally true. Attraction at first sight is mistaken for love, and character flaws or irritating idiosyncrasies are overlooked for the sake of the original infatuation. People feel that being thrown together at some time of crisis forges a lasting bond between them, although they have few common interests, beliefs or goals. Sometimes the fall is gentler, as acquaintance grows into friendship and friendship deepens into serious commitment. Good marriages have, in fact, begun in each of these ways, but wise counsel would suggest a firmer foundation. Falling in love can be quite passive and irrational, something that just happens. True love balances feelings of romance, mystery and unpredictable joy with active rational thought and planning. Falling can cause serious injuries. Stepping carefully ensures a safer journey together.

Counseling married couples would be much simpler if all engaged couples were counseled wisely. Engaged couples could be counseled more easily if all individuals contemplating courtship relationships were more adequately prepared. Marriage counseling and premarital counseling are well established practices. Pastors, counselors and parents should consider putting more effort into pre-dating counsel. What people find in their mates depends on what they have learned to look for. If they have absorbed the popular ideals of their culture, they will look for what the culture values at the moment. If they have been taught biblical criteria of character, they will look for qualities of lasting value.

In an individualistic culture the idea of an arranged marriage seems regressive and oppressive. The chilling days of yesteryear when everybody married who they were supposed to marry are gone forever. Men and women think for themselves now and make up their own minds. This elevation of individual choice has been called autonomy, which has the root meaning, "self-law." While it is true that no man or woman should be in absolute subjection to any mere man or woman, being a law unto ourselves has always had its drawbacks. The roller coaster moral chaos depicted in the book of Judges has a simple explanation and epitaph. There was no authoritative moral guidance, and everyone "did what was right in his own eyes (Judges 17:6; 21:25)."

What is right in the eyes of an individualistic culture is portrayed in its heroes. Films, television shows, news reports and stories swapped among friends paint a picture. The ideal man, the real man, has several identifying characteristics:

An impressive record. This gifted man can list abilities and achievements far beyond the capacity of most mere mortals.

Dynamic motivation. This man of action knows what he wants and how to get it quickly.

Strong self-image. This self-confident man knows what he is worth and demands the recognition and rewards he deserves.

Street smarts. This clever man looks out for himself, aggressively exposing frauds and putting con artists in their place.

A string of conquests. This man is a winner whose strength and shrewdness have overcome many obstacles and opponents.

These characteristics are admired in both men and women because they are perceived as necessary for successful living and personal advancement. The stories people tell about themselves often portray them as possessing these qualities. Lists of credentials and accomplishments are coupled with anecdotes which show how shrewdly they maneuver through life, their unconquerable selves emerging victorious from every conflict.

Two questions arise concerning cultural and biblical standards for personhood and marriage. Within a culture which exalts the autonomous individual, how can a man who is a law unto himself and a woman who is a law unto herself make a binding commitment to each other while retaining their autonomy as individuals? If biblical standards for marriage are respected, how can a self-made man or a self-made woman admit the need for a suitable helper or sacrifice personal rights and interests for the good of a partner? In fact, the individualistic mindset which gives rise to such questions is the very mindset behind many marriage problems. If people think God was wrong when He said Adam's isolated individuality was not good, they will have difficulty with His plan for connectedness in society and oneness in marriage.

What is right in God's eyes challenges human cultural ideals and transcends every cultural mandate. God's character, the character He wants to see in men and women, is revealed in Jesus Christ. His plan for humanity, including His plan for marriage, is grounded in love.[40] God the Father loved the world and sent His Son (John 3:16). God the Son brought the love shared within the Trinity into human relationships (John 15:9). God the Holy Spirit implants this divine love within the hearts of those who will receive it (Romans 5:5). In Christians, love can be an expression of the character of Jesus Christ. What does this love look like? Its characteristics contrast sharply with the cultural model of the autonomous man or woman. Aspects of love described in I Corinthians 13 indicate the shortcomings of the cultural ideal:

An impressive record is worthless if gifts have been used to bring glory to self rather than to help others (I Corinthians 13:1-3).

Dynamic motivation can be tainted with impatience, envy and arrogance (I Corinthians 13:4).

A strong self-image might make a person inconsiderate, irritable and suspicious (I Corinthians 13:5).

Street smarts can compromise morality and honesty (I Corinthians 13:6).

A string of conquests may be the mark of a bully. True victory in life is measured not by whom we beat but by who we become (I Corinthians 13:7). There will be no regrets over how we treated people or over how we finished.[41]

---

[40] People keep using the word "love" although it may not mean what they think it means. Ed Wheat distinguished "The Five Ways of Loving" as desire, romance, affection, friendship and the unconditional love empowered by God. Each way of loving should be evident in a marriage. (Ed Wheat, M.D. *Love-Life*, Zondervan, 1980, pp.57-66)

[41] My father and coach used to say, "Win without boasting and lose without excuses." My friend Bob says, "The best part of life is having few regrets."

The description of love in I Corinthians 13 delineates the character of Jesus Christ, the character God wants to see in all humanity. What should a man or woman look for in a mate? The biblical answer can be reduced to one word: Jesus. If a person embodies the character of Jesus, the love which proves God's presence in the world (John 13:35; 17:21), then marriage will be an excellent opportunity to demonstrate God's love in all the dimensions of human life.[42] God does not isolate His people from common human troubles. He demonstrates His presence and power in the loving ways His people handle the challenges of life. A man who loves his wife as Christ loves the Church will nurture and care for her, valuing her advancement more than his own (Ephesians 5:25-27). A woman of godly virtue will devote herself to the welfare of her husband and family (Proverbs 31:10-31). Life together becomes a contest to see who can out-please the other, and marriage becomes fun.

Conformity to Christ does not produce uniformity. Variety is the strength of the Church and of the richest friendships and marriages. The Bible recognizes the most basic distinction God built into humanity: "male and female created He them (Genesis 2:25)." A one-flesh one-mind union of a man and a woman does not diminish their distinct needs and responsibilities. God brought Eve to Adam because it was not good for the man to be alone. A sense of connectedness not only relieved Adam's aloneness, it also created his responsibility for Eve's welfare and fulfillment. He could not live a life of arrogant self-sufficiency, but would have to accept help from his wife and

---

[42] Theologians have pointed out that one of the purposes of the incarnation of God the Son was to "fulfill all righteousness," not only in the sense of perfect obedience to the law but also in demonstrating the perfect love which is the object of both law and grace. In the person of Jesus Christ, God Himself lived a human life of perfect obedience and love. Believers rightly emphasize the death, resurrection and intercession of Christ as the essentials of Christian faith, but must not neglect the fact that Jesus also provided a living human example of loving service and patient endurance (John 13:15; I Peter 2:21). The Man who is divine is also the God who became human.

care for her needs. Eve was deceived by Satan and overstepped the bounds of her role as Adam's helper. Adam chose to disobey God's direct command. After they had sinned, God said to Eve, "Thy desire shall be to thy husband, and he shall rule over thee." God told Adam, "in the sweat of thy face shalt thou eat bread (Genesis 3:16, 19)." Adam's work would be more arduous and Eve's attachment to him would subdue her. Distinctions which God decreed and created cannot be obliterated by human debate. Men and women have different needs and responsibilities.

A few generations ago, there was a general consensus regarding the different needs and responsibilities of men and women. Nothing has changed in the most basic distinctions between the sexes. God still forms male and female human beings according to His original pattern. What has changed is not in the physiological differences between males and females, but in the technological and sociological contexts in which they live.

The Industrial Revolution took manufacturing out of the home or family shop and into the factory. Men followed first and the exigencies of World War II accelerated the movement of women into the wage-earning work force. The concept of careers for both men and women being separate from household roles was an innovation with serious implications for the cultural ideals of marriage and the family. God's plan did not change; cultural perceptions changed. As it became apparent that a woman was often "the best man" for the job, barriers to newly aware "career women" were removed or broken through.

Issues of sexual equality in careers outside the home do not diminish the life-defining differences God builds into males and females. Theologians debate biblical role distinctions between men and women, but what the Bible says about roles is based on what the Bible assumes about more basic differences. God created humanity as male and female for good reason. There may be controversy over details, but the words "masculine" and "feminine" still have meaning. Those who wish to move beyond masculine and feminine into an androgynous homogenization of sexuality cannot get past the one difference which is at the heart of all the other differences between men and women. Women bear children.

Defending motherhood has become a radical thing to do—child-bearing is the last battlefield of the war to merge the sexes. God gave Adam and Eve the power of choice, and they chose wrong at the first opportunity. Now women are insisting on the power of choice in the last area in which they think God restricts them. It was not good for Adam and Eve to be alone any more than it was for Adam to be without Eve. God told them to multiply—their sexual compatibility was designed to be productive as well as pleasurable. Women who want to discard the privileges and responsibilities of child-bearing in favor of personal freedom miss the whole point of God's plan for human connectedness.

Child-bearing is the first and final distinction between men and women, and the root of many other differences. Pregnancy and nursing limit a woman's mobility—in tribal cultures men would do most of the hunting and gathering while women stayed home with the babies.[43] Nurturing their children, they had a vested interest in peace, safety and a stable society. Men could be adventurous risk-takers, even without the macho after-shave, but women needed security, and guarded their homes (Titus 2:5). The biblical teachings about the roles of husbands and wives are not arbitrary; they reflect the way things work when motherhood is given its true value.

Allowing for differences of culture and personality, women have three basic needs. First, they need security

---

[43] Some have suggested that these stay-at-home moms discovered and developed agriculture as they learned to cultivate seeds discarded from gathered foods.

emotionally, financially and geographically. Exemplary women of the Bible sought stability and a secure future for themselves and their families. The story of Ruth shows how God provides security for a woman who trusts him to supply her needs.[44] Beyond basic security, women need affection: regular loving touches, snuggling and cuddling as well as specific sexual contact. The Song of Solomon is filled with references to physical attraction and affection within marriage. Besides receiving security and affection, a woman needs to know she is needed. She needs to know that she is essential to her husband's life and well-being, a helper whose input and support are appreciated. Nabal did not appreciate his wife Abigail's wise counsel, and his foolishness cost him his life as well as his wife (I Samuel 25).

A woman needs security, affection and essentiality: a man needs respect, support and admiration. Since the fall, a man's prideful urge to conquer challenges by himself must be tempered by recognition of his need for his wife's help. Her first job is to show him respect. A wife who expects her husband to be the spiritual leader of the home will help him to grow into his responsibility. As a man exercises leadership, his wife will support his decisions with wise input and kind encouragement. Her loyalty and faithfulness will build his confidence and

---

[44] The vow in Ruth 1:16-17 is among the most radical statements in Scripture. Naomi's husband had left the place of blessing seeking greener pastures. His sons married pagan women. After her husband and sons had died, Naomi prepared to return to Israel. Ruth's vow is more than a commitment of loyalty to Naomi: it is a statement of faith. "Thy people shall be my people and thy God my God." She is renouncing her pagan heritage to join the household of the only true God. She demonstrates her faith by giving up the security of familiar surroundings to entrust herself totally to God's care. Her faith was honored by her marriage to Boaz and her inclusion in the genealogy of Jesus (see Matthew 1:5). Ruth's native people, the Moabites, traced their origins to a girl who committed incest with her father after getting him drunk (Genesis 19:31-38). The Moabites tried to get Balaam to curse Israel, and when he could not, they followed his counsel to lead Israel into immorality and idolatry (Numbers 22-25). A girl raised as a Moabite would be as far from the true God as anyone on earth at that time. Ruth's faith brought her out of that background to inclusion among God's people, marriage to a responsible man and a place in biblical history.

increase his sense of responsibility for the family's welfare. A woman who helps her husband grow in character, leadership and responsible behavior will frequently express her admiration for him. A man needs to be assured of his personal significance.

These basic needs are neither selfish desires nor signs of incompetence. God brought Adam and Eve together to bring connectedness and balance to the human race. As finite beings, a husband and wife accept and supplement each other's limitations and admit their own. Their connectedness is a model of the mutual ministry of diversely gifted believers in the Church and of the complementary social roles within a culture. The need for a suitable helper existed and was provided for before the fall.

Many Christian writers assume the validity of a whole list of perceived needs which are created by human cultural trends and have no basis in Scripture. With no biblical grounds for defining these needs, suggestions for meeting them are necessarily speculative and uncertain. Those who take this approach may be politically correct, but they are biblically incorrect, much like those who look at grief as a mental and emotional process rather than as the loss of a person.[45]

When the first pair sinned, their relationship changed. The positive aspects of connectedness remained. Adam and Eve maintained their mutually supportive roles. With the entrance of sin, their relationship took on negative aspects. Their basic needs became non-negotiable demands. The bitter root motivation of sin is to be as gods, to have unlimited power and authority, to be

---

[45] The Bible recognizes periods of "grievous mourning (Genesis 50:13)," weeks or months of dealing with the trauma of bereavement. The initial shock diminishes and mourners are able to rejoin society, but the reality of the loss remains. To be bereft is to be robbed of something essential, to have a precious treasure snatched away. Nigerians say of missed appointments, "I met your absence." Gordon Puls has said of his daughter Michele, "We're content with where she is. Our problem is with where she isn't." Meeting a loved one's absence extends beyond the first pangs of loss, and moments of intense memory can trigger the deepest levels of grief.

absolutely autonomous. To mitigate the damage such selfishness would cause, God adjusted the roles of husband and wife to fit the new situation. The man's desire for achievement would be checked by obstacles to easy success. The woman's desire for control would be challenged by man's dominance.

These modified marital roles are subject to abuse unless both husband and wife will accept and adhere to God's standards for marriage. The marriage covenant binds the couple together for life. They vow that nothing but death will separate them. They share a one-flesh union which comprehensively fulfills their sexual needs. Growing into a one-mind union restrains their competitive desires. Marriage is not a give-and-take contract between two autonomous individuals. It is a covenant commitment of two individuals to give themselves freely and completely to deepening oneness with each other.

A Christian marriage is a basic unit of fellowship in Christ as well as the basic unit of human society. Expressing Christ-like love within marriage shows the world the reality of God's presence and assistance. People will be attracted to Christ as they see His love in action. In a Christian marriage, God's love is enacted in unwavering commitment to the responsibilities of the relationship, upholding a vow to maintain the conditions of the marriage covenant. In a Christian marriage, sinful selfishness is set aside, legitimate human needs are met and both husband and wife grow in conformity to the character of Jesus Christ.

If Jesus is the standard for biblical character, a person cannot have the fullness of such character without having Jesus. The admonition against an unequal yoke (II Corinthians 6:14) is often invoked negatively to warn against marriage between a believer and an unbeliever. Light has no fellowship with darkness. As someone has said, "If you marry a child of the devil, you'll have in-law problems." A Christian who marries an unbeliever violates a fundamental command. Even dating an unbeliever raises the risk that the heart will overrule the head and the relationship will go where complete devotion to God cannot follow. Any hope of serving the Lord will be diminished by the reality of serving an ungodly partner.

On the positive side, the advantage of believers marrying believers is that Christ Himself is at the center of the marriage and both husband and wife are empowered by the Holy Spirit to share the love of God as the basis of their love for each other. It is possible to have a good marriage on the human-to-human level, but it is humanly impossible to have the full riches of a God-designed marriage without God. Believers have the Spirit of God to lead them in the way of God's truth as they grow day by day into conformity to the character of Christ.

This divine dimension is especially significant in the role of the husband. Husbands are to emulate the Lord Jesus Christ. They are to love their wives as Christ loved the Church and gave Himself for it (Ephesians 6:25). This cannot be done adequately by the natural human spirit. Some pagan husbands and fathers do a remarkably good job in their roles, but without divine empowerment the job cannot be accomplished at the highest level of God's plan. The key for the husband is Christ.

How did Christ love the Church? Christ so loved His people that He died in their place while they were at war with Him (Romans 5:8). He became the Savior of the Body of Christ. Therefore, a Christ-like husband will always put his wife and her interests first. Her welfare will be his primary concern, her comfort his greatest pleasure, her desires his highest goals and her protection his most urgent duty. He will seek to make her the most fulfilled person on the planet. A husband's love will be measured by what he is willing to give up for his wife, the time, energy and focus he gives her. He will give her abundant encouragement, tenderness and patience. A Christ-like husband will desire to provide whatever his wife needs or wants, whatever the cost to himself may be. His spiritual leadership will give her energy, confidence and hope for the future. She will be secure in the knowledge that he will never leave her or forsake her, but will always be at her side to provide security and affection and to assure her that she is important to him.

Leaving and forsaking are the logical consequences of autonomy, and, in their various forms, the causes of many marriage problems. A focus on individuality overshadows loyalty and oneness in marriage, and the self-actualizing individuals go their separate ways. Leaving and forsaking are different dimensions of abandonment. Leaving a spouse means maintaining physical distance with or without legal action to dissolve the marriage. Forsaking may include turning away, rejecting, withdrawing support or even opposing. As mental and emotional unfaithfulness precedes physical adultery, mental and emotional forsaking precedes physical leaving. A marriage can be chilled by lack of communication, sexual coldness, negative attitudes, selfishness and hostility long before physical separation.

Assurance that a spouse will not withdraw companionship or support establishes the basic trust needed to grow together in a one-flesh one-mind bond. When God said He would never leave or forsake His own (Deuteronomy 31:6; Hebrews 13:5), He assured them that His presence and assistance would secure their future. God's people can say confidently, "If God be for us who can be against us? The Lord is our helper, and we will not fear (Romans 8:31; Hebrews 13:6)." A relationship with God is not established through sporadic miraculous signs or dramatic divine interventions, nor is a marriage built on occasional exotic vacations or expensive gifts without day by day compassion and care. God's Word is His side of a living conversation with those who know Him, just as marriage is meant to be a lifelong conversation between best friends. When two believers marry, their ever-deepening conversation with God and with each other binds them together.

The love of God shed abroad in their hearts unites them in a shared life which puts the concepts of leaving and forsaking far from their thoughts.

It is crucial to remember that a relationship with God is a covenant relationship. Those who turn to God in response to His voice are assured that He will not forsake them and that their trials will not destroy them, because He "will not forget the covenant which He swore (Deuteronomy 4:30-31)." To give His people full confidence, God confirmed His promises to them with an oath, pledging Himself and His blessings to the household of faith (Hebrews 6:13-14). God commits Himself to be present to protect and to nurture His own. A relationship with God is a covenant relationship established by His vow.

Marriage is also a covenant relationship entered by vow. The vow guarantees commitment to the covenant which establishes the conditions of the relationship. The moral force of the vow and the legal force of the covenant confirm the permanence of the relationship. The quality of the relationship depends on but is not limited to adherence to the conditions of the covenant. Marriage vows express commitment to each other in both attitudes and actions. Upholding these vows by living according to the marriage covenant requires character and conduct which will build the marriage relationship.

The character of Jesus Christ, His incarnation of the love of God, is the standard for fleshing out Christ-like love within marriage. Jesus displayed this love in all of His contacts with people. He was always concerned with the welfare of those around Him, with their comfort and safety. He fed the five thousand rather than sending them away to fend for themselves. He helped Peter pay his taxes, and cooked breakfast for His disciples after they had worked hard all night. From the cross He told John to take care of Mary as he would care for his own mother. He always attended to anyone in need, supplying what they lacked and offering encouragement. He used every opportunity to share spiritual truth in the simplest, most effective ways. His constant focus was the spiritual growth of everyone he met. The things which angered Him were teachings which led people astray and practices which encumbered or displaced true worship and fellowship.

Husbands are to follow the example of Jesus Christ as the spiritual leaders of their homes. This leadership is expressed in service, giving up one's rights and self-interest for the good of others (Matthew 20:25-28). It involves a deepening understanding of one's wife, recognition of her specific needs and respect for her equal position in Christ (I Peter 3:7). I Peter 3:5-6 suggests that submission to a Christ-like husband protects a wife from fear and terror, possibly implying that fear and terror are possible characteristics of a marriage to an ungodly spouse. The Christ-like husband knows his wife thoroughly and provides the security she needs. Husband and wife live together quietly and peaceably, growing in conformity to Christ and trusting each other completely.

The demonstration of God's love in a Christian marriage removes the fear of being left and the terror of being forsaken. A commitment to never leave is a promise to stand faithfully together no matter what challenges or distractions may come. A commitment to never forsake is a determination to focus attention and resources on service to each other no matter what personal sacrifice may be required. The husband's leadership in the family spiritually is similar to all competent leadership and is characterized by the development of a certain capacity to tolerate a reasonable expectation of failure based on the individuality, nature, and maturity of the person in front of them; nothing is perfect or works perfectly in a fallen world.

The ideal for a wife is Christ-like character expressed in building up and defending her husband and her home. We do not live in an age when husbands and wives share tasks in a self-sufficient household which neither of them leaves for outside employment, or in an age when men compete in the work-a-day world while women stay home to bake cookies and mop floors. The Bible does not teach either of these models as the necessary pattern of marriage. The virtuous woman of Proverbs 31:10-31 is fully engaged in the family's dealings with the world as well as in its internal workings. Her husband, to be sure, has a position of leadership in the community (verse 23), but as keeper of her home (Titus 2:5) she has a full range of private and public activity.

The virtuous wife is priceless in her service to her husband, her family and her community. She is trustworthy and good-hearted, putting time, effort and careful thought into her work. She prepares food and clothing for her husband and children, purchases real estate for purposeful use,[46] provides goods for her family and for the poor and proclaims wisdom and kindness in all her conversations. She is rewarded for her ministry with both private and public praise.

The logical connection between a wife who builds and guards the home and a husband who is respected as a man among men must not be glossed over. When one man was asked to consider serving as a church elder, he said he would talk it over with his wife. His pastor said, "Oh, this has nothing to do with her." The qualifications for church leadership in I Timothy 3:1-13 and Titus 1:5-9 have everything to do with relationships within the home, specifically the oneness of husband and wife. Ideally, a Christian husband and wife will be united in ministry at home, in the church and in the world.

What should a person look for in a mate? For believers the clear answer is someone who is growing in conformity to the character of Jesus Christ, someone whose covenant relationship with God can support and nourish the covenant relationship of

---

[46] I have taken this reference seriously, and advise wives to get real estate licenses. One couple profited greatly through the wife's wise real estate dealings while her husband was in seminary. Many others have told me of similar blessings from taking this qualification of a virtuous woman literally.

marriage. Christ-like character is not only what to look for in a mate, but also what to be like to attract a mate. Relationship with God is the strongest possible foundation for relationship with a spouse.

In marriage counseling, I remind couples of God's plan for marriage and help them move from where they are in their struggles to where God wants them to be in His plan. As I counsel engaged couples, my goal is to prepare them for the biblical roles and responsibilities of husband and wife. I encourage pastors, counselors, teachers and parents to teach and preach God's standards for marriage to unattached young people so that they will have a clear understanding of what to look for in a mate, or even a date. Finding the right mate starts with being the right mate, being marriage material biblically by correct thinking, excellent behavior and choices made throughout the earliest years, up to and including marriage.

A Man or Woman in Christ

When counseling unmarried Christians, whether younger or older, I remind them to trust God to bring each of them the person He has especially prepared to be his or her helper. I believe there are an equal number of marriageable Christian men and marriageable Christian women in the world. The geographical distribution may be uneven but God can take care of that. Choosing one person out of billions of people can be a mind-boggling task, especially when considering the spiritual effects this decision can have for time and for eternity. God will give wisdom to those who ask (James 1:5) and He honors those who honor Him (Proverbs 1:7; 2:1-11). Part of the wisdom God gives concerns the elements of Christ-like character which will be present and growing in a suitable Christian mate.

Right beliefs provide the entrance into a relationship with God which makes Christ-like character possible. How people behave depends on what people believe. Those who profess to believe nothing still have basic assumptions which influence their actions. Those whose basic assumptions are wrong will not act rightly. Christians may differ from one another on many secondary matters but their core beliefs about how a righteous God relates to sinful humanity unite them. Biblical Christianity finds the truth about God, humanity and spiritual reality in the Bible's message of salvation through faith in the Lord Jesus Christ. Those who reject this message are subject to the errors of their own imaginations and to the lies of Satan.

I John 4:1-6 say that the Spirit of God, the Spirit of truth, proclaims that Jesus Christ came in the flesh and that those who receive this message are released from the spirit of error which deceives the world. Believing that God's salvation has come through the death and resurrection of God the Son in human flesh is the essence of Christian faith. The living Word became flesh and dwelt among humans so that His death for their sin could break the power of sin and death (John 1:14; Hebrews 2:14-18). The place of God's presence and blessing is in Jesus Christ, the only human who lived in perfect obedience, God the Son who brought grace and truth to humanity, the God-man who bore human sin in His death and now offers believers His resurrection power to live lives of righteousness.

The place where God now meets His people is in Jesus Christ. Meeting the God of the Bible in Jesus Christ brings a person into spiritual reality. Jesus is the way to God, the truth which sets free and the life which energizes His people (John 14:6). Faith in Jesus Christ brings rich blessing to believers. Rejection of Jesus Christ leaves people living by their own false assumptions, walking in a way that leads to destruction, dead in their sins. The Holy Spirit guides believers into the truth and stabilizes them with power, love and a sound mind (John 16:12-15; II Timothy 1:7). The power to enact God's plan, the love to enrich other people and a sound mind which rejoices in the truth: these are the foundations of conformity to the character of Jesus Christ.

A Christian's devotion to Christ will be evident in attitudes and actions. Knowing Jesus Christ means more than agreeing with a sermon or a tract which presents the Gospel in a few words. Knowing Jesus Christ may begin with a simple prayer of faith, but it grows throughout a life of deepening understanding of the implications of that faith. Faith in Jesus Christ is a way of life, not just a way into life. Everything a person has assumed about life must be questioned and corrected in light of this new relationship with God. All other relationships will be seen from a new perspective.

A person who seeks to stand where Christ stands will see as Christ sees and will act as Christ acts. As new creatures in Christ believers will be concerned about the spiritual condition of those around them and will seek to present Christ to them. Conscious of their part in Christ's ministry of reconciliation, they will give His interests higher priority than their own (II Corinthians 5:16-21). The contrast between worldly wisdom and God's wisdom sets believers apart (II Corinthians 6:16-18). Their renewed minds transform them into people who display the richness of God's plan (Romans 12:1-2). Personal ambition and achievement will be subservient to a desire to know and serve Christ better (Philippians 3:7-16). As followers of God believers growing in conformity to Christ will forsake all forms of sin in thought, speech, and action. They will find contentment in lives of self-sacrifice and thanksgiving (Ephesians 4:10-5:20). Devotion to Christ reorders a believer's life as obedient faith responds to God's plan.

A person devoted to Christ will have right priorities. In a culture where many people assume that the meaning of life is found in money, pleasure and popularity, conformity to Christ creates radicals. If God is in control and only what is done for

Christ has eternal value, life is no longer a mad dash for the finish line. He who dies with the most toys does, after all, die. Riding in a stretch Hummer or driving a Ferrari does not change where the road ends. A believer recognizes that material wealth and worldly accomplishments are temporary, destined for destruction (Ecclesiastes 2:1-11; I John 2:15-17; James 1:9-11).[47]

We are who we are and we have what we have in order to serve others, not to please ourselves (Ecclesiastes 5:8-17; II Corinthians 9:6-9). Some people who admit that money cannot buy happiness use it to buy everything else, as if "living large" could compensate for inner emptiness. Many who live large die very small.[48]

A celebrated promoter had a waterfront mansion built for millions of dollars. Before it was finished he bought land next to it and began construction of another one. Another mansion-dweller had a problem when he was placed under house arrest and the range of the transmitter in his ankle bracelet did not allow him to walk through his whole house.[49] When the billionaire, John D. Rockefeller, was asked, "How much is enough?" he supposedly replied, "Just a little more." It is better to live in simplicity and contentment than to pursue an insatiable desire for riches, excitement and fame. God will supply what His people need as they pursue His purposes (Matthew 6:25-34). Believers are transformed into instruments of God's will rather than being conformed to the culture around them. God's presence and assistance bring true contentment. Nothing else can.

---

[47] See "Ash Heap Lives," in Francis Schaeffer's book of sermons, *No Little People, No Little Places*. After hearing this sermon, I made a habit of going to the dump with my son Jacob each year to see what people work all their lives for. I would say, "Son, don't live for the ash heap, live for Christ and His Kingdom." Jacob is now on the mission field.

[48] "Fifty years have passed since first I was Caliph. Riches, honors, pleasures – I have enjoyed all. In this long time of seeming happiness I have numbered the days on which I have been happy – fourteen!" – Last words of Caliph Abd-er-Rahman III (961 A.D.) Sultan of Spain

[49] He might have fared better if he had been given the range of "a Sabbath-day's journey," about one thousand yards, the prescribed distance a Jew could travel on the Sabbath. The legalistic Pharisees would have delighted in

monitoring ankle bracelets every Sabbath day.

Contentment is at the center of the inward beauty of Christ-like character (I Timothy 6:1). In a culture which worships narrowly defined images of ideal humanity, many people value jogging over Jesus and Botox over the Bible. A company which supplies uniforms to service workers is called "Image First," an apt term for a popular attitude. Personal hygiene and appropriate clothing are as necessary for Christians as for anyone else, but obsession with a perfect face and a perfect body in brand-name packaging makes it clear why celebrities are called idols and fans could be called fanatics.

Good appearances can be deceptive but internal goodness pleases God (I Samuel 16:7). A six-year-old girl told her dad that one of the boys in her class said he liked her, "But he doesn't really know me. I think he just likes what I look like." More than one young man who has dated girls because he liked what they looked like has wisely realized that the other girl, the one with "a great personality," was really the most beautiful. External beauty may be attractive, but it cannot hide a lack of internal beauty (Proverbs 11:22). Many women and men who spend large proportions of their income and hours of their time to get the right look have invested absolutely nothing in the development of their souls. Getting one's look right is an empty pursuit compared with getting one's soul right.[50]

Among Christians, there has been renewed interest in spiritual disciplines, programs of Bible-reading, prayer and meditation designed to develop the soul. The most effective of these simply supply a framework for biblical principles of discipleship which have always been implied in a full response to the Gospel. Knowing Jesus Christ is meant to change lives from the inside out as the beauty of His character is worked into the believer's personality.

---

[50] Mrs. Wheat used to say; "If a girl at sixteen is not beautiful, it isn't her fault, but if she isn't beautiful at sixty; it is her fault"!

The inner beauty of goodness and discretion produces praiseworthy service, as illustrated in the description of a virtuous woman in Proverbs 31. The truly beautiful person is the person whose inner character is expressed in ministry which brings beauty to the lives of others. True beauty is not the decoration of the external but the development of the internal.

Honesty is among the most appreciated facets of inward beauty. Given open access to God in Jesus Christ, Christians have nothing to hide. Their inner motives as well as their outer actions are all known to God and constantly cleansed by the blood of Jesus. They know that no secret sin can be hidden from Him. Even in the world, the truth eventually comes out. Some of the most pitiable members of the human race are those who live with the illusion that they can fool enough of the people enough of the time to get what they want. Disregarding the fact that what they want is also an illusion, their deceptiveness hardly fools anyone but themselves.

Total truthfulness may seem as undesirable as it is rare, but lies are deadly. As a young woman, Iris hardly knew what to ask for in a husband, so she prayed only that he would be honest. God brought her John, who was all she had asked for. She was often embarrassed by his candor. Yet everyone John met was challenged by his truthfulness, and many came to the truth as it is in Jesus through his ministry.[51]

God Himself acts according to the truth, rejecting all lies (Proverbs 12:22). Satan works through lies, rejecting God's truth (John 8:44). Most of Satan's lies are not direct contradictions of the truth. They are distortions, deviations and deflections designed to create doubt and indecision. "Did God really say that? He couldn't have really meant it that way. What do you think He was really trying to say? What was He really

---

[51] Another woman, after relationship failures, prayed in desperation "Lord, give me a good man." God answered that prayer with a good man, named Mr. Goode.

thinking?" This is the line of reasoning the serpent used in deceiving Eve (Genesis 3:1-7).

Jesus came to proclaim the truth which liberates all who receive it (John 8:31). Those who abide in Christ speak the truth in love (Ephesians 4:15). Those who depart from God speak lies in hypocrisy (I Timothy 4:2). Those who are indwelt by the Holy Spirit are good, righteous and truthful (Ephesians 5:9). A truthful person is a faithful person.

Self-control is another evidence that the Holy Spirit is working in a believer (Galatians 5:23). A believer controlled by the Holy Spirit will not come under the control of anything else (Ephesians 5:18). Addiction to drugs, alcohol, sex, work or recreation destroys the capacity to act responsibly in building relationships. Leadership in the home or in the Church requires friendliness, respect for others, thoughtfulness, righteousness, holiness and self-control. Self-control balances and directs a person's good traits and restrains unproductive or sinful impulses.

Responsible relationships grow when self is controlled and others are served. Relationships are destroyed when the goal is to control others and serve oneself. Believers are not to be selfish, short-tempered, greedy or pleasure-seeking (Titus 1:6-9). Lack of self-control unleashes impulsive speech and action which spreads disorder and disunion. The balanced character of a Christ-like Christian brings stability to personal life, to families and to churches (I Timothy 3:1-5). Self-control makes balanced character possible by resisting any distractions from the goal of greater conformity to Christ.

Self-control includes sexual purity. Honesty, contentment and self-control preclude any unfaithfulness, promiscuity or lustful schemes or fantasies (Romans 13:13-14). It may seem naïve to expect both males and females to maintain virginity until marriage, but that is God's standard. In I Thessalonians 4:2-5, fornication (all forms of sexual indulgence outside marriage) is contrasted with honorable use of one's "vessel" — the body, the genitals, or a spouse.

Sexual purity is not merely abstention from specific physical acts, but a purity of heart, speech and behavior in regard to sex. Ephesians 5:3-4 says that sexual impurity should not be a topic of conversation and that all obscenity (gestures, behavior, appearance, actions, words, entertainment) should be avoided. Romans 1:32 has a pointed message to believers with television sets, computers, and phones. God's judgment is against those who are entertained by the sins of others as well as those who actually commit the sins. In Psalm 101:2-3 a wise walk with God includes what goes on in a believer's house. Keeping the heart pure requires a commitment to quit putting worthless, wicked, ruinous images before our eyes. Naughty pleasures of the visual media are, in fact, ungodly evils. In the ancient world there was far less opportunity for vicarious rape, seduction and perversity.

The so-called sexual revolution of an earlier generation did not liberate sexuality, but demeaned it. Portraying sex as a bodily function to be performed at will with or without a consenting partner removes the glory of a one-flesh covenant union. When the glory has departed, sex is emptied of its significance for human connectedness. Sexuality becomes a weapon of conquest or control rather than a gift of affection and trust. As depicted in much of what passes for humor and entertainment, sexuality has been reduced to depersonalized lust.

A biblical view of the place, purpose and pleasure of sex makes it an expression of the whole-person whole-life oneness of covenant marriage. Sexuality can be expressed freely and fully only within marriage. It is an honorable gift from God which must not be tarnished by misuse or abuse (Hebrews 13:4). Physical pleasure, affectionate companionship and faithful love give sex within marriage a context of lifelong exploration and enjoyment of each other (Proverbs 5:15-19; Song of Solomon).

Sexual purity is a matter of constant vigilance in a culture obsessed with sexual impurity. People without dark pasts are more likely to have bright futures. The grace of God which forgives sin is equally powerful in preserving from sin. Believers who are growing in Christ will consider sexual purity a valued treasure in them and in prospective spouses.

A loving attitude will permeate all of a believer's relationships. The love Christians share is the mark which proves their union with God in Christ (John 13:35). The primary evidence of the Holy Spirit's indwelling is that the believer is characterized by love rather than by sin (Galatians 5:19-26). Conformity to Christ develops inner qualities which are expressed in actions and relationships. Love is more than a feeling of attraction or affection. It is the motivating force behind patterns of action which benefit others. A loving attitude is a mindset which values and elevates other people. The inward beauty of devotion to Christ brings honesty, self-control and purity into relationships.

The love produced by the Holy Spirit is an unselfish concern for others. It is demonstrated in the character qualities listed in Galatians 5:22-23. These are not just internal perfections, but the effects that a Christ-like character produces in relationships. A loving attitude brings joy to others. A conscience at peace with God creates an atmosphere of security and tranquility. Patience, perseverance and forbearance ensure commitment and constancy in relationships. Moral goodness is expressed in courtesy and consideration for the needs of others. A kind person is characterized by tenderness and a readiness to do good. Love acts gently, in a calm, balanced attitude of true humility. The love of God brings moderation in all things, the self-control which manifests the Holy Spirit's control. Sacrificial love among believers contrasts sharply with worldly selfishness, even while enduring ridicule and persecution (I John 3:11-20).

This loving attitude will be noticeable in a good relationship with parents. God will bless children who are a blessing to their parents (Ephesians 6:1-3). Parents are responsible to give their children loving care, training and correction. In return, children should give their parents respect, obedience and affection. Children are God's gifts to parents and should bring them joy and satisfaction. A household established in obedient faith will be a household in which family relationships are harmonious and productive, passing the peace of God from generation to generation.[52]

Broken relationships between parents and children call forth the wrath of God (Malachi 4:6; Romans 1:30). Stubborn rebellious children become stubborn rebellious adults.[53] The way we treat the people we live with in youth sets the pattern for the way we treat the people we live with as adults (Deuteronomy 21:18-20). A young person will be affected by the example of his or her parents and will carry patterns of interaction from the childhood home into the home established with a spouse. Common wisdom advises a young woman to consider well how a young man treats his mother. Young men should be equally observant of the pattern of relationships in families they might want to join.

Although parents are fallible at best, a Christian child will show due respect for their roles and display Christ-like responses to them. Ideally, parents will enjoy raising children who become their close friends as adults. Jesus set the pattern

---

[52] There are only two heritages we leave to our children: a spiritual heritage and a financial one. Both are spoken of in the Bible and are important, but the financial without the spiritual is a disaster.

[53] It has been my observation that at whatever age a child rebels against parents, he or she remains emotionally that age throughout life, or until he or she repents.

for believers, accepting the parental authority of Mary and Joseph as He grew in favor with God and men (Luke 2:51-52).

Willingness to serve is a primary element of character which finds favor with God. As Jesus washed the feet of His disciples He told them they should follow His example of humble service (John 13:1-17). God the Son set aside His glory to become a servant, becoming flesh to dwell among humans. He submitted to the humiliation of ridicule, abuse and crucifixion (John 1:14; Philippians 2:5-8). Believers are told to have the same mindset, the same servant mentality. They must not compete for recognition, but should set aside self-serving ambition and serve the least of their brothers and sisters (Romans 12:9-16).

The ministry of reconciliation to which believers are called is primarily about reconciliation to God, but being reconciled to God brings the responsibility to carry out the implications of this new relationship. Whenever we can bring reconciliation and restoration into the lives of troubled people, we are following God's plan and Christ's example. More than a good work ethic, a willingness to serve is motivated by gratitude to God and compassion for people.

Conformity to the character of Christ involves the realization that just as Jesus Christ did not come into the world to be treated royally, believers are not here to be pampered and entertained. Like Him, His followers are here to serve and to dedicate their lives to bringing God's blessings to others. Acts of common courtesy and kindness will characterize a person who is willing to serve others. Young men and women should observe how their dates treat the people around them. Are they helpful, encouraging and ready to go the extra mile?[54] Are

---

[54] The "extra mile" is an interesting concept. Any Roman soldier traveling through Jerusalem could command any boy 12 years of age or older to carry his pack and equipment one mile or face death for refusal. The Jews hated them for that burden. Jesus, without questioning the authority of the Romans, indicates that the first mile is an obligation, but going the second mile is an opportunity to demonstrate and share one's faith in the ultimate authority of God (Matthew 5:41).

they sensitive to needs and creative in meeting them? Is their conversation uplifting and optimistic? Willingness to serve will find ways to express itself in positive speech and action.

A Christ-like believer will have a strong sense of responsibility. Faith in God inspires faithful provision for one's own family (I Timothy 5:8). Devotion to heavenly goals is accompanied by diligence in earthly work (II Thessalonians 3:7-12). Personal responsibility goes far beyond meeting minimal demands. Whatever a Christian finds to do should be done thoroughly and well. God brings decency and order, beauty and arrangement to everything He does. So should we. Ephesians 6:5-7 repudiates the idea of doing only what is required, only when someone in authority is watching. Every aspect of a believer's life is under the watchful care of God. Everything must be done as service to God, even if no one else is watching.

Two young Christians were scraping dried lacquer from a spray booth when some of their fellow furniture workers decided to cut out for an early break. When the Christians did not accept the invitation to go along, someone asked, "Why not? Does your father own the company?" One of the Christians pointed upward and replied, "As a matter of fact, He does."

Responsibility involves more than diligence in work. A responsible person lives an orderly life, making wise use of resources and opportunities to be productive and purposeful.[55] Responsibility includes foreseeing the possible consequences of decisions and actions rather than giving in to impulses. Living responsibly does not mean living a regimented life with no room

---

[55] At a somewhat exclusive private school, maintenance workers had to be careful when mowing the grass near the bookstore entrance. Students who made purchases would throw away any coins they had received in change. They seemed to have little respect for the responsibility their parents had shown in building the careers that fed their supply of paper money.

for fun and adventure.[56] It means having a good grasp of reality, the thoughtfulness to plan well, and the determination to follow through.

In looking for a possible spouse, it is important to consider whether a person's life is well-ordered and firmly grounded. A date can be an exhilarating escape from responsibility for an evening. Marriage means taking responsibility for the day by day challenges of a lifetime together.

These qualities of Christ-like character are what a person should look for in a mate, and what a person should be like to attract a mate. It is unnecessary and unwise to expect too much of a mere human being, but by the power of the Holy Spirit every believer should show significant growth towards conformity to Christ. The ideal marriage would be the union of an ideal husband and an ideal wife. The ideal is not a selfishly defined measure of attractiveness or usefulness but "the measure of the stature of the fullness of Christ (Ephesians 4:13)." If both husband and wife are growing in conformity to the character of Jesus Christ, their marriage is well grounded. The faithful trusting love described in I Corinthians 13 will sustain an atmosphere of trust and nurture which will endure the challenges and distractions of life.

When Luther called marriage a training ground for spirituality, he knew what he was saying. As a former monk married to a former nun, he could no longer pursue spirituality through isolation and private meditation. He and his Katie were

---

[56] I have spent three summers searching for Noah's Ark on Mt. Ararat in Turkey. The experience was very exciting, and required an adventurous spirit. Real courage was found in a Pakistani friend who, with five children to support, refused to work on the printing of a bartending book because he felt it blasphemed the name of God by using Jesus' name as a slang name for a drink. His company kept him on board because of his work ethic and allowed him to work on another book which would not offend his conscience. He truly felt he might lose his job of eight years, but would not compromise his beliefs. That is real courage.

thrown into the daily concerns and confrontations of family life. Godliness and love cannot be contemplated abstractly by husbands and wives. Their conformity to Christ must be lived out in their daily interaction.

Objective biblical criteria show what it means to conform to Christ and describe characteristics which identify a man or woman in Christ. In seeking a spouse, biblical principles and admonitions must be followed. Believers may sense spiritual promptings in this, as in other life-defining matters (Acts 8:29; 11:28; 13:2; 21:11). These promptings will be consistent with biblical truth and wisdom. Personal thoughts and feelings must also align with the truth. Instruction, advice, encouragement or warnings from credible sources must be considered soberly. The final validation of God's choice comes when a man in Christ and a woman in Christ agree that they belong together for life.

Pastor Sam told the story of how he met his wife Nancy in the cafeteria of a Christian college. He saw a pretty girl across the crowded room and was immediately interested in meeting her. He kept looking at her until he saw that she had also noticed him. In that brief first moment of eye contact he did what his heart told him to do. He winked. His mind immediately told him that was a silly thing to do, but then something amazing happened. She winked back! With that confirming wink, they both ended their search for a spouse.

I would not advise anyone to go around winking at members of the opposite sex as part of a search for a mate. It is more to the point that Sam and Nancy were looking in the right place. They were in a place where believers were growing in conformity to Christ and actively equipping themselves for ministry. Their faith made them aware of God's call to service and they obeyed. In that place of obedient faith, God brought them together quickly and simply. I pray that others may follow their example in being men and women in Christ who respond with their whole hearts and minds to His guidance.

In marriage counseling, believing couples can be reminded to help each other be more Christ-like and to return to their commitment to show His love in their marriages. In premarital counseling, couples considering marriage can be encouraged to consider their decision carefully and biblically, with special attention to how they can plan a lifetime of ministry to each other and, together, to the world. People who are still looking for suitable marriage partners can be shown the advantages of following God's plan from the start.

Choosing to serve the Lord, seeking His kingdom first and desiring to be an exemplary man or woman in Christ puts a person in position of obedient faith, the place of God's blessing where God's presence and assistance will supply every need. If the need is a suitable helper through the joys and trials of life, God will provide a person who is similarly committed to Him.

The Place of Blessing

God's thoughts about marriage are higher than our thoughts. When Jesus proclaimed God's standard for marriage, His disciples said, "If the case... be so, it is not good to marry (Matthew 19:10)." The standard is high because the stakes are high. "Choose you this day whom ye will serve (Joshua 24:15)." A covenant relationship with God brings commitment to build our households according to His plan. "Seek ye first the kingdom of God, and His righteousness (Matthew 6:33)." Submitting to God's sovereign power means letting Him rule over our lives and overrule our wrong choices. "Be ye not unequally yoked with unbelievers (II Corinthians 6:14)." Identification with Christ and partnership in His ministry of reconciliation lead to choosing a mate with similar commitment. "Blessed with all spiritual blessings in Christ (Ephesians 1:3-14; Colossians 1:9-18)." When a man in Christ and a woman in

Christ marry, the blessings of God can fill and overflow their home.

I would be out of work if every marriage followed God's plan. As a Christian, I accept and proclaim God's standard. As a counselor, I try to help those whose marriages fall short of that standard. In fact, all marriages fall short of God's standard because all people do. "All have sinned, and come short of the glory of God (Romans 3:23)." We all fall short of God's standards in every aspect of human life.

The first three chapters of the book of Romans reveal God's summary indictment against the human race. All have sinned: the openly immoral (Romans 1:18-31), the morally judgmental (2:1-16) and even the judgmentally religious (2:17-28). All humanity lies under the control and condemnation of sin (3:1-19).[57] At the conclusion of this catalogue of crimes against divinity, thoughtful readers will feel breathless and awestruck as the gavel comes down and we hear the Judge call out, "Guilty!" We have nothing to say for ourselves: "every mouth [is] stopped, and all the world [is declared] guilty before God (Romans 3:19)."

The root of the problem is in rejecting the concept that there really is a God whose character determines what is right and wrong. When Adam and Eve focused their attention on God, knowing Him was all they needed to know. Eve was deceived into distrusting God, and Adam chose to identify with her in disobeying God. The primal reality of sin as disbelief and disobedience is noted repeatedly in Romans 1.

---

[57] The accusations of Roman 3:10-18 are drawn almost entirely from Psalms, the Bible's prayer and praise book. Is this sense of sin present in our prayer lives? Do we confess it in our worship songs?

Refusal to believe in God (Romans 1:18-20). Although Creation (including human personality) gives evidence of God, people choose to ignore it.[58]

Refusal to respond to God (verse 21). Rather than turning to God in grateful worship, people choose to explain and exploit Creation without acknowledging Him.

Exalting the creature over the Creator (verses 22-25). Following godless assumptions to their logical conclusions, people abandon all restraint and idolize whatever captures their interest or brings them pleasure.

Exiling God from their thoughts (verse 28). Living in unbridled sin, people do not like to think of the fact that there is a God who will judge them. Because of this rebellion, God is said to leave sinful humanity under the control of their own impurity, vile passions and rebellious thoughts (Romans 1:24-28). This is the sad state of people without God, although He mercifully holds them back from the total wickedness which would destroy them (II Thessalonians 2:7; II Peter 3:3-9).

How can such people expect to be blessed by the God whom they deny? How can they ask a God in whom they do not trust to show His presence and power in their lives and marriages? As a counselor, I have to help couples deal with offenses against each other which have poisoned their marriages. As a Christian, I know that the root offense is sin against God in not believing and obeying Him. I know that God has provided redemption from sin and remedies for the consequences of sin. Turning to God and entering the place of

---

[58] A careful reading of the first chapter of Romans will reveal that God's wrath is primarily against deliberate disbelief — unbelievers are not ignorant (agnostic) concerning God, they just refuse to include Him in their thoughts. Gross sins are simply the consequence of choosing to live without God. When the Hubble Telescope finds one-third more stars than we previously believed to exist, or a galaxy which seems older than any previously known, the current scientific establishment takes its default position in evolutionary explanations. (According to CNN it turns out we were wrong about how many galaxies there are as well. There aren't 200 billion galaxies in the universe, it's more like 2 trillion!) I have known members of the extended family of Dr. Edwin Powell Hubble — and they are godly believers who give the Creator glory for His wonderful works which have been seen through the telescope.

His blessing is as "simple" as turning from rebellious unbelief to obedient faith.[59]

Turning to God begins by believing that He is really there and that He wants us to meet with Him (Hebrews 11:6). We are all created as spiritual beings who need to relate to our Creator. Even a casual glance at the history of humanity reveals a spiritual quest, an inextinguishable desire to connect with the eternal. Human religion has been described as the attempt to reach God, know God and please God by man's own effort. The Unknown God of the Athenians (Acts 17:23) may have represented the unreachable, unknowable truth beyond the limits of human comprehension, the possibility of a God beyond the gods of human imagination. Some have emphasized the transcendence of God — the fact that He crosses the boundaries, the feeling that He is not only more but also totally other than what we can think. Rudolf Otto's classic work concedes that this "numinous" quality cannot be defined by any human mind although it has been felt by every human heart.[60] If God transcends our comprehension, our one-sided efforts to reach Him must ultimately fail.

Assuming that God is too distant to be reached, many people view Him as a cosmic watchmaker who set the laws of nature in motion and then left them to take their course without Him. He may be really there, somewhere, but we cannot find Him, and He is too self-sufficient to have any interest in us, and any attempt to communicate with Him would be futile. Kafka described the frustration of being unable to get through to someone who could determine the course of one's life. In *The Castle*, the main character keeps trying to telephone his prospective employer, but the town has a chaotic phone system.

---

[59] In many years of witnessing and counseling, I have seen some people come to faith quickly and easily, others only after much struggling and reflection, and still others almost persuaded, but lost.

[60] Rudolf Otto, *The Idea of the Holy*, Oxford Galaxy, 1958, pp.5-7.

All phones ring simultaneously and almost constantly, and are answered randomly at the whim of petty officials. The answerers are indifferent to the callers' concerns and provide no useful information.[61] We may laugh at the realization that we have bureaucracies and machines that do this, but there is a more sobering parallel. The real ruler of the town, the main character's employer, lives in the Castle, and, as the Mayor explains, "There's no fixed connection with the Castle, no central exchange that transmits our calls further." What if that is how prayer works, or rather does not work, for most people? They keep calling, and someone is really there, but He might not answer, He does not care about us, we cannot be sure who He really is and we cannot rely on the connection, if it exists at all. People who invent their own ways to approach God become ensnared in Kafkaesque rituals. Human religion keeps calling wrong numbers until it concludes that God does not exist, is not at home or refuses to answer. This leads many desperately religious people to give up on God.

The good news is that God does not give up on us. Yes, God is transcendent. His self-existent holiness separates Him from our creaturely limitations. We are further separated from Him by our sinfulness, which taints even our religious efforts. God is not merely a spirit being or a higher power which can be manipulated by our rituals. He is really God, really there, and He really cares. Our problem is in thinking we have to do something to get His attention. Elijah mocked the prophets of Baal who screamed, lacerated themselves and leaped around their altar on Mount Carmel. Was their god sleeping, traveling or otherwise too occupied to respond? Bottom line: "there was no voice; no one answered, no one paid attention (I Kings 18:26-29, NKJV)." Wrong number! The fact is that God gives us His answer before we call Him. He is really there, and though He is

---

[61] Franz Kafka, *The Castle,* Schocken Books, 1974, pp. 26-28; 93-95.

infinitely transcendent, He is also intimately personal. God cares enough to communicate His love and His plans to us.

All have sinned and fall under God's condemnation and wrath, but God's grace is greater than our sin. Jesus Christ is the place and the means of reconciliation. He provided satisfaction of God's wrath against sin and deliverance of believers from sin through His blood (Romans 3:23-25). God's justice is maintained by the outpouring of His wrath upon Jesus Christ, the perfectly righteous One who took our sin upon Himself on the cross. The whole indictment against our sin was charged to Jesus Christ in His death, and now those who entrust their salvation to Him can live in His righteousness (II Corinthians 5:17-21). Simple faith, recognizing our hopeless sinfulness without Christ and accepting the righteousness offered us in Christ, brings us into a relationship with God.

Faith in Jesus Christ is not only the way into the life of God; it is a way of living enriched by the presence and power of God. By faith, we come to know God in Jesus Christ. We will never know God exhaustively, but we can know Him truly. His self-existent essence as Father, Son and Holy Spirit is beyond the comprehension of any created being. We cannot know God as He is within Himself, but we can know Him as He reveals Himself to us. "The secret things belong to the Lord our God, but those things which are revealed belong to us and to our children forever (Deuteronomy 29:29)." God's existence and character as revealed in the Bible determine the meaning and purpose of all Creation, including our lives and marriages. The mystery of the Trinity surpasses our highest thoughts, but tells us something about the God whose image we bear. God subsists as personality in relationship. That suggests that we should reflect the character of God as personalities in relationships.

Conformity to God's character is God's purpose for us. His moral law was given to show us how to live as personalities in relationships, how we should live together and how we should treat one another. Any breach of God's law hurts us. Rather than restricting us, His law actually frees us to live as we were meant to live. If we were looking for a more contemporary title for the Bible, we might call it, "What Works."

Those who reject God's plan in the name of personal autonomy are not merely unwise, they are foolish. A quest for freedom without moral restraint will bring disaster. Suppose the conductor of a passenger train came to your seat with a rather worried look and told you that the engineer had decided to experiment with personal freedom. "When he gets to the next sharp curve, instead of slowing down, he will accelerate in order to be freed from the stifling restraint of the track." For a train, freedom to be all that it can be depends on staying on the track laid out for it. Getting off the track may give a momentary illusion of freedom before inevitable catastrophe. For human beings created in God's image and for His purpose, true freedom is in staying on the track laid out for us in God's Word.

Moses, who received the Law, and Paul, the preeminent minister of the Gospel, emphasized the clarity of God's message. We do not need to rise to states of mystic ecstasy or sink to the depths of occultism to find spiritual guidance. What God commands is readily accessible in the Bible. We are to respond in righteous action (Deuteronomy 30:10-14). What God offers in the Gospel is readily accessible in the Bible. We are to receive righteousness by faith (Romans 10:6-13). Faith receives God's righteousness in Jesus Christ. Obedience demonstrates God's righteousness in our actions. The place of blessing is the place of obedient faith.

This is not to say that God's presence and power are restricted to providing the blessings of faith to believers. What theologians call the providence of God includes His holding all Creation together and sustaining the existence of every created being (Colossians 1:15-17; Acts 17:24-26). Some speak of common grace bringing all humanity a certain level of security and comfort through the reliability of the physical universe and the relative stability of social institutions. Beyond this, the Creation indicates its Creator in general revelation which makes us responsible to acknowledge God's omnipotence and sovereignty. God has communicated more directly in special revelation: the words of the Bible and the person of Jesus Christ. All of these are blessings God presents to all who will receive them.

God's richest blessing is for those who know Him. There is no guarantee of undisturbed physical security or unlimited material comfort. Neither health nor wealth is the greatest gift God offers us. When God said to Abraham, "I will bless you, and in you shall all the families of the earth be blessed (Genesis 12:1-3)," He had something greater than earthly prosperity in mind. Later, the Lord explained, "I am your shield, your exceeding great reward (Genesis 15:1)." God gave Abraham His greatest gift: Himself. In Isaiah 41:8 God gives Abraham the highest title a human can hold: "my friend."

James 2:22-23 explains what this title implied: "faith was working together with his works, and by works was faith made perfect ... Abraham believed God, and it was accounted unto him for righteousness. And he was called the friend of God." Abraham did not come to God to present an agenda. He did not propose a wonderful plan for his own life and ask God to endorse it. Abraham presented himself to God. He believed what God said and acted according to God's plan. This is the path of blessing. Much contemporary religion emphasizes bringing God into our plans to assure our personal success. Biblical faith brings us into God's plan, where success is measured by conformity to His purposes, not to our own whims.

Friendship with God is established in and by Jesus Christ. He presented Himself to us as our God, our shield and our great reward, and our friend: "Greater love has no one than this, than to lay down one's life for his friends (John 15:13)." He went on to set the terms for friendship with Him: "You are my friends if you do whatever I command you (John 15:14)." The obedience of faith is not legalistic subservience, but spiritual liberty: "No longer do I call you servants, for a servant does not know what his master is doing; but I have called you friends, for all things that I heard from my Father I have made known to you (John 15:15)." The pattern for friendship with God has not changed. God opens communication with us, and we respond in obedient faith.

Abraham's experience and ours has another dimension. We can speak to God and expect Him to respond to us. If we speak to God about how what He has said affects our lives, He will help us understand what He is doing and how we can participate in His plan. God is not a silent partner in this relationship, and neither is any believer. When God was planning to judge Sodom and Gomorrah, He said, "Shall I hide from Abraham what I am doing (Genesis 18:17)?" Because of His plans for Abraham, He gave Abraham insight into His plans for Abraham's world. Significantly, Abraham negotiated with God in behalf of Sodom, and God accepted his proposal. Ultimately, God's planned judgment fell, but God was gracious to Abraham's nephew, Lot. As God's Word shows us His plans for our world, we can pray about our participation in them.

Friendship with God, like any friendship, is a lifelong conversation. We need to hear from Him through His Word, and He invites us to speak to Him in prayer. Christian marriage planning will include plans for deepening this friendship. Theologians may debate whether it is possible to be a child of God without being a friend of God, but it is clear that God intends for each of His children to grow into responsible friendship with Him.

Conversations and friendships between spouses will grow richer as they develop their friendship with God together. "As for me and my house, we will serve the Lord," said Joshua as diverse false religions tempted his people (Joshua 24:15). May the Lord empower us to move others to base their marriages on friendship with God. "Unless the Lord builds the house, they labor in vain that build it (Psalm 127:1)." Even if we have to teach some basic theology to our clients, we need to let them know the importance of building on the firm foundation of obedient faith in order to build their marriages in the place of blessing.

In the World

According to an old story, an itinerant preacher visited an isolated rural church one Sunday morning, and found only one man there, a cattle farmer. They exchanged greetings, prayed briefly, and the preacher said, "Well, I'd better do what I came here to do." He took his place behind the oaken pulpit and preached for forty-five minutes. At the end of the sermon the farmer looked dazed. "What's wrong?" the preacher asked. "Well, that was a lot of talkin' for my hearin' to take in," the farmer replied. The preacher said, "Think about it this way. When your cows are in the field during a dry spell, you take a wagonload of hay out to them, don't you?" "Well, yes, I do," answered the farmer. The pastor went on, "And if there's only one cow out there, you would still go out, wouldn't you?" The farmer stroked his chin for a few seconds and then said slowly, "Well, yes, but I wouldn't dump the whole load."[62]

In counseling, I never lose sight of my own presuppositions about marriage, but I seldom dump the whole load on a couple during our first counseling session. God's standard for marriage includes the perfect love and purity found only in Jesus Christ. I have to work with imperfect people who have difficulty loving each other in a corrupt world. The farmer in the story struggled to digest a long sermon (which may have

---

[62] My faithful Uncle Tom teaches a Sunday school class of three or four each Sunday. Seminary trained, at 87 he still studies all week for his lesson. He does not dump the whole load, but gives his class a few things to ruminate on.

been packed with vital truth). Maybe what he needed was a few words of comfort and a helping hand to deal with the sickness or other circumstances which kept his family and neighbors from church that morning. I have elaborated on my marriage manifesto because the full sermon needs to be preached publicly. In the privacy of the counseling process, I try not to say more than my clients are ready to hear.

What clients need to hear are helpful words which will enable them to make better choices and plan more wisely. Abstract ideas about marriage may be accepted intellectually without any application to real needs. People need to see the truth about their situations as well as the truth of God's standard for marriage. The standard is high and we are not there yet. What can we do right now that will be a step in the right direction? My friend Mickey Holiday once said, "I know why life is so hard. Jesus said, 'In the world you shall have tribulation.'" The rest of John 16:33 tells us to be cheered because Jesus has overcome the world, but Mickey's point is valid as far as it goes. Life in this world can be full of pressure, distress and affliction. People overwhelmed by the troubles of the world need counsel which speaks directly to their condition.

When a funeral director told Gordon and Joyce Puls, "Remember to breathe, remember to eat," his words were more helpful than many of the things friends said to comfort them in the loss of their twenty-seven year old daughter, Michele. Amy, twenty months younger, knew that God had killed her sister, and that none of the reasons well-meaning Christians suggested made any sense. Lisa, the youngest sister, had been sharing Michele's home, and the shock of losing Michele was compounded by the disruption of her own life. T.J., the twelve-year-old brother, had enjoyed Michele's visit just five days earlier, and was confused by the turmoil around him. Never mind the kind words about enduring, accepting or understanding. These people needed to be reminded to eat and breathe.

Couples who come for counseling do not need to have a load of wisdom dumped on them. They need to be reminded of the basic functions which breathe life into a marriage and bring it nourishment. Even in premarital counseling, where there is usually less sense of crisis, couples can be so blindly in love that a little eye salve to clear their vision is more appropriate than a load of advice which rubber-stamps their intention to marry each other. Counseling should be based on a clear and comprehensive understanding of biblical principles, but it also requires sensitivity to the specific needs and capacities of clients. Couples need to know that biblical principles not only address their specific problems, but also teach the way to the happiness they seek. Jesus invited people to accept the way of life which He offered, a good, pleasant, manageable life guided by His own gentle presence (Matthew 11:28-30).

God's plan for marriage makes the home a place of blessing for the husband and wife, their children, their community, and ultimately for all humanity. Marriage is the foundation of all institutions of society. Structures of government, economics and education are built on the interdependent connectedness of humanity which finds its basic expression in marriage. The family home establishes a context for growth in spiritual and intellectual maturity, development of economic and social responsibility, and appreciation of the joys of living as a personality in relationship.

Even the Church, the called-out community of believers, is viewed as an extended family. The image of the Church as a family is alluded to throughout the New Testament. In the Church, those who have met God in Christ gather as His adopted children. The household of God (Ephesians 2:19; Galatians 6:10) provides a nurturing atmosphere which draws its members together. As David wrote, "God setteth the solitary in families (Psalm 68:6)." The Church provides fathers, mothers, sisters and brothers for its members (I Timothy 5:1-12). If God describes His Church as a family, Christian families should display the love, acceptance, care, growth and forgiveness which are marks of the true Church. Relationships in the household of faith and in homes of believers should show the pattern of love which should govern all other relationships.

I Timothy 2:1-2 suggests that other institutions of society are designed for the benefit of the family home: "that we may lead a quiet and peaceable life in all godliness and honesty." Prayers for those in authority need not mention advancement of national or local political interests; emphasis should be on preserving a social environment in which families and individuals are secure. A secure home is a place of blessing where people can live quietly, peaceably, reverently and honestly. A home should be a place of tranquility in the midst of the world's confusion, a place of rest in the midst of the world's hyperactivity, a place of godliness in the midst of the world's sinfulness, and a place of purity and honesty in the midst of the world's corruption and lies.

A home secured by obedient faith will establish a baseline of blessing. There will be a pervading sense of calm acceptance and mutual affection which can weather any storm. When a crisis comes, it will not threaten the basic soundness of the bonds among family members. Psalm 1 says that the blessed person, the truly happy person, is the person whose life is rooted deeply in obedient faith. Obedient faith in God lets a person settle down and dwell securely, without dread of catastrophe (Proverbs 1:33). Reverence for God refreshes life, brings satisfaction and protects from calamity (Proverbs 19:23). Even in times of distress and weeping, God strengthens and guides His own (Psalm 84:5-7).

These blessings are applied to the family in Psalm 128. Reverence and obedience ensure God's blessing: "Blessed is every one that feareth the Lord that walketh in His ways (verse 1)." Work will bring satisfying results: "Thou shalt eat the labor of thine hands, happy thou shalt be, and it shall be well with thee (verse 2)." The home will be a place of joyous companionship: "Thy wife shall be as a fruitful vine... thy children like olive plants (verse 3)." Blessings upon the family will overflow into the surrounding society and continue for generations to come: "Thou shalt see the good of Jerusalem all the days of thy life (verse 5)." "Thou shalt see thy children's children, and peace upon Israel (verse 6)." This baseline of blessing is God's intention for every marriage.

In families where the baseline of blessing is well established, there is a solid foundation from which to face every crisis. The Puls family felt shock, perplexity, anger and a profound sense of loss when Michele died, but there was no fear of ultimate evil. They did not turn against God and they did not turn away from each other; their foundation was firm. Their various temperaments and positions in the family meant that there were incommunicable differences in their grief, but their baseline relationships with each other and with God remained secure. As Gordon says of their loss, "People can't know how bad it is unless they know how good it was." How good the unity and joy of a family is depends on their baseline relationships.

Planning can help establish a baseline of blessing in a marriage. Every couple will experience their own tribulations in the world, some of them completely beyond their control. Planning can keep them of one mind in responding to these unexpected crises. Other problems are more predictable, and planning can prevent or minimize them. Establishing a baseline approach to challenges improves a home's security in potential problem areas. Couples who have run into seemingly irreconcilable conflict need to rethink their patterns of behavior in problem areas. Starting from where they are, they can make corrections and move ahead with more unified planning.

When couples say they are planning to get married, they usually mean they are making plans for the day of their wedding, not for the lifetime of marriage which follows it. Premarital counseling which focuses on life-long commitment helps clients think more soberly, and sometimes leads them to change their plans. Couples may decide to postpone marriage in order to work out issues they had not considered thoroughly. Some may reconsider even their choice to marry each other, and conclude that it was ill-advised. Believers may respond to biblical warnings against marrying unbelievers.

Couples thinking about courtship and marriage should think about key predictable challenges:

Spiritual matters, including theological beliefs, devotional habits and involvement in church and personal ministries.

Husband/Wife relationship, including couple time, dating, sex, and decision-making conferences as well as daily conversation and displays of affection.

Relationships with friends and extended family, including shared activities, holiday celebrations and reciprocal visits, and possible sources of conflict.

Financial security, including career expectations, budgeting, and short-term and long-term investment.

Educational goals, including lifelong learning by husband and wife as well as appropriate training for the children.

Recreational interests, including hobbies, vacations, projects, entertainment and weekend activities.

Cultural, ethnic or racial differences can complicate these issues, most notably regarding relationships with friends and family. A balanced marriage requires thoughtful planning in each of these areas to ensure that individual differences will not threaten a couple's oneness. I challenge engaged couples to consider carefully their existing differences over matters which can make or break a marriage.

Spiritually, the unequal yoking of a believer with an unbeliever is not the only issue. Depending on church and family response, a marriage between believers of different Christian denominations can enrich or cripple their faith. Where oneness in Christ is more than an empty motto, there is richness in diverse understandings and experiences of the one true faith. Where a sectarian attitude reigns, differences in non-essentials can become stumbling-blocks to a free expression of faith. Couples must consider whether they can agree on a church affiliation in which both of them can worship and minister without compromising their basic convictions.

Relationally, the way a couple gets along before marriage may or may not indicate their ability to get along within marriage. Dating tends to emphasize positive impressions: courtesy, kindness and charm. If there have been disagreements during courtship, it is important to note the issues involved and how they were handled. Marriage is more than dinner and a movie, and being one flesh is more than physical sexual compatibility. The relationship between husband and wife is a bond between two whole persons involved in the full spectrum of human experience. Couples should consider whether the euphoria of courtship has given them an inaccurate picture of their ability to face life's challenges together.

Relationships with family and friends affect a couple's relationship with each other. The leaving and cleaving of Genesis 2:24 mean that all other loyalties are redefined by their marriage. The two are to become one, undivided in their relationship to all others. Friends and extended family now relate to a married couple, not to Daddy's girl, Momma's boy or just one of the gang. On the other hand, marriage does not abruptly end all other human connectedness. Marriage binds

111

husband and wife together in unique oneness: it redefines but does not necessarily break all other legitimate human connections. Couples must consider how the continuing influence or opposition of friends and family members might affect their marriage.

Financially, there are issues other than responsible use of income. Where differences in family background or career create a wide gap in financial resources, the prospective husband and wife will have widely different experiences and perceptions of the value of money. In a materialistic culture, both wealth and poverty can produce their own varieties of covetousness. The relatively wealthy can feel self-sufficient and trust money more than God; the relatively poor can feel oppressed and grasp for more than God has given them (Proverbs 30:8-9). Couples should consider whether differences in economic resources will bring misunderstanding and suspicion over financial matters into their marriage.

Educationally, the issues include capacity, achievement and goals. To be of one mind a couple needs to be able to think together. If their thinking skills or patterns of logic are very dissimilar or if they have different levels and fields of academic achievement, they may have difficulty thinking alike. A couple should consider whether educational gaps might create problems, and whether plans for further education for either or both of them will bring them closer together or only magnify their differences.[63]

Recreationally, diverse interests may require some adjustments. A NASCAR fan and a quilter can coexist, but they might spend some Sunday afternoons apart. Dating and courtship usually revolve around shared recreational activities, so some adjustments already will have been made. Diversity of

---

[63] A pastor/counselor told a male counselee, "You should not have married a girl with a PhD.—you should have picked a high school graduate like I did, and she would worship you." Insecure people need worship; godly people want to serve.

interests can broaden a couple's range of conversation or pull them in different directions. They must consider whether they will be able to develop common interests while accepting their differences.

God's plan for marriage is not a load of theology to be dumped on couples. It is the way to make a home a place of blessing in the world. When the perils of life in the world threaten a marriage, the husband and wife need to know what their next step should be. As they begin going in the right direction together, they can learn to apply biblical principles to all aspects of their marriage. They do not have to do everything at once. Just agreeing to work together to improve their marriage is a big step.

Sometimes small changes can signal willingness to tackle the larger issues. Problem solving and planning are learned skills: it is important to begin with choices which can be put into action immediately. Agreeing to pay bills on time is easier than formulating a five-year financial plan, but it is a necessary first step.

Building a baseline of trust and affection begins as couples learn to be considerate of each other, resolving minor differences and agreeing to work through major disagreements with mutual respect.

Blueprint for Blessing

Marriage, as God planned it, is a relationship maintained in decency and order, beauty and arrangement. As the basic unit of human society, marriage connects a man and a woman in a unified approach to the full range of human needs, interests and experiences. The security and growth of the husband, wife, and children requires a conscious effort to meet needs and pursue interests calmly and peaceably, honoring God and living honestly in the world. Careful planning can reduce confusion and conflict over basic issues and provide a stable baseline from which to meet unforeseeable challenges. A well-planned marriage totally involves the couple in seeking God's best for each other and for their children. Heart, soul, mind and strength will be fully committed to making the home a place of blessing.

Planning to Marry

The most important task in premarital counseling is to help people see the importance of establishing a solid foundation for marriage. I am never concerned about the age of a couple as much as I am about their stability as a couple and their maturity as individuals. I always want them to be engaged for at least one year. Love is blind for a time, and it is possible to fool someone about who you really are at the core of your being.[64] A relatively long engagement period gives a couple time to observe each other's responses to a wide range of circumstances. Of

---

[64] Trying to make a good first impression is a high priority in dating, and courtship continues the effort to be as attractive as possible. As someone has said, a person is like a glass filled with liquid: what's inside is what comes out when they're bumped. A whirlwind courtship minimizes the valuable lessons bumps can teach. It is better to find out what's in a person during a long engagement than to risk an extremely bumpy marriage.

course, with elderly couples I have to consider how much time they might have left for marriage after a long engagement.[65]

The selection process which precedes engagement is very important. Planning at this stage will determine a couple's capacity for planning together later. Hasty courtships lead to early divorces, setting off a chain of negative thoughts, emotions and behaviors which take years to correct. Some people in their twenties have spiraled downward through two, three or even more failed marriages. Instead of carefully analyzing wrong choices, they jump with both feet into another relationship, irrationally certain that the new choice is right. Instead of seeking help in making wiser choices, they desperately pursue anyone who will have them. They feel rejected and every failed relationship makes them feel more worthless. This syndrome makes me question the intelligence of an allegedly enlightened generation. Perhaps the vast majority of people entering marriage today are ignorant of God's requirements and provisions, and blind to their own irrationality. Poor planning in the selection process leads to bondage, either within a miserable marriage or in a cycle of miserable relationships. Poor choices do not produce good results.

Poor choices produce nightmares. I tell clients that people choose their own nightmares and then must live with them. People who are rude, stingy and self-centered create a climate no one would relish living in. Frankly, this is the reason for most early marriage problems. Young people trained in self-

---

[65] Usually six months is sufficient time for the engagement of older couples, but careful pre-marital counseling is still very important. An older couple's assets should put money in trust for their separate children and what they bring into the marriage or make during the marriage (whether equal or not) should be agreed upon and shared equally between them and divided between families when the survivor dies.

esteem have difficulty overcoming sinful self-centeredness.[66] Men and women seem commitment-phobic. How can you be a helper or nurturer when you think only about yourself? From a biblical standpoint, the autonomy idealized in Western culture has no place in a marriage. Two must become one. Marriage is designed to keep a couple together for a lifetime, while careers and other interests come and go. Nightmares arise when our eyes are shut. The time to open a couple's eyes is during the selection process, before the nightmare becomes a reality.

Vision testing is part of a counselor's ministry. Are these clients going into marriage with their eyes open? At some point in premarital counseling, I separate the couple and speak with each of them individually. I ask whether there are any unresolved questions between them. I have heard such things as:

"He's so secretive about his business. It seems to be doing well, but I feel like I'm intruding when I ask about it."

"Whenever I speak of redoing some rooms in his house, he says we'll talk about it after we're married."

"Her apartment is a mess, and she says she just doesn't have time to clean it up. She says that after we're married, she will have more time because we won't always be going places."

"She is always bouncing checks and making excuses for it."

"He never seems to want to go anywhere any more, and we end up making popcorn and watching television."

"There are certain topics he/she avoids like the plague: future plans, education, money, exercise, opposite-sex friends."

Unresolved questions may have been glossed over during courtship. I try to stimulate discussion of hitherto forbidden

---

[66] One well-known Christian speaker makes sure that flowers are delivered to his hotel room when he is on a speaking tour. I respect him as a speaker and a decent person, but this is the kind of self-serving attitude which permeates all levels of our society. A security guard parked in a restricted area within sight of his desk rather than in a distant lot which he was supposed to patrol because, "I have valuable things in my car." Some of the cars out of his sight in the lot were worth about ten times his annual income.

subjects. Many couples end their engagements when one partner refuses to be open and honest.

Premarital sex is an issue which absolutely must be discussed. If the couple's relationship has been sexually pure, has either of them had sex with other partners? Are other relationships continuing, simmering on a back burner, or have they been decisively and irrevocably ended? Biblically, confession and repentance are mandatory. The increasing risk of HIV/AIDS and other sexually transmitted diseases adds medical and legal urgency. If the couple has had sex with each other, they should be encouraged to commit themselves to making things right and maintaining abstinence until their marriage, even if it means going back to just holding hands. Repentance brings them out of fornication. Abstinence restores them to the place of God's blessing, the place of obedient faith.

If there has been extreme immorality in either person's life, I strongly advise that after repentance at least three years should elapse before the couple enters an engagement. I recommend a five-year waiting period if either of them has been involved in a homosexual lifestyle. This does not imply that true repentance and God's forgiveness are not instantaneous. The problem is that the strength of sexual impulses is so strong that breaking sinful patterns of thought and behavior in this area usually takes considerable time and effort. Some have suggested that early sexual experiences become the "norm" for a person, even if they are clearly sinful and destructive. Temptation to sin is especially dangerous in areas where we have already fallen, especially in sexual matters. Abstinence and redirection of desires are difficult steps in a cleansing process which must be completed to establish a pure foundation for engagement and marriage.

Besides sexual and moral issues, finances are often a sore spot or can quickly become one. People who do not have a clear view of their resources and expenses risk doubling their

117

financial problems by marrying each other. Two most certainly cannot live as cheaply as one. Combining two insecure financial situations does not create financial security. Does the couple have a financial plan? Are there extreme differences in their incomes or spending habits? Is either of them deeply in debt? What choices can they make to stabilize their finances? Do they have a budget? As their counselor, I want to know whether they are prepared to share the financial responsibilities of marriage. I make it my business to look into their business in order to help them think clearly and plan realistically. As my hard working friend Bob is fond of saying, "young couples today do not seem to realize that opportunity and success are often disguised in dungarees'."[67]

Sometimes, couples bring a number of unresolved doubts or concerns into their relationship. Any problems encountered while dating or engaged can be multiplied by a thousand in their potential impact on a marriage. What might seem like minor offenses during courtship can add up to a very undesirable character profile. It is important to watch for evidence that a prospective mate might be characterized as having negative qualities which could jeopardize a marriage. Attitudes about money, friends, and spiritual matters are especially important indicators of possible problem areas. Idiosyncrasies which seem charming sometimes are symptomatic of an unstable or abusive personality. During courtship, couples should be alert to warning signs as they observe each other in various dimensions of life.[68]

In personality: A person who is extremely passive tends to turn inward and to be subject to sometimes crippling moodiness. A

[67] My pastor's uncle Bobby is an interesting character, he amassed a fortune. While on a recent visit I asked Bobby how he earned his money, he walked me into his "home office" and pointed to a picture on his wall and asked me what I saw. I replied, "An old guy sitting on a donkey." He said, "Well I got off my as..." (donkey)

[68] One extremely wealthy widow was dating a fellow in another state. She was eager to get married after many years of single parenting, but the longer they dated, the closer to marriage they came, the more he talked about spending her money on vacations in exotic places. His pastor had recommended him to her

but forgot to mention that he had been a gigolo for many years and had only been a professing Christian for two years. The engagement ended.

person who is overly aggressive may be harmfully judgmental of others.

In relationship: A proud person will exaggerate his or her own importance and be unappreciative of others. A selfish person will be inconsiderate, seeking his or her own satisfaction with little regard for the needs of others.

In society: A forgetful person will neglect responsibilities; a person who is routinely late will be unreliable. A person who is messy at home and ill-mannered in public will be an embarrassment to family and friends.

In conflict: A head-strong person will be stubborn in pursuing his or her own way, and quick-tempered with anyone who disagrees. A bitter person will be offensive and sarcastic.[69]

It is important to remember that marriage does not magically change a person. In fact, it sometimes only removes the façade, and reveals even worse character flaws. Concerns in these areas should be addressed as early and as thoroughly as possible.[70]

Make sure you provide plenty of opportunities for opening every can of worms and dealing with its contents. Be the one person in the couple's lives who will keep asking the hard questions. They need to know that nothing they might reveal will shock you and that you are there to help them face difficult issues without unnecessary embarrassment. As they come to trust you they will feel freer to speak openly about their concerns.

How much should they tell, and when? Are there limits to self-disclosure and mutual questioning? Aggressive

---

[69] A bitter person is incurably negative. Whatever you do for them is not enough—not good enough, not soon enough, not thoughtful enough, not costly enough. Nothing pleases them. Bitterness is the acid that consumes the container.

[70] In all honesty and in recognition of the grace of God, Gordon and I admit that if Joyce and Joanne had chosen mates solely on the basis of this list, they

would not have married us.

interrogation or defensive evasions signal core problems in the relationship. Suspicion and secrecy are equally effective in sabotaging a marriage, but a need to know creates a right to know. Should a couple tell all before marriage, or wait until after the wedding to clear the air? How much should be revealed before or during the engagement? My suggestion is not to unload too early: if the relationship breaks apart, feelings of being exposed and violated may be matched by abuse of confidences. Mutual self-revelation should deepen with mutual trust. If there are deep dark secrets, it is best to bring them into the light early enough in the dating period to provide time for recovery from any shocks. Premarital counseling should make the engagement a progressive deepening of trust, so that the couple can enter marriage with no barriers to the total oneness God intends for them. To not reveal all before the wedding not only violates general decency: it is against the law and grounds for annulment.[71]

I also ask a couple what they think of their own and each other's parents and siblings. Misunderstandings and feelings of hostility or distrust need to be addressed. The couple needs to open up and deal with any ongoing issues or current conflicts. Some problems can be traced to differences in how their families functioned:

How was anger dealt with in each family of origin? Were there temper tantrums? Did screams and threats carry too much weight? How were conflicts resolved? Did the loudest and most powerful usually win? How were issues discussed and reviewed? Was there a routine process for negotiation and compromise? How were arguments stopped? Were there

---

[71] Sadly, it is necessary to alert people to evidence of questionable motives for engagement or marriage. If a potential mate seldom talks about the past except in general terms, avoids certain topics, is secretive about old friends and keeps family visits short and controlled, red flags go up. I recommend a professional background check. This is also a wise move where one partner may profit financially from a marriage.

121

cooling-off periods followed by calmer consideration, or did disagreements create permanent divisions ("Oh, we just don't talk about that any more," or, "Don't go there!").

Did the parents accept biblical roles or did they follow other patterns? Were they models of good parenting, or bad examples? Was the family emotionally and physically close? Was warm affection displayed in frequent hugs and gentle touches? Were the children brought up, or did they just grow? Was there moral guidance, training in responsibility, and attention to all areas of development? If these matters are not brought to light before marriage, they will be at the root of unpleasant surprises later. The home a couple builds is strongly influenced for good or ill by the homes which built each of them.

What if parents do not approve of the marriage? If the parents are wise and thoughtful believers, their counsel should be considered carefully. If they are kind and dearly love their children, their objections will be meant to benefit rather than control their son or daughter. Discussing their concerns patiently will bring better understanding, and possibly lead to their approval. Not all parents are believers, and not all believers are wise and thoughtful in launching their children. What if agreement cannot be reached because the parents refuse to release an adult child from their control? Does the twenty-something daughter or son blindly obey their wishes?

When the Bible says, "Children, obey your parents in the Lord (Ephesians 6:1)," two qualifying considerations apply to major decisions. First, obedience is to be "in the Lord," respecting the God-given role of parents as nurturers and admonishers (Ephesians 6:5), and following their counsel as it follows God's Word. Second, obedience is required of "children," the dependent offspring of a father and mother. Jesus was subject to Mary and Joseph while growing "in wisdom and stature, and in favor with God and man," even after He told them, "I must be about my father's business (Luke 2:49-52)."

A Jewish boy was considered an adult "son of the law," bar mitzvah, at age thirteen. Girls were considered women when they married, often in their early teens. Family ties would always be close, but establishing a household as a law-keeping adult meant leaving father and mother behind for the sake of oneness in marriage (Matthew 19:5). There was no prolonged "adolescence" to blur the distinction between dependent children and responsible adults, although age-appropriate respect for parents adjusted to the changing circumstances of life. As an adult, Jesus indicated that His spiritual family, those who responded to God in obedient faith, took precedence over His physical family (Matthew 12:47-50).

"Obey your parents in the Lord." Mothers and fathers who know the Lord and live according to His Word deserve more than the respect due to their roles as parents. They are to be esteemed highly in love for the sake of their work as God's ministers to their children (I Thessalonians 5:12-13). If their nurture and admonition have been consistent with biblical principles, decisions which contradict them may also offend God. Even on the human level, parents have seen more of life than their children, and lessons they have learned give their advice a measure of wisdom which should not be rejected lightly. God's plan for the family includes the provision of loving adults who protect and train their own children. Children should be grateful if their parents have done their job well.

In Colossians 3:20-21 the command to children to obey is balanced by a corresponding admonition to parents. They are not to provoke or discourage their children. Inconsistent discipline, unreasonable demands and verbal or physical abuse make loving obedience impossible. Under such conditions children are not being trained to face life responsibly. They are being neglected or exploited according to the moods and whims of irresponsible adults. Provoking children, using parental authority to "show them who's boss," teaches them that life is a struggle for physical or social power, and that power is useful for controlling people rather than for helping them. Constant criticism discourages children, teaching them that their intentions, actions and their very lives are inconsequential. As someone has said of the effects of leadership, there are lifters who facilitate free and full development, and there are limiters who stifle all expressions of creativity and personal aspiration. If parents are lifters, children are launched from home to fly to the heights. If parents are limiters, children escape with their lives, at best.

After coming of age, and particularly when considering the life-defining step of leaving father and mother to cling to a spouse, children should accept wise counsel from their parents but must make their own decisions. Honoring one's father and mother means to not do anything to bring them public shame and to help them financially when they are old. Showing them respect is a bonus some children can give to honor their parents. Respect for parents includes respect for their thoughts and feelings. Some parents give wise counsel—children blessed with such parents deeply appreciate their godly advice. Mel Johnson, co-founder of *The Children's Bible Hour* and long-time youth worker, used to say, "Don't put your parents down: they brought you up." Parents who have equipped their children to live responsibly deserve thankful appreciation. Their greatest joy is to launch their children successfully.

Parents who are reluctant to release the moorings are like a man who builds a yacht in his basement, with no way to get it out to the water.[72] I once counseled a woman who told her son's doctoral committee not to confer the degree on him until she had her own doctorate because she was smarter,

---

[72] Many years ago a man in Saugatuck, Michigan built a boat on the roof of his house, apparently expecting a flood. If his expectations had proven true, he would have been considered wise. As time went by, it became clear that he had built on the wrong premises. Parents whose expectations limit or misdirect their children also make a smooth launch unlikely.

better qualified and, after all, his mother. She was definitely a limiter, refusing to rejoice in her son's success. Another mother brought her son for counseling because he had been talking about experimenting with homosexuality. After counseling he wanted to date girls but could not find one who could meet his mother's expectations. In this case, the mixed signals suggested that the mother was more concerned about controlling her son's behavior than about contributing to his happiness. A mother who disapproved of her daughter's groom showed her spite even after the wedding. Entrusted with the wedding gown while the couple was honeymooning, she sold it. Sometimes leaving parental control is unnecessarily painful and painfully necessary.

Parents may try to influence premarital counseling by interrogating and coaching their children or by contacts with the counselor. Legally, ethically and biblically a counselor must not give up responsibility (or authority) for setting the agenda of the counseling process. If counseling is to be directed towards a goal, rather than sinking to the level of a pity party or a "feel good" session, the counselor must call the shots and direct the questions. Premarital counsel should be carefully designed to prepare a couple to enhance and enrich each other. The stage should be set for a marriage that will be filled with good memories from the beginning, and for all the years to come. If you run someone off because they refuse to accept your guidance, so be it. You will be loved by some, hated by others and abandoned by many who wanted nothing more than your approval for what they wanted to do. Just do your job fearlessly, and remember that you minister under God's authority and are required to be a faithful steward of the gifts and opportunities which He gives you.

Couples may resist your best efforts to point them in the right direction. What if you give all the right counsel, and they go through all the assignments and discussions, but you are still convinced the marriage is doomed from the start? You can express your concerns, but be careful not to give the couple a self-fulfilling prophecy to live down to. Tell them the truth as you see it, in a loving, "I don't know everything" fashion, but do not attempt to play God in their lives. The decision to marry is their own responsibility. Joanne and I received both good and bad counsel, and went through some very difficult years before our marriage began to stabilize. Tim LaHaye, who performed our wedding ceremony, advised us to move a thousand miles away from our parents for the first year of marriage, pray together daily, have Bible study together, and call him if we ever thought of separating even for one night. We tried that, and still fell so far short of the heart of marriage that two reputable Christian counselors told us to give it up and get a divorce. By God's grace we eventually came to a better knowledge of the truth, and our marriage was saved. It is surprising and, in cases such as ours, clearly miraculous how God redeems lost marriages as well as lost souls.

Planning to marry, of course, includes planning a wedding day. No matter how simple or elaborate wedding plans may be, certain pitfalls can cause unnecessary conflict and lasting bad feelings. The groom should remember that in our society wedding planning is primarily the domain of the bride and her mother (not necessarily in that order). The ritual of a father "giving away" a daughter, aside from anachronistic proprietary connotations, acknowledges male responsibility for the well-being of the family. But it is really the mother who is most closely identified with a daughter and most deeply affected when her little girl leaves home to establish a new household. The bond between a mother and her daughter is extremely strong. A man who hopes to build an even stronger oneness with his wife wisely accommodates her mother's wishes concerning the wedding day. In healthy families, mothers and daughters are best friends for life. A man can be greatly blessed by a friendship with his mother-in-law from day one.

Something must be said about the pagan custom of immoral partying on the night before the wedding (the so called bachelor party). It is sinful and dangerous to trivialize sex just before solemnizing a marriage union. Going beyond chaste limits during a stag party or a girls' night out leaves lasting scars. Only a fool would start marriage on the basis of distrust or mutual permissiveness. Lies and secrets about promiscuous celebrations contaminate marriages. Starting with uncompromised faithfulness confirms a lifetime commitment and delivers souls from endless pain.

Premarital counseling sorts through the couple's thoughts and questions, and gives them a clearer idea of what they are getting themselves into. Thinking through issues of concern together trains them to communicate and resolve future problems. The counselor's task is to prepare the couple to function as a couple, rather than as separate individuals who may be going in different directions. Information gathered by thorough questioning will equip them for thorough planning.

In The Beginning ...

Adam and Eve began their marriage perfectly. Theirs was a case of love at first sight, with no desire for anyone else and no memories of lost loves. God Himself introduced them to each other at their wedding. There were none of the uncertainties of dating and courtship. Their home had no mortgage, no taxes and no utility bills. Their pets were well-mannered and there were no obnoxious neighbors. They never made a trip to a grocery store and never had to shop for clothes. Their picnics were never rained out. They did not have to go to church: God made house calls every day. All they had to do was express their love for Him in obedient faith.

They blew it for all of us. Other than creating a market for marriage counseling and other helping professions, their disobedience was calamitous. Our participation in their sin makes a good marriage a hard-won rarity. God still graciously provides the resources we need, but we insist on looking out for ourselves. Sin makes the human race needy, fearful and distrustful. We are needy because we have broken our connections with God and with each other. We are fearful that we will be cheated out of the affection and support we need. We are distrustful of others, considering them competitors who will stop at nothing to make sure their own needs are met. Love, which began in unselfish innocence, is now encumbered with doubting, defensiveness and even mutual deception. Unless God lifts this load, we all bring baggage into every relationship.

Adam and Eve found that sinful selfishness in itself is sufficient cause for failure to follow God's plan. Only sinful selfishness interfered with their perfect happiness in the place of God's blessing. Couples entering marriage now find their own selfishness reinforced by misdirected spirituality, competitive individualism, inconsiderate ambition and sin-tainted relationships. The bad news is that all humanity is hopelessly enmeshed in sin and its consequences. The good news is that God provides redemption from sin and amelioration of its consequences to those who are united with Him through obedient faith. Obedient faith is still at the heart of Christian marriage, making the home a place of blessing, a place where God meets with His people and dwells with them and in them.

We cannot go back to Eden. Until the times of refreshing and restitution of all things, the whole creation groans under the weight of sin and its consequences (Acts 3:19-21; Romans 8:18-33). Believers are motivated to live spotlessly and blamelessly as they look forward to a new heaven and a new earth where righteousness is at home (II Peter 3:13-14). Reconciliation with God brings a taste of the power He will reveal in the world to come (II Corinthians 5:18-21; Hebrews 6:5). Christians are set apart from this present evil world and placed under the kingship of Jesus Christ (Galatians 1:4; Colossians 1:13). Lutherans speak of the "already" and the "not yet" of Christian faith and life, Calvinists cite the "Creation mandate," and fundamentalists sing, "Brighten the Corner Where You Are." The Christian mission is not a race to the lifeboats: the blessings of reconciliation with God are to spread outward from each believer through gospel witness and righteous living. The world has been corrupted by sin, but those who have received the righteousness of Jesus Christ claim the ground they stand on for Him, making their lives, their marriages and their homes places of blessing.

God has given believers all they need to live godly lives and to build godly marriages (II Peter 1:3-4). He has given them Himself. God is not the author of confusion and instability but of peace and security (I Corinthians 14:33). The Holy Spirit gives believers power, love and a sound mind, enabling them to face challenges with compassion and self-control (II Timothy 1:7). Jesus Christ becomes the believer's wisdom, righteousness, sanctification and redemption. Believers are enriched by God with true speech and knowledge (I Corinthians 1:5). They are filled with goodness and knowledge, equipped to admonish one another (Romans 15:14). With all the resources of God Himself available to meet their needs, a Christian couple has no more reason to fail than Adam and Eve had.

This is not theological abstraction. Christian marriage does not take a couple back to Eden. They live in a sinful world as redeemed sinners, but their life as believers is enriched and empowered by God. Their marriage should demonstrate their position in Christ not through passive isolation but through active involvement. Their confidence in Christ should make them proactive in overcoming challenges and setting aside distractions. Finding the real purpose of life in their knowledge and enjoyment of God, they need not be discouraged or defeated by the common trials of life. Adhering to God's intention for marriage, they can surrender themselves to Him and to each other, not as an act of stoic resignation but as a joyous, energetic lifetime commitment. As they make plans according to biblical principles and put hard work into their radical commitment to Christ and to each other, God's blessing will fall upon their marriage.

Blessing falls upon a marriage as a couple fulfills the purpose of marriage. The purpose of marriage is to establish the most basic and comprehensive human connection. God created us for companionship. He intended that we would be bound to Him and to each other with bonds of love. For most of us that means finding a person to share intimately any and all experiences of life. Marriage is a life partnership designed to move onward and upward as oneness becomes more and more complete. There is no escape route, no going back, no Plan B. God's plan for marriage still includes His provision for success. Especially for believers, it is inexcusable to begin or end a marriage without fully appropriating and using the resources that God provides.

One of the most serious threats to marital success is selfishness. A society which teaches self-esteem to infants and tells adults to "look out for number one" can hardly expect anybody to love, honor, cherish or obey anybody else. The greatest antagonist against happiness in marriage is self. Conversely, the greatest antidote to unbridled self is happiness in marriage. God said it was not good for Adam to be alone. Isolated human beings tend to turn in upon themselves or strike out at others.[73] Their unmet needs include the need to serve

---

[73] How little focused attention time is given to each other in a household where the computer is treated like a sacred cow. Hours can pass at home or even in restaurants as couples set across from one another in computer isolation. The computer is also used as a "teacher" to children and interaction between children and parents is now rare unless the child does something outrageous to get the parent off the computer, Youtube, or computer games.

others. Eve not only met Adam's need for a companion, but she also met his need for ministry and responsibility. He needed someone to need him. In fact, the heart of marriage and of society is the God-designed interdependence of humanity. The individual human self is fulfilled through serving others.

Ironically, the best way to enjoy the benefits of any relationship is to be unselfish. Seeking to please another person draws out his or her appreciation and affection.[74] It is, of course, possible to be selfishly unselfish, accommodating someone in minor ways to get concessions regarding more major issues. Love does not keep double-entry books to make sure that all investments are cost-effective. Such hypocrisy is quite transparent. When a man brings his wife flowers or candy, she should be able to say, "How thoughtful!" Without wondering, "What does he want?" or, "What did he do now?" Unselfishness must be consistent, including major issues as well as minor ones.

Selfishness can be unlearned by accumulating shared experiences and developing shared interests. In whatever point of contact a couple is brought together, their common ground should be expanded. If their only shared interest at the beginning was physical attraction, their courtship should have explored hobbies, projects, skills and ministries to share. A marriage founded on sex, entertainment and eating is doomed from the start because it lacks the dimension of service which is essential to unselfish companionship. A couple needs to develop shared interests which reach out to others, whether in community or church activities, creative projects or performances, or simple social contact. A husband and wife who have many interests in common will find themselves bound together firmly. Being absorbed in shared pursuits will make them increasingly absorbed in each other.

[74]The expression, "Honesty is the best policy," does not refer primarily to a moral and theological judgment that honesty is intrinsically right and good. It is a pragmatic, utilitarian observation that honesty is the most effective way to achieve goals. Similarly, saying, "Unselfishness is the best policy," in relationships can fall short of acknowledging that unselfishness is good and right in itself because it is an aspect of Christ-like character. No virtue should

be pursued solely for its cash value in positive returns.

Compatibility and understanding will grow as they deliberately develop areas of common interest. Spouses who care little for each other's passions eventually lose their passion for each other. The oneness which brings true happiness must be cultivated constantly and consistently.

Happiness in marriage is very closely correlated with the desire and determination to live life at its best, according to God's plan, seeking His blessing. Mutual and equal spiritual growth enriches a couple's relationship, each stimulating the other into greater conformity to Christ. A low level of Christian life produces a low level of marital life. A Christian couple needs to be enriched and empowered by attending and participating in a church which preaches and teaches the Word of God and facilitates mutual ministry and great Christian relationships. They need to study the Bible together, and pray for wisdom and courage to apply its truths to the details of their life together. They need to grow together in conformity to Christ, and to demonstrate His work in their lives through their love for each other. The world needs to see that marriage based on purity and oneness brings the greatest lifelong satisfaction. As both husband and wife develop Christ-like character, the bond of love between them will demonstrate the presence and power of God in their marriage.

Even in a healthy Christian marriage husband and wife will have differences of opinion caused by differences in perception. Misunderstandings arising from cultural, social and economic issues may be rooted in the couple's different backgrounds. If their marriage brought significant changes in environment and status, each will be trying to maintain a former lifestyle and standard of living. The manner of life to which each has become accustomed may not be the manner of life their marriage can sustain. The only unequal yoke the Bible mentions is the union of a believer with an unbeliever, but marriages which cross humanly-perceived barriers require special consideration. Cultural differences due to regional, ethnic or family background can cause friction within a marriage and make it difficult to accept each other's relatives and friends. Cultural differences due to regional, ethnic or family background can cause friction within a marriage and make it difficult to accept each other's relatives and friends. This may be especially problematic where differences in race or nationality are subject to prejudice from either side.[75] Extreme differences in economic background can make household finances an area of conflict. If God has clearly brought a man and a woman together to accomplish His purposes, all other issues are secondary. What God puts together, He can keep together, but some couples will have to work harder than others to accommodate each other and to maintain a fruitful witness.

Serious maladjustment in marriage stems from failure to live with each other according to accurate knowledge of each other's needs and expectations. Besides differences in background, there will be differences in personal temperament, taste and habits. An argument over which way to hang the toilet paper or which way to squeeze the toothpaste only symbolizes irritated mystification over the idiosyncrasies of a spouse. A person brought up as an only child and taught to speak only when spoken to will have a tough time dealing with a spouse who had to compete with a houseful of jabbering siblings (their table manners are likely to be radically different, for one thing). The simple things individuals do differently can be exaggerated

---

[75] Gordon spent the summers of 1968-1969 tutoring at Rust College, in Holly Springs, Mississippi, what was called "a traditionally Black college." He was surprised at the indifference and even disapproval of Christian friends and family members in Michigan. Racial tensions were high just after the murder of Dr. Martin Luther King, Jr., and the emerging Black Power movement added what some call "reverse racism" to the mix. Riots at the Democratic Convention in Chicago exposed nerves people didn't know they had. Gordon's close friendship and teaching partnership with a female Rust College student brought warnings of God's judgment bringing harm to others through Gordon's Jonah-like defiance of God's will. How far have we come since then, really?

into judgmental conflicts. If there must be conflict, it should be over major issues where the outcome really matters. Accepting harmless idiosyncrasies may even add charm to the relationship between husband and wife.[76] Troubles and trials will come often enough: there is no need to invent them. The realities of life can disturb domestic tranquility, and balance is difficult without a united approach to issues. Intimate living demands purposeful love: the purpose is the determination to enhance the happiness of the other through adjustments and sacrifices in areas of potential conflict. Thorough understanding of each other must be applied logically, analytically and without expressing or evoking negative emotion.

It may seem paradoxical to speak of showing love logically and analytically, but that is precisely how common courtesies of society developed. Necessary human contact creates the need to treat each other civilly. People have learned that living with each other is more comfortable and productive when mutual respect is maintained through gestures of acceptance and encouragement. The Golden Rule (Matthew 7:12) has its parallels in almost all cultures: treat people the way you want to be treated, and they may return the courtesy. Conflict can be minimized by mutual restraint and avoidance of unnecessary offense. What we call "common courtesy" is simply an accumulation of wisdom which lubricates relationships and keeps society running as smoothly as possible.

The common courtesies of society are especially important to the love-life which is at the heart of marriage. The romance of courtship, when he and she were almost excessively considerate of each other, should extend into the romance of marriage. Consideration, appreciation, gratitude and basic politeness recognize the shared humanity of everyone we meet.

---

[76] Joyce Puls is amused, not upset by Gordon's frequent oversight of leaving the third button on his shirt unbuttoned. Her father, it must be said, almost always wore a rubber band around his wrist. Go figure.

It is incredible how inhumane we can be to those we claim to love. Words of greeting, questions about thoughts and feelings, thank you's, apologies, forgiveness and encouragement are all necessities, not luxuries. Common courtesy builds the loving atmosphere of an orderly home. In marriage, common courtesy extends to frequent hugs and kisses of greeting, farewell and simple affection. The opposite of love is not hatred, but indifference. When the spark goes out of a marriage, it has not been fanned and fed by common courtesy.

Courtesy is essential in dealing with failures, frustrations and freak occurrences which challenge a marriage. In the course of life, each spouse will have disappointments, off days and dismal failures. Supporting each other when things go "for worse" is at the heart of a strong marriage. When both husband and wife are cast down by cares and catastrophe, their marriage is as vulnerable as they are. If they are not held in God's hand, their own strength will fail them. Marriage vows express a radical, courageous commitment. Husband and wife are joined to stand together and, if knocked about by the adversities of life, to help each other up to stand again. Among the greatest blessings of a strong marriage is the fact that at least one other human being understands and shares all the struggles of life.

Happiness in marriage rests in trusting confidence; confidence depends on understanding; understanding has its basis in frank and objective review of issues and options. Couples should not allow anything to poison their confidence in each other. No misunderstanding should be allowed to degenerate into misgivings. Distrust and suspicion can be countered by absolute openness.[77] Every misunderstanding or

---

[77] Ultimately, there are no secrets. In healthy marriages and families there is a cycle of self-revelation. Husband and wife learn to see through each other's defenses, and dare to live transparently in each other's sight. Living transparently in their homes, they rear children who are able to see through other people.

disagreement should be addressed courteously before the close of each day. If conclusive resolution is impossible, the couple should find some common ground of understanding from which to resume the discussion later. Every issue between them should be laid to rest before they lay themselves to rest for the night. At least they can agree on a good-night kiss.[78]

Even when going to bed, courtesy is important. The oneness of marriage is not one-sided ownership. Unrestrained intimacy gives rise to disrespect. Selfish behavior, insistence on privileges and uncleanness in conversation demean the purity and trust of oneness. Both husband and wife are entitled to a degree of privacy which maintains their personal identity and value as human beings. Knocking before opening a bathroom or bedroom door and giving each other masculine and feminine space in the dresser is more than logical and analytical courtesy: it heightens the romance of marriage by preserving the mystique of sexuality.

There is little mystique in getting along with in-laws. Respect for husband or wife includes respect for in-laws. In arranged marriages, the choice of in-laws was a predominant factor, and the bride or groom had to be accepted as part of the bargain. Now the situation is reversed, and the in-laws are the surprise behind the veil. If dating, courtship and engagement have progressed according to biblical principles, accepting a spouse's family has begun well. Each family has its idiosyncrasies; each has an eccentric or criminal relative nobody talks about when a date is brought home for dinner. These are not secrets to anyone born into the family, but can be quite shocking when discovered by an uninitiated spouse. Appreciating the positive qualities of in-laws and accepting their

---

[78] Ed Wheat used to say, "Couples should never go to bed back to back." Their relationship should be reconciled nightly, even if all issues between them cannot be perfectly resolved. Obviously "back to back" is metaphorically used. Over 90% of couples sleep back to back because of oxygen deficiencies sleeping face to face causes.

quirks should be among the most valued gifts the bride and groom give each other.

Maintaining a congenial attitude toward in-laws may be made easier by considering that this family of strangers (some stranger than others) produced a perfectly wonderful bride or groom.

At the beginning of a marriage, a couple needs to be reminded to be guided by their minds as well as their hearts. There may be stars in their eyes, but behind the stars there must be something more than the vast emptiness of space. In this chaotic world, we are attracted to sports and the arts at least in part because they exhibit a measure of order and arrangement in human effort. Sixty minutes of well-executed basketball or three hours of precisely-played classical music leave us feeling that there is control and purpose somewhere in our world. A well-crafted play or novel can make it seem that, at least for a few characters, life eventually makes sense. A couple entering marriage does not need to depend on athletes, musicians, authors and actors to make sense of life. That space behind the starry eyes usually contains a brain which can be put to good use for exactly this purpose. Couples need to get beyond admiring order and arrangement in sports and the arts, and to start thinking about how to arrange for more order in their lives and marriages.

A couple's commitment to make their marriage work can be facilitated by short-range and long-range planning. Since many people reach the biblical lifespan of seventy or eighty years, a bride and groom in their twenties can expect their marriage to last fifty years or more. How can they plan for all of the possibilities of such a long time together? Their limited experience and the uncertainties of their future make solid counsel imperative. In my practice, I begin with three basic principles in mind:

Be biblical. I look to the Bible for answers to problems and sources of joy. The Bible contains all we need to know to enjoy happy, productive lives. Those who turn to the Bible only in times of crisis miss the stability and encouragement it gives to those who fill themselves with its wisdom.

Be practical. I start where people are and work with them on what can be done. Small steps which can be taken immediately demonstrate the effectiveness of planning. Resolving minor problems builds confidence to tackle major issues.

Be complete. I try to get to the root of issues to make sure plans cover as many details as possible. When a couple has acquired skills in problem-solving and planning, I expect them to apply what they know to all areas of their marriages.

Being biblical means making biblical principles and values the basis of all plans. Being practical means beginning with short-term plans to clear up existing issues and prepare for challenges of the immediate future. Being complete means long-term planning to provide for as much of the future as possible. In the beginning, a couple needs to know how to apply all the resources God has given them to all the life experiences they will face as husband and wife.

Getting Started

The best way to build a good marriage is to begin well. Beginning well in the basic elements of marriage establishes a strong foundation of oneness in meeting life's challenges. In premarital counseling, I present biblical principles which can be put into practice immediately to bring order and arrangement to a wide range of marital issues. I believe that problem-solving skills are rootless and fruitless without a clear view of what marriage is supposed to be and how it is supposed to work. Putting band-aids on a five-year-old's knees every few minutes does not teach the child how to ride a bike. Teaching a child to ride a bike saves both knees and band-aids. No, I am not going to say that marriage is just like riding a bike: it is never so mechanical that all the right moves become automatic. What I am saying is that certain elements of marriage are so essential that they must be the focus of planning and hard work from the very beginning, and that if they are developed well they will give the marriage stability and direction.

These fundamental elements of marriage are leaving, cleaving, roles, relationship and resources. Leaving and cleaving are biblical words for attaining independence as an adult and establishing oneness with a spouse. Roles of husband and wife are also clearly delineated in Scripture, and deal with procedures and attitudes of an effective marriage. Relationships with God and with each other must also be developed according to biblical guidelines. Resources outside the home will supplement and support the couple's efforts to live together peacefully and joyfully.

Leaving

Independence from parents is essential to establishing a couple's identity as a married couple in their own new household (Genesis 2:24; Mark 10:6-9). It is God's order for a man to leave father and mother to establish a household with his wife. When is a young man ready to marry? When he is emotionally, socially and financially secure enough to no longer depend on his parents (or in-laws) for basic needs. This independence honors parents for their success in preparing him for the responsibilities of adulthood and marriage. A close adult friendship with parents is a wonderful blessing, but continued dependence on them violates biblical roles of parents and children. Parents are to care for the needs of their dependent children, but adult children are to care for the needs of their parents, if necessary (I Timothy 5:8).

Financial independence from parents cannot be achieved through indebtedness to others. A couple beginning marriage should have no outstanding debt and should not incur debt to establish their household. The only ongoing debts believers should be paying are the debt of love owed to one another and the debt of evangelism owed to the world (Romans 13:5-10; 1:14-15). I tell couples plainly: borrow no money. Marriage vows do not say, "Until debt do us part," although that is what happens all too frequently. Money is the number one cause of marriage break-ups. Patterns of indebtedness at the beginning of life together establish habits which eventually bury a marriage under an avalanche of bad debt. Bad debt includes not only indebtedness beyond the foreseeable capacity to repay, but also overinvestment in quickly-depreciating items which are destined for the ash heap.[79] Dependence on parents brings obligations to them into every decision a couple makes. Dependence on creditors intrudes into a marriage even more forcefully. Husband and wife should be obligated only to each other. If they are also married to a bank or a loan company, their connection with each other will suffer.

Cleaving

Connecting with each other is the primary task of newlyweds. In Deuteronomy 24:5, a full year of exemption from public responsibilities is prescribed so that husband and wife can rejoice in their new union. I tell couples to set aside enough money for at least a few weeks of honeymooning. They need this uninterrupted time together to relax and get to know each other. Being physically available to each other twenty-four hours a day gives them opportunity to develop patterns of affectionate contact which form an enriching context for sexual

---

[79] Francis Schaeffer strongly warned against ash-heap lives based on accumulating material wealth which ultimately depreciates into nothingness.

intercourse.[80] Investing in the beginning of their life together is more important than spending money on an elaborate wedding. I even suggest that their honeymoon destination should be more of a hide-away than a tourist attraction. The main attraction on a honeymoon should be each other. A quiet place to talk, share intimacy and simply be comfortable with each other is all they really need. In fact, a vacation which focuses on just being together refreshes a marriage at any time. Even after many years together a couple can profit from getting away together without a list of places to go, things to do and people to see. So much of life is consumed in doing what we think we have to do that it has become necessary to set aside time to just be who we are meant to be. The oneness of marriage should reach to the core of each spouse's being. Careful attention to strengthening and enriching connections between husband and wife is at the heart of marriage from the very beginning.

Disconnecting from distractions facilitates connecting with each other. The biblical provision for a distraction-free first year of marriage goes beyond the usual perception of a honeymoon as a brief escape from reality, a romantic interlude followed by the sobering obligations of married life. If the couple spends a few weeks concentrating on each other rather than on a theme park or an exotic resort, they will be on their way to forsaking all distractions in order to build their marriage. Spending time face to face talking about everything and nothing opens communication lines which will help them be of one mind. Back at home, early evening is usually a good time for a leisurely meal and free-ranging conversation. Clearing the schedule of errands and outside activities for as many evenings

---

[80] The one-flesh union created by sex within marriage involves more than physical sexual release. The word "intercourse" is a synonym for "conversation." Some dictionaries still include "sexual intercourse" as a secondary definition of "conversation." Thinking of sexual intercourse as a lifelong conversation between husband and wife comes close to the meaning of being one flesh. The conversation begins during the honeymoon, when all aspects of sexuality can be addressed at leisure.

as possible should be a high priority, especially during the first year together. Without intimate self-revelation, husband and wife limit their ability to be true partners and helpers to each other.

One of the greatest threats to spending quality time together each evening is so called "prime-time" television. I advise couples to have no television in their home for at least one year. This is not only because of the low morality of much programming, but more importantly because television's prime time cuts into a couple's prime time for getting to know each other better.[81] Our culture's addiction to all media makes us think we cannot live without being connected to all the world all the time. Television presents an illusion of being connected to the world's reality while actually disconnecting us from the reality of our own lives. Medically, a dramatic test of a patient's survivability is to remove all artificial means of life support. The same principle applies to the survivability of a marriage. To determine whether a couple has a real, living relationship, pull the plug on their life support system: the television, the computer, in many cases the phone. If they cannot survive without it, they need to get a life. Beginning marriage without a television set gives a couple opportunities to invest their prime time on their primary objective, building their life together.

Roles

Responsibility and respect characterize the biblical roles of husband and wife.

They are not just roommates who adjust to each other and learn to share the same living quarters. They are not just business partners sharing legal responsibilities and liabilities.

---

[81] This applies to couples of any age, at any stage of marriage. Vegetating in front of a television or computer is often culpable escapism and sometimes a form of idolatry. Couples who have serious issues to resolve, or who have just drifted away from each other, cannot rebuild their relationships during commercials.

Marriage is more than cohabitation and obligation. The covenant of marriage is a commitment to fulfill the biblical roles of husband and wife. Although the concept of the husband's headship (I Corinthians 11:3; I Peter 3:1-7) has been misinterpreted and abused, the truth remains that the husband bears primary responsibility for the stability and viability of the marriage. Dwelling with his wife according to knowledge of her needs, he carries the weight of decisions which affect the quality of their life together. Facing challenges and resolving conflicts, the husband bears the burden of major decisions. The wife's role is to respect her husband's acceptance of this responsibility, encouraging him through gentle counsel and support. The wife also takes on responsibilities as keeper of the home (Titus 2:4-5), and deserves her husband's respect for her efforts in maintaining an atmosphere of order and nurture. Both husband and wife are to meet their responsibilities in ways which deserve respect.

Love and submission are the attitudes behind the actions of a healthy marriage. Biblically, husbands are reminded to love and wives are reminded to submit (Ephesians 5:22-28; Colossians 3:18-19). This is consistent with their roles and may also suggest that these are the attitudes males and females may be most likely to neglect. Love actively seeks what is best for the other; submission humbly accepts the preferences of another. When two Christians marry, their yoke is equal. All believers are told to love one another and to submit to one another (John 13:34-35; Ephesians 5:21). Love and submission are complementary characteristics of people growing in conformity to Jesus Christ.

Relationship

Relationship with God distinguishes Christian life and marriage from life and marriage without God's presence and guidance. Couples need to know God before they can live for God. They need to know God's plan for marriage before they can follow it. Living for God according to His plan necessitates meeting with Him in His Word. Christian couples should follow the example of the believers in Acts 2:42, giving unremitting attention to doctrine, relationship, shared meals and prayer. Daily Bible study together seems a minimal requirement. God leads according to knowledge of His Word: there is no other authoritative source of guidance. The blessing of God comes through meeting Him in His Word and living according to the truth He reveals there (Psalm 1; Joshua 1:7-9). Ignorance of God's Word leads to disorder and disaster. The truth of the Bible is demonstrated in our homes daily, whether we know it or not. We are "known and read" by everyone who knows us, especially those with whom we live (II Corinthians 3:2; I Corinthians 7:14-16; I Peter 3:1-2). Our relationship with God is demonstrated by the amount of attention we give to His Word.

Relationship with each other is also at the heart of marriage. As couples learn each other's desires and objectives, they will discover differences which could grow into conflicts. In adjusting to each other, husband and wife must be proactive rather than falling into patterns of reluctant compromise or codependency.[82] As issues arise they must be resolved conclusively as soon as possible. When resolution of a problem cannot be achieved without considerable time and effort, reconciliation of the couple to each other must be sought daily. They can agree to maintain civility and mutual respect while continuing to work on their differences. Resolution of the issue may take weeks or months of candid discussion. Reconciliation

---

[82] In Arkansas, I learned about hounds and ticks. Some marriages are a hound-tick relationship, where one spouse is out to suck the other dry. In a tick-tick marriage, both spouses are parasitical, and their whole relationship really sucks. In a hound-hound marriage, there is howling, growling and occasional nipping at each other, but once they catch the scent of what they're hunting for, they run straight after it together.

with each other should be almost immediate. A couple should
never go to bed unreconciled to each other. The bedroom is for
sleeping and love: nothing which interferes with those purposes
should be allowed through the doorway.

Resources

Spiritual counsel should be sought if a conflict cannot
be resolved satisfactorily in one week. I suggest that couples
consult their pastor or another Christian of proven maturity
and compassion. Ideally, they will know a Christian couple
whose home life is exemplary, radiating tremendous love.
A couple with an excellent marriage relationship has better
qualifications to help a troubled couple than a counselor with
only professional credentials. Mentoring programs which
recognize this priceless resource are being developed in many
churches.[83] In a healthy church, preaching, teaching and
purposeful conversation will create an atmosphere of mutual
ministry which opens many channels of effective support
for couples, families and individuals. All believers should be
available to help each other. A professional counselor's training
and experience are nothing more (or less) than a specialization
in particular aspects of the ministry of reconciliation entrusted
to all believers. The best counsel comes from believers whose
spiritual gifts and growth qualify them to speak the truth in
love to accomplish God's purposes in the lives of their brothers
and sisters in Christ.

Sexual counsel may be necessary if there are hindrances
to full enjoyment of intimacy. I Corinthians 7:2-4 teach that both
husband and wife owe each other a good sexual relationship.
If the wife is consistently unable to attain satisfying sexual
release, the husband should try to find ways to please her. In

---

[83] As in many ministries, priceless results are often achieved at no cost to the
recipient. The price of professional counseling is not always justified by the
results.

early marriage sexual freedom between husband and wife may be hindered by learned attitudes towards sex as well as by physical or emotional difficulties. An old cartoon shows a young couple sitting together on a bed, staring straight forward in fear and guilt as the portraits of their parents on the wall behind them stare down in disapproval. Conservative Christians have sometimes reminded couples that, once they are married, everything that was "No, no no!" becomes "Yes, yes, yes!" That is a rather simplistic way of saying that the marriage vows commit a couple to entrust their bodies to each other as completely as they have already entrusted their hearts and minds. The sacredness of the spiritual bond of marriage exalts the physical bond of sex. As Proverbs 5:18-19 indicates, sexual ecstasy is closely associated with total infatuation with the partner. In marriage this complete absorption in shared pleasure is the highest expression of romantic love. Mutual sexual fascination and satisfaction throughout a lifetime together: this is the one-flesh union the marriage covenant makes possible.

There is no prudery or dualism in the Christian approach to sexuality within marriage. Outside marriage, as Paul says in I Corinthians 7:1, "It is good for a man not to touch a woman." Sexually-charged contact evokes the desire to possess, cling to and unite with the other person physically and romantically. Outside marriage such touching is spiritually and morally dangerous. Within marriage, it is at the heart of the relationship between husband and wife. If there are problems in this area, counsel may be needed to help the couple make adjustments. To ensure confidentiality, objectivity and well-informed advice, sexual counsel should be sought from reputable sources. Pastors, medical doctors and marriage counselors have devoted their lives to dealing with problems people bring to them, and will not be shocked by any appeal to their expertise.

Getting a good start in marriage requires careful attention to the basic elements of the marital relationship. Leaving, cleaving, roles, relationship and resources are the heartbeat of marriage. A living, growing marriage is kept healthy by planning and hard work in each of these areas from the very beginning.

The Keys to a Good Marriage

A Christian home is a laboratory in which to demonstrate how people can love each other. In effect, God could say to an unbeliever, "If you want to know what my kingdom is like, look at that Christian family across the street. The way they love each other, the way husband and wife relate, the way the children respond, the structure and stability of their family life — that gives you a picture of the relationship between Christ and His Church."[84] The only Bible some will ever read is the revelation of God's presence and power in the lives and homes of believers.

It is possible for Christians to love as God loves because we have His Spirit and His Word to direct us. In the home, Christ-like love creates an atmosphere which teaches family members how to relate to other people. A person who has seen and experienced love at home will know how to love. A Christian home should be the most attractive place in the world. Biblically as well as traditionally, a nurturing mother will be at the heart of the home, and therefore its greatest attraction. Her husband's love for her will be his most important gift to their children.

But what is love? A person who tries to define love faces the dilemma of a caterpillar trying to figure out how to walk. Thinking about which step to take first can be paralyzing, but once started, progress becomes automatic. Getting started

---

[84] *Love-Life Seminar,* created by Ed Wheat, MD, now conducted by Dr. Dow Pursley.

correctly determines the direction and effect of progress. A man who adamantly argued in defense of his own "rational definition of love" ended up with a bloody nose from someone he probably considered irrational and unloving. At some risk then, I propose that love involves both attitudes and actions, and that biblical principles and examples indicate that the highest expressions of love include planning, hard work, and God's blessing.

God's blessing, of course, is primarily for those who know Him. Love is at the head of a list of qualities described as the fruit of the Spirit in Galatians 5:22-23. II Peter 1:3-7 lists characteristics believers should develop in themselves, culminating in unconditional love. An attitude of death to self is to be followed by daily acts of dying to self and living for others.[85] The mystery of godliness, God's work in and through believers (Colossians 1:27), involves divine empowerment for human responsibility. Love is a fruit of the Spirit which must be cultivated by every believer. In the Galatians passage, love can be considered the primary quality which includes the other qualities empowered by the Holy Spirit. In II Peter, love may be seen as the summation of the other character traits for which the believer is responsible. By any interpretation, the Holy Spirit's fruit and the believer's work result in Christ-like love.

God's rule in a person's life is neither an aura of other worldly religiosity nor a regimen of meticulous ritualism. A person ruled by God will exhibit righteousness, peace and joy in the Holy Spirit (Romans 14:17). The effect will be freedom to love purely, confidently and joyfully. Marriages and homes filled with purity, faithfulness and joy demonstrate God's power and presence. Obedient faith makes a home a place of God's blessing.

God's blessing comes first and last in a Christian home. The fruit of the Spirit grows as living in God's love empowers a family to express love. Christ-like character is cultivated as

---

[85] II Corinthians 4:10-16; 5:14-17 make this abandonment of self to the purposes of God the initiatory requirement of a true ministry of reconciliation.

believers accept responsibilities which express love. Revivalist Charles Finney defended his methods by a simple agricultural analogy. A farmer plants seed, then waters and cares for it as God makes it grow into a rich crop. A farmer who plants no seed or neglects what he has planted has no right to expect God to bring him any increase. Similarly, love is a gift from God which requires responsible nurturing.

Planning and hard work are clearly associated with God's blessing in II Peter 1:3-7. Believers are given "all things that pertain unto life and godliness" and are "partakers of the divine nature," yet they are told to earnestly nourish their faith, furnishing it with character qualities which bring glory to God. These character qualities demonstrate God's rule in the children of His kingdom. A believer's life, marriage and home are where God shows Himself on earth, and should be ruled by righteousness, peace and joy in the Holy Spirit.

Righteousness is prominent in the first two qualities mentioned in II Peter 1:5. Virtue, or right action, comes first. Obedient faith does what God says to do, regardless of the reluctance of human emotion or the objections of human reason. Knowledge, accurate understanding of the truth and right thinking about its applications, anchors action in what is true, right and good. Christ-like character is expressed in virtuous, knowledgeable love. Right action and right thinking are foundational to righteous love.

Peace is exemplified in the qualities of temperance and patience. Self-control keeps a person balanced — not enslaved to personal desires, not prone to irrational outbursts. Patience keeps a person calm in the face of trials not discouraged by stress or emergency, not prone to panic or escapism. Self-control and patience are foundational to peaceable love.

Joy is expressed through godliness and kindness. Godliness serves God through heartfelt worship — when righteousness and peace are united in God's love (Psalm 85:10), they motivate joyous love for God. Kindness serves others out of a heart which enjoys spreading justice and mercy (Micah 6:8). Godliness and kindness are foundational to joyous love.

God's blessing comes to those who seek it. Peter admonished his readers to give diligence to developing Christ-like character. Marriage is a laboratory which tests character and shows it for what it really is. Developing Christian love in a marriage requires planning and hard work. Being righteous as a lone individual is not the biblical model: God designed us to live as persons in relationships. Being at peace as a lone individual bypasses all the biblical references to "one another" ministry and witness to the world. Being truly joyous as an isolated individual is absolutely impossible. Marriage, as the most intimate human relationship and the basic unit of human society, challenges the husband and wife to accept responsibility for developing and displaying Christ-like love.

The keys to a good marriage are planning, hard work and God's blessing. People come into marriage with high expectations not only for themselves, but particularly for their mates. They soon despair over the poor performance levels attained. What began with such high hopes can seem a very wrong decision just a few months after the wedding. The problem is poor planning of the marriage itself. Most people plan their wedding day with more care than their future years together. People plan their education, occupation and wedding celebration, but expect the details of the marriage relationship to take care of themselves.

After working for many years with thousands of couples, I am convinced that there is nothing magical about the success of a marriage. It may be true that some couples seem to get along better by accident than others do by design, but the key is not in appearance but in perseverance. Success in conforming to an ideal requires conscious focus on the ideal and determination to do what is necessary to achieve it. Giving all diligence to virtue means doing the planning and hard work to behave well. In *Anne of Green Gables,* Anne imagines herself in certain ways and then acts out what she has imagined in order to reach her goals. She uses language, poise and grace beyond her natural inclinations to accomplish great things. She plans all the details of her imagined acts in a delightful, although not always successful, manner.

I do not endorse a "fake it until you make it" mentality. Acting artificially does not change reality. Hypocrisy is antithetical to the intimacy inherent in a one-flesh one-mind marriage. But we can choose to do what is right just because it is right, regardless of feelings or circumstances. Peter says that the first abounding addition to living faith is virtue, action of moral excellence which is the first step towards unconditional love. Faith produces works of faithfulness; love acts unselfishly for the good of another. When we know what is right, we must choose to do it: "To him who knows to do good and does not do it, to him it is sin (James 4:17)."

Choosing to do good within marriage means planning to do good. A couple must have a clear view of what marriage can be and set realistic goals to achieve that vision. Goals for marriage should be jointly established yet independently carried out. A couple may make it a general goal to encourage one another. One of them might decide to take the specific step of saying five encouraging things to the other each day. The independent implementation of the plan is chosen behavior unrelated to moods or previous habits.

A good marriage is a work of art. Any valid art form requires planning and hard work. Painting, music, poetry, choreography — satisfying and enduring creative works are neither random nor rigid. The artist makes choices, selecting materials and arranging them purposefully. As they discern what works in a marriage and what does not work, couples can choose to emphasize the good and eliminate the bad. They can choose to bring order out of chaos by getting organized and arranging their life together more purposefully.

And what is their purpose? To form a more perfect union, to be of one mind so emphatically that their one-flesh union will never be threatened. In marriage the foundation of any action must have the benefit of the other partner in mind as well as the general good of the marriage itself. When problems arise they must be dealt with together as a one-flesh unit attempting to be of one mind. Thinking or acting as separate competing individuals is contrary to the purpose of marriage.

Selfish behavior and attitudes must be eliminated. It is impossible to develop a constructive relationship while tolerating destructive habits. All forms of unfaithfulness and abuse violate the total trust needed to clear up misunderstandings and resolve disagreements. Even less threatening offenses can erode trust and block progress. Life together falls into a routine as a couple develops patterns for dealing with day-to-day issues. Their lifelong conversation and their life together can deteriorate into unwritten scripts and hidden agendas instead of deepening in understanding and acceptance. As they discover negative elements in their marriage, they must decide and plan to replace them with more positive patterns of interaction.

For example, if a couple's decision-making process has been short-circuited, they can analyze its faulty elements and at least imagine how it could be made more productive. The expressions, "I'm not having this conversation!" "End of discussion!" and "Don't go there!" are absolutely destructive. Communication within this most intimate relationship must go anywhere that matters to either partner. Barriers which cut off communication shut each spouse out of the other's thoughts and feelings, blocking the understanding and acceptance which could make them of one mind. These walls also shut each spouse in, leaving frustration to fester into bitterness

153

and division. If a couple's communication has sunk to this level, seeing what they have been doing wrong will motivate them to look for better ways to communicate. As they learn to communicate more effectively, they can plan to avoid unnecessary conflict by steering away from conversational dead-ends. Planning a marriage presupposes healthy communication. To formulate and implement plans for other aspects of their marriage, a couple must be able to talk about them rationally and considerately. Planning itself is hard work, and there is hard work in the communication and commitment necessary to carry out a plan.

Good premarital counseling goes beyond preparing a couple for their wedding: it includes helping them to plan their marriage. Couples who seek counsel later will see that better planning would have made their marriages stronger from the beginning. What is planning? It begins with a clear view of the current situation and a clear goal. Dissatisfaction with a marriage usually can be traced to dissatisfaction with a short list of problems within the marriage. Planning begins by defining existing or potential problems and determining what is unacceptable or unproductive in a marriage. Couples who desire to change may have different perceptions of what is wrong and what would make it right. The counselor's task is to guide them to a working consensus. Once they agree on how to describe a problem, they can begin to envision how to correct it.

Once we have gained a fair understanding of a couple's situation and have assessed their resources for handling it, we can help them plan improvements. At this stage we can introduce planning models which are also appropriate to premarital counseling. Square one is square one for everybody. The biblical definition of marriage establishes an absolute standard. Living up to that standard requires being aware of challenges and being prepared to meet them. This is the essence of planning.

In a society in which the reinforcing structures of extended family, community and church are not united in supporting marriage, couples need to work harder to prepare themselves for the challenges they will face. Every couple can profit from good planning. Planning a marriage before the wedding gives a couple a firm foundation for their life together. If they cannot agree on a comprehensive plan for their marriage, I might question the wisdom of planning for their wedding. Couples with strong marriages can make plans which maximize what has united them and cut down on less productive behavior. Couples in crisis need plans to repair damage caused by what has gone wrong and to prepare for more to go right.

Communication is the beginning of good planning. The hard work of carrying out a marriage plan involves learning to communicate clearly and patiently. Speaking the truth in love, the couple grows in their ability to understand and accept each other. To agree on a plan, they must reach consensus through open expression of thoughts and feelings. When they have agreed on a plan, free communication will work out the details of living according to the plan.

Commitment is the lifeblood of good planning. Planning and communication succeed when they are grounded in commitment. Saying "I do" and "I will" in their wedding vows commits a couple to continue choosing and acting together for the rest of their lives. It is more than a commitment to endure a marriage no matter how bad it gets. It is a commitment to actively pursue a one-flesh one-mind union to see how good it can get. Commitment opens up the trusting communication needed to plan effectively. Once plans are made, commitment ensures their implementation.

Marriage counselors cannot consider themselves successful when their clients merely stop destroying each other. A home damaged by fire must be rebuilt. To diminish future risks, better building methods and better materials might be necessary.[86] Marriage counselors, whose ministries go beyond putting out fires, will give couples tools for more effective communication and planning. As couples succeed in their renewed commitment to each other, those who have assisted them may rightly share their joy.

Planning a Marriage

Are adventures a sign of poor planning? Can our lives and marriages be stabilized so securely that nothing can go wrong? Or is life what happens while we are making plans? Are we victims of circumstances and events beyond our control? What we cannot control often interferes with our plans, but what we can control should not be left to chance.

Some marriages seem to succeed by accident, with minimal deliberate planning. The best of these are marriages in which love thrives, commitment is taken seriously and the example and support of family, community and church is exceptionally strong. Others are marriages in which one spouse dominates decision-making and the other acquiesces without arguing. Some seem to succeed only because they have not been tested.[87]

The tests of a marriage may come at the critical mile markers where changes in circumstances alter aspects of a couple's relationship, or at times of crisis anywhere along the road. Traditional marriage vows include a commitment to endure sickness, financial hardship and "worse." But loss of

[86] When Gordon and Joyce Puls needed a new roof after two hurricanes hit their house, repairs had to be made according to stricter codes than the original construction. Similarly, building a marriage which is biblically "up to code" requires correcting flaws in the original construction if the marriage was built on faulty presuppositions.

[87] Joanne and I were forced to analyze what was wrong with the early years of our marriage. Our struggles taught us the necessity of planning. Gordon and Joyce Puls were surrounded by examples of biblically grounded marriage. Their solid Christian families taught and demonstrated the value of following God's plan from the beginning of their marriage.

health, loss of income and other crises can be catastrophic if the comforts of health, wealth and happiness are valued more highly than commitment to marriage vows. Marriage is more than comfortable companionship in the best of times: it is compassionate commitment through the worst of times.

Couples can hope for the best and rejoice in times of relative ease, but they must plan for the worst and strengthen each other in times of distress. Adventures, distractions and disruptions which break the pattern of their lives test their character and their commitment. They also test a couple's faith in each other and their faithfulness to each other, and even their faith in God. Changing circumstances and unforeseen events disturb a couple's lives even while they are making plans, but solid commitment and open communication can hold their marriage together.

I emphasize planning as a continual refinement of the marriage relationship. My premarital sessions, crisis counseling and marriage seminars always include formulating plans to establish, preserve and enrich marriages. Some couples have sought counsel after only a few days or weeks of marriage. A few have called for advice while on their honeymoons. It is much better to get help on the honeymoon than to let issues simmer for fifty years. Adjusting plans to problematic circumstances and events should be an ongoing means of improving the marriage. Right from the start and through all the mile markers of marriage, planning to make the marriage better will keep it from getting worse.

Insights gained in the counseling process must be translated into actions which will reinforce or rebuild a marriage. Knowing where they are on their marriage journey, a couple can make necessary course corrections and move forward. Taking stock of their spiritual and personal resources, they will see where they can get help and how they can be helpful to each other. If the assessment of their situation has been thorough and accurate, they will have gained a realistic view of themselves, their marriage and their place in the world. Seeing more clearly, they will be able to make wiser decisions and to implement them more effectively.

The best way to handle marriage problems is through preventive measures. Observing thousands of couples over years of ministry at the Wheat Clinic, I saw the need for more comprehensive premarital counsel. Many of these couples had gotten into serious trouble through inadequate planning. People are often surprised at the extensive premarital package I developed out of the experience of those years. The program consists of seventeen sessions, complete with homework assignments each week. And, yes, as I have stated, there is a proportionately high drop-out rate of couples who discover that they are not ready to commit themselves to the hard work of preparing for a strong marriage. Better to stop the wedding plans than to have no plan for sustaining the marriage. Marriage is more than standing facing each other, gazing dreamily into each other's eyes. It is standing next to each other, facing in the same direction with a clear vision of how to move forward together. Sooner or later a couple will learn that that is how a marriage works. Planning turns them in the right direction and clarifies their vision.

Every couple needs to plan. A marriage planning model will include common areas of concern where decision-making and response to changing circumstances can be facilitated by careful preparation. Good intentions and high expectations are actualized as a couple sets goals and develops practical plans to reach those goals. Some people lack clear goals and refuse to put time and effort into short-term or long-term planning, then blame circumstances, other people or even God for their failures. Most of the marriages which fail within the first few years are goalless and were entered without wise counsel or careful planning.

Where is the romance in planning a marriage? What about falling in love? Songs, movies, novels and advertising perpetuate our culture's emphasis on emotions associated with love. We feel the chemistry, catch the spark, hear fireworks and see stars. Strangers in the night falling in love with love, boy meets girl and they live happily ever after. When he saw her standing there he wanted to hold her hand in strawberry fields forever. She was sixteen going on seventeen, holding out for a hero, when he came out of her dreams and into her arms, and now nothing in this world can come between her and her guy. More recent popular music is too obscene or profane to qualify as romantic, but it still exalts the feelings of the moment over wisdom and planning.

Love is more than the sum of its accompanying emotions. Love is a total and unconditional focus on the good of the other person. It does not focus on the good feelings the other person gives to me, the good feelings I give to the other person, or the good feeling of being together. Feelings of connectedness disappear if the connections are not well secured. Connections are secured through the hard work of clear communication and detailed planning.

Does this take the fun out of marriage? Does a planned marriage resemble the arranged marriages of other times and places more than the romantic ideal of our own pop culture? Where is the spontaneity, the excitement, the romance in all this? Arranged marriages were meant to reinforce the prosperity, security and traditions of subcultures. Viewed as a fundamental structure of society, marriage has great significance for the welfare of the extended family, the stability of the community and the perpetuation of beliefs and values. Where these societal concerns predominate, tribal elders or heads of families choose who should marry whom. Any romance in the marriage depends on how the couple responds to the arrangement.

According to the Genesis account, the marriage of Adam and Eve created human society. There was no preexisting social context other than their relationship with God. Modern concepts of marriage often leave God out of the picture and depict marriage as a voluntary commitment between individuals with little or no reference to their family and societal context. The ritual of a father giving a woman away is perceived as glaringly anachronistic and sexist. If parents have any place in the wedding ceremony, it is to give their assent to the independent choice the couple has made.

Traditional societies view marriage quite differently. Arranged marriages are not arranged by the bride and groom. In fact, the bride and groom may have little or no part in making the arrangements.[88] A kinship group of family, tribe or clan decides on who should be married based on communal tradition. Economic, social and religious values of the community determine suitable pairings. The kinship group, rather than the married couple, is considered the basic unit of society. Marriages are considered fundamental to the welfare of the group, and corporate interests take precedence over individual choices. Inheritance rights, political alliances and religious taboos dictate which pairings are best for the future of the group. Individuals enter marriage for the good of the group, and the group fully supports the couple in living out their assigned roles. The stability of the group provides identity, security and purpose for its members as long as adherence to its

---

[88] We have a wonderful Pakistani family living a few doors down the street. Both Danny and Parveen were from generational Christian families. Danny's father was a pastor, and bore on his body the marks of standing up for his faith in a Muslim culture. He was beaten and jailed numerous times for being a Christian. Danny moved to America, and his parents eventually arranged a marriage for him. His wife had never met Danny before their marriage, but both of them trusted the faith and wisdom of their respective parents. They now have five children and a blessed marriage and are among the most courageous Christians I have known. They now "adopt" poor Christian children and provide educational opportunities for them (www.visionforpeace. com).

160

traditions keeps it self-contained and self-sufficient. Maintaining the internal balance of the group assures that members will be protected, governed, educated and provided with physical and spiritual nurture. Arranged marriages preserve the group's internal balance and facilitate the group's survival.

Recent Western culture has become so individualistic that the patriarchal structure of its historical roots is forgotten. The Roman familia encompassed more than husband, wife and children or even what we might call extended family. One sense of the word referred to a family line, all the descendants of a noted progenitor. This defined a person's place in history and status in society. Familia also referred to the household, all the persons living together in one home, whether related by blood or resident servants. The Greek word oikonomia includes a similar meaning, referring to the arrangement of a household. This etymology is consistent with the picture historians and sociologists present: The family gives a person a way to live with others in a mutually beneficial arrangement, an economy.

We no longer live in totally self-sufficient households or tightly bound kinship groups. The complexities of our society make us look elsewhere for identity, security and ways to live with each other. The functions of the kinship group or household have been delegated to the institutions of modern society which govern, educate, and employ us. The institutions of society can define us and circumscribe our range of choices just as surely as simpler societies did for their members. As the benevolence of these larger social structures deteriorates or as we reject "the establishment," we face another prospect: although society still provides for basic survival, questions of personal purpose, character and happiness are left for individuals to define and pursue. Autonomous individualism leaves us without the support of a kinship group's compassion, wisdom and encouragement.

Compassion, wisdom and encouragement? Where can couples find these lost foundations? I hope these are characteristics of pastors and marriage counselors, but our shoulders cannot carry all the weight. Must couples let depersonalized institutions determine the meaning of their lives together? Is marriage what the government says it is? Or is it whatever an individual wants it to be? Does personal self-interest determine the quality and durability of a marriage? These were purely rhetorical questions when religious, political and personal values were identical. Now there are serious attempts to separate a legal definition of marriage from the biblical definition, and individuals are seriously concerned about gaining legal status and religious approval for whatever misunions they choose to enter. Where there is no absolute authority, consensus over ethical and moral issues evaporates, and society disintegrates. [89]

Traditional kinship groups and households integrated individuals into viable societies. The advantage of arranged marriages was precisely the fact that they were arranged. Family and community placed the couple in a context where few major decisions would be necessary, and where social catastrophe would be nearly impossible. Inheritance determined what they would have, tradition determined what they would do and local resources determined where they could go, who and what they would know and even what they would eat. Lack of choices might have made life uneventful, but a secure, clearly defined role in the society precluded whole categories of marriage problems.

Society no longer offers such security, and few couples would want it if it meant such limitation. But if society does

---

[89] This disintegration is not only the current push that the Sodomite community is trying with some success to ram down our unsuspecting gullets; It was present in the hippie days when people were living nude in communes. Recently a young man, now a lawyer, told me his naked communal living mother traded him for a pair of boots during that social experiment.

not plan marriages, couples must plan them. Identity, security and purpose can be built into a marriage by a couple's choices and actions even where external support is lacking. Husband and wife can strengthen the foundation of their own marriage by agreeing on shared values and goals. They can build on that foundation by planning how to achieve their goals and then living out their plans. Rebuilding a family from the ground
up, a couple can provide a context of compassion, wisdom and encouragement in which they and their children can thrive.

Counselors and church leaders should realize that helping couples plan and build their marriages could revitalize all the structures of society. We must be construction workers as well as firefighters. There would be fewer marriage problems to solve if couples were prepared to handle the responsibilities of marriage more systematically. That means planning. An inspiring teacher told her students to "Fasten your dream to a star and climb, climb, climb!" Lofty advice. Daring to aspire to the highest goals is truly commendable, but to climb toward them confidently, the first concern might be to build a ladder. Couples need to know not only where they want to go but also what steps they can take to get there. A journey of a thousand miles begins with the first step, but if you get off on the wrong foot you can go a thousand miles in the wrong direction.

Metaphors aside, there are at least six areas of marriage which call for careful planning. Each area should have a one-year plan, which outlines specific actions to be taken to reach measurable short-range goals and a five-year plan describing long-range goals. Each plan should be evaluated annually to check progress and consider improvements. Adjustments and revisions may be necessary to keep on target. The six areas of marriage which need to be planned are:

Relating to God. Spiritual growth of each spouse and of the couple's spiritual fellowship and ministry begins with relating to God. Seeking God's rule in their lives will bring His presence and power into their marriage to bless their home.

Relating to each other. The intimacy of a one-flesh one-mind union grows through open communication on all levels: conversation, decision-making, problem-solving and sexuality.

Relating to family and friends. Oneness as a couple takes priority over all other relationships. The exclusive intimacy of marriage does not sever legitimate connections to other people, but these must be secondary to the connection between husband and wife.

Regulating finances. Couples who know where they are going know where their money is going. Clear understanding of financial resources and expenses can keep a marriage on track, but mismanaging money can destroy a marriage.

Reinforcing knowledge. An education for husband, wife and children will enrich their lives and equip them for the challenges of life. Being proactive about learning keeps a couple alert and interesting to each other.

Relaxing. Recreational activities give couples and families opportunities to interact with each other in refreshing ways. Hobbies, sports and travel provide new contexts in which to get to know each other better.

Each of these six areas carries its own issues. The plan for relating to God might include reading the Bible through during the next twelve months and establishing family devotions and prayer time. The plan for regulating finances should include a one-year budget to be renegotiated at the end of each year. There should be an educational plan for both husband and wife as well as for each child, including reading for personal enjoyment and enrichment as well as classes and workshops. Relational plans acknowledge that good relationships take careful planning for quality time together, and for maintaining appropriate connections with friends and relatives. A recreational plan is necessary because the body is not a perpetual motion machine, and breaks from routine responsibilities rebuild the whole person.

Where is the romance in all this planning? Not just

in the good feelings, but in feeling good about the strength of the marriage. Not just in the excitement of a moment, but in the security of a life-time of productive years. In all areas of life together, the trust and safety that planning builds into a marriage actually increase the freedom and joy which are the keys to true romance.

Relating to God

Advising people about friendship with God might seem presumptuous. As counselors, we confess with Paul that we have not attained perfection, but are reaching forward to understand and follow God's purposes for our lives (Philippians 3:12-14). Admitting fallibility does not mean accepting failure. As Paul says, "to the degree that we have already attained, let us walk by the same rule, let us be of the same mind (Philippians 3:16, NKJV)."

We can avoid slipping backward and take steps to move forward in our spiritual lives. Recognizing our weakness, we can encourage others to walk forward with us in the strength of the Lord.

A wise church officer prayed for his ambitious pastor, "Lord, don't let him try to lead us someplace he's never been." We cannot export what is not working in our own lives. A counselor whose own marriage is at risk will be pessimistic or hypocritical in suggesting what might work for others.[90] If our own spirituality is more formality than power, our clients will question our credibility. The first step towards helping couples create a spiritual plan is to make sure we are growing spiritually ourselves.

A family's spiritual life can be very active and exciting. Having a family ministry can teach children the value of commitment and service. The Pursley family has been involved in the pro-life movement from the time the children were very small. Some of the Pursley children's earliest memories include

---

[90]Early in our marriage, Joanne and I were counseled to give up our struggle and get a divorce. The pastor/counselor himself was involved in an affair, and left his wife a short time after we saw him.

involvement in sit-ins, marches, rallies, picketing, mass mailings and Operation Rescue activities. Family devotions included prayer and Bible study related to public events and issues. Arrests, court cases, jail time for Dad, and the positive results of persistent, uncompromising, activist faith showed the children the real-life consequences of friendship with God.[91] According to their capacities, the children shared in these expressions of faith, and developed strong convictions of their own. They learned that conforming to Christ means not conforming to the shifting values of the world.

A family's spiritual strength may be tested in other ways. When Michele Puls was two years old, she liked to sing "Put Your 'Jamas on in a Sailboat." The song Mom and Dad taught her in toddler's church was really about Peter, James and John, but Michele's middle name was Joy, and she showed it in her singing. As a child, she enjoyed singing at church and listening to Christian recordings at home. When she grew up and worked as a pharmacist, she sang, "If you're happy and you know it, count your pills," and was known to dispense hugs to patients as she prayed with them. When Michele was twenty-seven, an explosive sound startled a horse she was leading, and the horse stepped on Michele's chest. The family knew three of her favorite songs had to be sung at her funeral: "Joyful, Joyful, We Adore Thee," "I Have Decided to Follow Jesus" and "Shine, Jesus, Shine." Two of Michele's friends decided to follow Jesus while singing Michele's songs that day. The joy goes on.

Spiritual planning is not about a "pie in the sky" or a "castle in the air." It is about receiving power, love and sanity from God Himself and being carried along by the Holy Spirit to do and endure what would be overwhelming without Him. As Peter says, God "has given us all things that pertain to

---

[91] A reporter quoted Joanne as saying she "was not surprised" when I was arrested and tazered for trying to take water to Terri Schiavo, whose feeding tube had been removed by a court order. That is a considerable understatement, considering our track record on right-to-life issues.

life and godliness" (I Peter 1:3). The exceeding riches of God's grace are not just for heavenly places or the age to come. These resources are for the good works, which God prepared for us to do (Ephesians 2:6-10). Peter says that virtue, knowledge, self-control, perseverance, godliness, brotherly kindness and love are outgrowths of real faith. The faith we take to church on Sunday morning should be the same faith we take to work on Monday morning.

A family's spiritual growth goes beyond Sunday-go-to-meeting Christianity. Real Christianity comes with a price of service, not for salvation, but out of love for the Savior (I Corinthians 6:20; 7:23; II Corinthians 5:14-15). It may mean political and legal activism, being valiant for the truth in a culture which proceeds from evil to evil as it ignores God (Jeremiah 9:3; 5:4). It may mean helping twenty-one toddlers take their turns at the drinking fountain while their parents are listening to a sermon. At home in the living room it might mean making plans for an amendment to the state constitution to protect the unborn, or reading about Narnia and Middle Earth with a child on your lap. A good spiritual plan outlines a couple's growth and ministry at home, at church and in the world.

The purpose of a spiritual plan for the home is to stir a hunger for closer friendship with God. This plan is separate from individual prayer and devotional life. Unless personal duties are established and maintained, it will be impossible to lead a family in spiritual growth. This is especially crucial for counselors and their families. Regardless of professional credentials, the biblical standard for leadership begins with the recognition that ministry begins at home. Public ministry is an outgrowth of faithful private ministry (I Timothy 3:1-5, 12; Titus 1:5-6). Beyond individual devotions, it is essential for husband and wife to develop a spiritual plan for themselves and their family.

A good place to begin is to pray for each other together every day, calling down God's blessing and favor on each other. Giving thanks for your marriage and for each other's part in its success, the prayer should include requests relevant to specific challenges of the day. It might be useful to follow patterns found in the Bible. Paul's prayer in Colossians 1:9-14 asks God for wisdom, power and awareness of our riches in Christ. Couples can ask that for each other:

Father, I pray that Joanne might know your will and have the wisdom and understanding to do it. May she represent you well today, getting to know You better as you make her good works effective in the lives of others. Show your power in Joanne, energizing her to deal with difficult situations and people she faces today. Make her joyfully thankful that you have delivered her from darkness into light. Let her live on earth as a citizen of heaven.

Paraphrasing portions of other biblical prayers and blessings can prompt us to more meaningful spontaneous prayer. Paul's prayers, some Psalms and other Scripture passages are well-suited for usage in prayer at home or in the counseling office. The benediction in Numbers 6:25-26 is just as appropriate at home as it is in church:

Lord, bless Joyce and protect her. Let her know you are with her today. Refresh her with your kindness. Show her your face; give her restful confidence.

This is how God teaches His people to bless each other. Certainly husbands and wives should be faithful in asking for God's blessing upon each other.

Does this sound artificial? Perhaps we have short-circuited communication so completely that taking time for more content-laden conversation seems burdensome. A quick goodbye at the door and our thoughts turn from each other to the cares of the day. The goodbye itself exemplifies the problem. Originally it was, "God be with ye," and carried some of the intention of biblical blessing formulas. It has been a custom within Christendom to acknowledge that God cares for loved ones who are parted from each other. The Spanish "adios" and the French "adieu" commit friends "to God" until they meet again. Restoring "goodbye" to "God be with you," and expanding that into more specific and comprehensive prayer is neither artificial nor burdensome. It expresses the reality of relationship with God and with each other, and leaves our real-life burdens in His hands.

Praying and reading the Scriptures together strengthens the marriage bond. The cares of this world distract us from each other as well as from God. Addiction to entertainment and recreation tempts us to seek pleasure rather than commitment. Satan poses questions about what God has said and prompts us to act out our sinful desires. We need to open God's Word to hear Him speak, and we need to open our hearts to speak freely to Him. Jesus tells His friends that as they stay close to Him and obey His commandments, He will stay close to them and their prayers will be effective (John 15). John 15:7 is the mandate for spiritual growth in an individual, a couple or a family: "If you abide in me, and my words abide in you, you will ask what you desire, and it shall be done for you."

What do we desire? Home is where the heart is, and our hearts are where our treasures are (Matthew 6:19-21). What do we treasure? What do we really want, what do we live for? What our flesh desires, what our eyes covet and what our pride craves can lead us far from God. Physical pleasure, material wealth and proud self-satisfaction are temporary. Lasting treasure comes through wanting what God wants (I John 2:15-17). If what we treasure is friendship with God, our hearts will be most at home in God's presence. If our home is in God, God will be in our homes. What we really want will be what He wants for us, and He will provide it abundantly.

Searching the Scriptures to discover what God wants to do in and through us involves more than ritualistic reading and perfunctory prayer. The concept of family devotions as a few minutes for God is another example of how our instant-everything culture pares down and shrink-wraps our lives. Yes, short Bible readings and spiritual exercises at set times are helpful in keeping in touch with God and with each other. A verse or two at breakfast and the day's reading from a devotional booklet at the evening meal might seem an unattainable goal in our busy lives. But what are we busy about? If our hearts are set on friendship with God and with each other, why do our work and play leave only a few minutes each day for seeking our real treasure?[92]

It is especially important to focus on our real treasure as we accept the responsibility of rearing children in the "nurture and admonition of the Lord (Ephesians 6:4)." Half a century ago a gospel song said, "Don't send your kids to Sunday school — get out of bed and take them!" During most of church history there were no Sunday schools. The first one was started in 1780, primarily for poor, uneducated children whose families had few resources for training them. A rescue mission director has observed that before World War I, professing Christians nourished the faith of their families through "religious practices in their homes." Evangelists could refer meaningfully to a mother's prayers and an unbroken family circle when presenting the Gospel." But when Protestantism in America became more formal and church-centered, religious instruction largely disappeared from the home. The Sunday school was

---

[92] When counseling those who are dying, I have never had a man say to me, "Dow, I wish I had spent more time at the office or on the golf course." Almost without exception the conversation has to do with regrets over not having spent enough time with family and the agonizing consequences of missed opportunities with their wives and children.

171

an extension not of the church, but of the home."[93] Going back even further, William Barclay explains why the New Testament church did not include a New Testament Sunday school: "The New Testament is certain that the only education which really matters is given within the home, and that there are no teachers so effective for good or evil as parents are." He summarizes the view of early Christians: "The training of the child is a parental duty... The whole task of education is laid squarely on the shoulders of the father."[94]

Historical precedents and cultural accommodations can be debated. Has God said anything about how parents should share His Word with their children? Timothy's mother knew something about it. Paul commended the sincere faith of Timothy's mother and grandmother, the same faith he saw in Timothy (II Timothy 1:5). Timothy was Paul's "own son in the faith (I Timothy 1:2)," but from early childhood he had "known the Holy Scriptures, which are able to make wise for salvation through faith which is in Christ Jesus (II Timothy 3:15, NKJV)." Timothy's mother had taught him God's Word. Did she teach him the Scriptures simply because it seemed the right thing to do? Did she sit him down for a few minutes each day to pray and learn a Bible verse? Possibly. It was customary for Jewish boys to memorize key passages of the Hebrew Scriptures. Usually this would have been done with their fathers in preparation for participation in synagogue services. But according to Acts 16:1. Timothy's father was a Greek and there is no reference to his conversion to either Judaism or Christianity. So a godly mother accepted responsibility for the spiritual training of her child. A Christian parent with or without a Christian spouse bears the same responsibility.

---

[93] Arthur Bonner, *Jerry MacAuley and His Mission*, Loizeaux Brothers, 1967, p. 101.

[94] William Barclay, *Educational Ideals in the Ancient World*, Baker, 1974, pp. 236, 238.

Timothy's spiritual training would not have been limited to a brief time for family devotions each day. The responsibility of godly parents was much more comprehensive. The primary passage a Jewish boy would memorize would be Deuteronomy 6:4-9. This passage declares faith and devotion to the one true God and commitment to His Word. The evidence that God's commandments were in the hearts of His people was shown as they taught God's Word to their children in all the activities of life: sitting in the home, going for a walk, bedtime and breakfast were all places to speak and teach God's Word. What was done with the hands or seen with the eyes was subject to God's commandments. God's Word was to be the foundation of both family life and business dealings.

In our culture, this means that our children should not rush through a *Keys for Kids* devotional and then go web-surfing unsupervised. It means Mom and Dad cannot pray for God's will to be done on earth and then go off to employment or amusements which compromise biblical principles or corrupt the lives of others. Family devotions, brief times with God together, grow out of family devotion, total life commitment to God. Successful devotions involve both the husband and the wife and, later, the children. A whole family devoted to knowing and serving God can be quite innovative in their devotional exercises. Taking turns reading the Scriptures, asking questions and praying gives everyone opportunities to minister. The transition from couple devotions to family devotions is much easier if the couple started their life together with a commitment to shared Bible reading and prayer.

Sharing responsibilities for devotional activities helps families establish a consistent schedule. Everyone will be involved in preparation. The parents will not feel overworked and the children will not feel bored. A family prayer journal can record the date of each request and the date the prayer was answered. Missionary biographies and communication from current missionaries can enlarge the family's vision. Devotional times might begin as ten or fifteen minute periods and expand as the family's spiritual interests diversify. The length of devotions may vary widely and they might not be done daily. Consistency and quality are more important than ritual.

The relation of regular family devotions to a family's lifetime devotion is clear. A family devoted to God will devote time to knowing Him better. The time spent together in God's presence will confirm their commitment to Him at all times. Reading God's Word regularly convinces His people that the Scriptures are relevant to all the challenges of life. Seeing prayer answered encourages family members to bring all their cares to God. Learning about missionaries motivates them to speak boldly about their Savior.

Regular church attendance facilitates a family's worship of God. Again, the reality of meeting God together is essential. Being in church every time the doors are open is unnecessary. Church activities should not be allowed to bring stress or division into the family's spiritual development. Commitment to a church provides opportunities for a family to grow together through discipleship, fellowship, worship, ministry and evangelism. A well-balanced church will help its members grow in conformity to Christ. Bonds of love will grow to include the family of God as well as the family at home. Gathering to offer praise to God and encouragement to His people will invigorate believers to share the faith with everyone they meet.

A spiritual plan for one year begins with a commitment to pursue friendship with God within the home and within a local assembly of believers. Specific goals might include a schedule of Bible reading, mission projects and trips, ministry at church and in the neighborhood and personal growth goals for each family member. Beyond praying together, the family will stay together through studying God's Word and doing what it says. Regular spiritual disciplines will equip family members for extraordinary ministries and missions as their abilities, opportunities and interests are devoted to God. More ambitious goals may be stretched over longer periods.

Evaluating spiritual progress after one year or five years helps keep the family on track, but it does not tell the whole story. The object of family devotions within a devoted family is to prepare a new generation of committed Christians. Christian husbands and wives are concerned not only with their own spiritual growth and the immediate spiritual needs of their children. The highest satisfaction of Christian parenting is to have a part in equipping people who will be the godly husbands, wives and parents of the future. Parents can have no greater joy than to see their children walking in the truth in homes of their own.

Relating to Each Other

Ed Wheat, M.D. pointed out a fundamental truth: "you are commanded by Scripture to have a love affair with your marriage partner." He was referring to Proverbs 5, which warns that adultery destroys a person "sexually (vv.9-11), spiritually (vv.12-13) and socially (v.14)."[95] The explicit commandment in verses eighteen and nineteen indicates that the intimacy of marriage should be so rich and complete that there is no room for fatal distractions: "Let thy fountain be blessed: and rejoice with the wife of thy youth. Let her be as the loving hind and pleasant roe, let her breasts satisfy thee at all times; and be thou ravished with her love." The Hebrew is quite candid and forceful. A couple who are blessed, satisfied and ravished with

---

[95] Ed Wheat, M.D., *Love Life for Every Married Couple*, Zondervan, 1980, pp. 63f. Chapters five through ten of *Love Life* describe what Dr. Wheat called "the five ways of loving," which I have adopted from him. His best-selling *Intended for Pleasure* presents more detailed counsel regarding sexual fulfillment. My work in twice revising *Intended for Pleasure* and in conducting *Love Life* seminars indicates my indebtedness to Dr. Wheat, as does much of *Radical Heart/Radical Marriage*. Dr. Wheat also spoke of making your mate your best friend using the formula B. E. S. T. Blessing, Edifying, Sharing and Touching.

each other will not be looking elsewhere. Finding the fullness of love in the one right place will keep them from looking for it in any of the wrong places.

Relating to one another in marriage is a matter of rejoicing in the wife or husband "of thy youth," the companion who shares a lifetime of spiritual, social and sexual fulfillment. The place of God's blessing is in the one-flesh, one-mind union of a covenant marriage lived out in obedient faith. The place of satisfaction is in the security of a commitment to uncompromising faithfulness. The place of ravishing ecstasy is in the freedom of total abandonment to a lifelong partner. In a promiscuous culture, the concept of forsaking all others seems alien and negative. Those who are alienated from the life of God (Ephesians 4:8) can have little understanding of the positive joy of clinging to only one totally trusted marriage companion.

The blessing, satisfaction and ecstasy of the one-flesh one-mind union of a Christian husband and wife is the innermost of five circles of love. The outermost circle includes all humanity, and is the circle of unconditional acceptance and service. The next circle, the circle of belonging, embraces community and extended family. Within that circle, a circle of friendship develops among kindred spirits who enjoy shared activities and interests. Before marriage, a circle of romance may grow between a man and a woman whose friendship is enlivened by mutual attraction. The most intimate circle, the circle of desire, is reserved for marriage, since it involves total oneness. The strongest, happiest marriages are those in which husband and wife have gone through each of the outer circles together to find each other at the bulls-eye of the target of love.

The five circles of love are described by different Hebrew and Greek words in the Bible.[96] The outermost circle,

---

[96] I adopt the transliterated Greek words discussed by Dr. Wheat. In my description of circles of love, I am indebted to his description of five ways of loving.

agape love, is an unselfish mental attitude which always chooses the highest good for others: the standard for believers is the grace of God expressed in the sacrificial love of Jesus Christ (Philippians 2:1-8). The circle of belonging, storge love, is a comfortable relationship based on bonds of natural affection. Philia love in the circle of friendship is a relationship of mutual affection, trust and sharing. Eros describes the feeling of being strongly drawn towards another person, creating a circle of romance. Epithumia is a longing for, a strong desire to possess.

Sadly, epithumia, which is never translated "love" in the Bible, has become an acceptable basis for sexual activity: wanting each other is sufficient grounds for having each other. Marriages based primarily or only on desire for each other are doomed. Without guidance from the other circles of love, desire is simply lust. What happens when lust finds another object? Wanting and having someone else is considered sufficient grounds for divorce. In counseling and teaching, it is now necessary to tell people that there are other aspects of love, and that sexuality is designed to bring greatest satisfaction in a context enriched by unselfishness, belonging, friendship and romance.

Romance (eros) is also unreliable in itself. Flirtation and infatuation which brings a couple together can keep their marriage full of excitement and mystery. If the chemistry goes flat, spouses will find romance elsewhere. At work or among mutual friends, innocent camaraderie and teasing can be charged with sexual tension. There will always be someone ready to maximize this. Romantically vulnerable people are at great risk of being manipulated. In the musical *Into the Woods*, Prince Charming confesses: "I was raised to be charming, not sincere." That is too true of too many "self-actualizing" members of our individualistic society. Romance without unselfish acceptance and friendship is too often merely a sugar-coating for lust.

Friendship (philia) is the middle circle of love, the personalization of the bonds of community and shared humanity, the entrance to the circles of romance and desire. True friendship should be treasured. The mutual affection and trust of kindred spirits is the fundamental expression of human connectedness, as marriage is the fundamental structure. Sharing interests and activities throughout life can make husbands and wives best friends. Going separate ways in employment and recreation gives spouses separate circles of friends, which may be cause for concern if their friendship with each other has been neglected. Healthy friendship which moves into the circles of romance and desire is probably the basis of the majority of marriages which could be considered successful. When the friendship begins with unselfish acceptance and a sense of belonging, the family circle is blessed by all the circles of love.[97]

A sense of belonging (storge love) provides a context in which friendship can grow. The comfort of natural affection and basic trust is built in the reliable relationships of a stable family and community. The potential stability of a marriage is greatly enhanced if husband and wife come from similarly nurturing backgrounds. Shared values, traditions and lifestyles will help them make their house a home. Familiarity with each other's habits and idiosyncrasies can make a marriage as comfortable as an old shoe. But familiarity can breed boredom, and old shoes eventually are discarded. A marriage in which friendship, romance and desire are neglected is also missing the point of agape love.

Agape love patterned after the love of God for His people goes beyond a mental attitude of unconditional

---

[97] Joshua Harris takes "a new attitude toward romance and relationships" which is really a biblical defense of true character as the basis of friendship and true friendship as the basis of "principled romance" which may lead to marriage. (Joshua Harris, *I Kissed Dating Goodbye*, Multnomah Books, (1997). Joshua Harris, I now understand, has kissed his book goodbye. But understanding the cultures radical departure from Christian and historical Biblical courtship may not be caused by his view anymore than

he can take credit for the homosexual movement. Ideas mean something, historical context needs explanation.

acceptance of all humanity to a passion for unselfish service to individuals. Minimally, every human being should feel connectedness with all other human beings. In the story of the Good Samaritan (Luke 10:25-37), Jesus made it clear that the command to "love thy neighbor as thyself" extended to anyone in need with whom resources could be shared. A neighbor is any human being, regardless of ethnicity or kinship, who is cared for simply on the basis of common humanity. Conventional greetings carry little information, but acknowledge the presence and value of fellow human beings. Concern for human needs motivates unselfish actions which bring comfort and security to others simply because they are valued as persons. For believers, agape love is the love of God, which flows through His people in ministries of reconciliation. Believers will be helpers and facilitators rather than manipulators and exploiters. Their position as ambassadors for Christ will affect their choices of employment and recreation as well as their relationships in the world, the local community, the church and the home.

A plan for relating to one another as husband and wife is inadequate unless all five circles of love are given due consideration. Development of the relationship, from the broadest to the most intimate connectedness, builds a solid foundation for marriage. Within marriage, a relational plan should include strategies for maintaining oneness in all levels of the relationship. Plans for relating to God and to the world give a couple opportunities to experience and share agape love together. Connection with a local church and plans for relating to their community and extended family keep their marriage on target within a supportive context of storge love. Plans for relating to friends give priority to the husband/wife friendship in an enriched philia love. Plans for relating to each other romantically keep the excitement and mystery of eros love thriving. When a couple is well-connected in these outer circles of love, their epithumia love will be a strong desire for sexual union between partners who are already united in all other ways.

Their one-mind union in the outer circles of love will fortify their one-flesh union in the innermost circle.

Planning ways to express agape love as a couple may include choosing to support ministries and charities as well as serving in the church and community. Involvement in issues such as the pro-life movement or disaster relief connects a couple to humanity in helpful ways. Losing themselves in great causes helps them find themselves as agape lovers. The old motto, "Only one life, 'twill soon be past: only what's done for Christ will last," has many corollaries.[98] Whether by evangelizing thousands or offering a cup of water to an individual, the cause of Christ is to bring His love to the world. Bringing agape love to the world presupposes having agape love at home. The Church has grieved over believers who have cared so much for the world that they have neglected their own families. Agape love at home will be expressed in acceptance of each other's humanity through common courtesy and mutual respect. Each spouse should marvel at living in the same home with one of God's image-bearers, and each should reflect the image of Jesus Christ so clearly that the world will marvel at the love they have for each other. Their plans to express agape love must begin at home.

Belonging to a community and family implies mutual obligations. Storge love fulfills these obligations out of appreciation for the comfort and security of membership in the group. Values, traditions, familiar surroundings, and even favorite foods, make a home a home, and most of these are established in childhood by belonging to a distinct community. Ethnic, regional and sub-cultural distinctions provide people

---

[98] Ed Wheat had this motto engraved over his office door as a reminder of where to invest. I now have a copy over my office door. Gordon remembers it as a favorite saying of a couple who operated a small urban mission for over forty years.

with a feeling of belonging, a sense of community with those of similar backgrounds. Marriage does not isolate a couple from community and family. Plans for maintaining connectedness on this level help husband and wife act together for the benefit of the group which provided the training and context for building their home. This could mean volunteer work, political involvement and neighborly kindness, all of which can be planned to coordinate with the couple's shared interests and concerns.

For believers, the shared faith and practice of a local church or a denomination can build strong bonds of community. A Christian couple should make specific plans to strengthen their ties to God's people. The fellowship of believers, koinoinia (Acts 2:42), is a participation in a new community grounded in the grace of God. Believers recognize not only their shared humanity but also their shared standing in Jesus Christ as His community on earth. This should be reflected in assembling together for worship and ministry, and in a high level of mutual respect and service in the church and at home. Church attendance and active participation in ministry establishes the sense of belonging to the community of faith. If possible, a couple should find ways to serve together at church. They should also plan ways to open their home as a place of ministry and an example of Christ-like love. Both husband and wife should use every gift and opportunity for ministry, and grow together as Christ uses them to build His Church.

Friendship develops among people when they have similar ways of relating to humanity in general and to their communities. Through prolonged contact or through a shared crisis, they reveal their character to each other and find that they are kindred spirits. Philia love, mutual affection and trust, grows through shared interests and experiences. Husbands and wives are committed to sharing life with each other, and their friendship should grow through the joys and trials which come their way. They should also be proactive in planning shared activities, which bring them closer together in this circle of love. Plans could include time for quiet companionship and conversation as well as shared projects, hobbies and recreation. Whether working, playing, traveling or just "hanging out" with each other, building a friendship between husband and wife requires planning to spend time together.

Friends appreciate each other not only as fellow human beings and community members, but as unique individuals. They accept each other's idiosyncrasies and support each other against challenges. The value of connectedness with friends is integrated with the connectedness of marriage in Proverbs 4:8-12. Friends and spouses not only enjoy each other's company but also strengthen each other in times of trouble. For believers, all of the "one another" references in the New Testament define the Church as the mutual ministry of people who are friends with each other because they are friends of Jesus Christ (John 15:12-15). This should be the foundation for service to each other at home as well as in the Church. A couple's devotional life should include ministering to each other in all of the ways they engage in mutual ministry with other believers. The community of faith begins in the koinoinia shared in Christian homes.

The circle of eros love is restricted to husband and wife, although it may have ranged further before marriage. Once the romance of emotional interest in a person of the opposite sex moves deeper than the circle of intense friendship, a biblical barrier goes up, and the couple is committed to leave all others behind and share this new circle of love with no one but each other.[99] Within the circle of romantic love, sparks should keep flying throughout a marriage. There should be a sincerely

---

[99] Heather Paulsen suggests an earlier safety barrier, telling singles to guard their hearts, pursuing holiness and honesty in relationships and saving emotional as well as physical intimacy for marriage. (Heather Paulsen, *Emotional Purity*, Vinepress Publishing, 2001).

charming atmosphere of fascination with each other.[100] Glances, touches, notes, small gifts and favors keep the chemistry active. Besides surprising each other with such romantic gestures, couples should plan romantic activities. Continuing to date each other regularly keeps romance fresh. Spending a few hours or a weekend concentrating on pleasing each other with no distractions reminds husband and wife of why they got together in the first place, and lets their romance grow with their shared experiences. Too often puppy love and romance are left to the young and to memories.[101] The innocent playfulness of true romance still has a place at the heart of a thriving marriage. Husband and wife should not allow their mundane responsibilities to overshadow their first love for each other.

Epithumia love, the love of strong desire, is the innermost circle of marital love. This circle of love contains an honorable and undefiled bed. The Greek of Hebrews 13:4 is much more explicit than most translations. The word for the marriage bed is koite, which is easily recognized as the root of the word, "coitus," sexual intercourse. Marriage is held in honor as something precious, of great price, held dear and supremely worthy of defense. Sexual intercourse within marriage is to be undefiled, free of any deformity or debasement and exercised with unimpaired force and vigor. This is God's word about sex, and should be posted on every married couple's bedroom door (on the inside, of course).

Both positive and negative aspects of being "undefiled" are significant. Marital sex is not and should not be deformed or debased in any way. It is not "dirty" and should not be tainted or twisted by anything distasteful or demeaning to either partner. There should be nothing which diminishes pleasure for either

---

[100] Gordon's Uncle George repeatedly asked about his wife, "Isn't Bertha beautiful?" She was, because he said she was.

[101] It is said that puppy love often leads to a dog's life, but youthful love can remain vibrant if a couple plans it so.

husband or wife, but everything which maximizes pleasure for both. Sexual fulfillment for both husband and wife should be pursued vigorously. Total physical abandonment to each other in mutual ecstasy is God's standard for marital sex. Post that on the bedroom door, too.

Husband and wife can plan to have a satisfying and ravishing sexual relationship. If they are connected in all of the circles of love outside the bedroom, they will be fully charged to take possession of the treasures they offer each other behind that last door. If it is good to avoid provocative physical contact with members of the opposite sex before marriage, physical contact (provocative or otherwise) within marriage must be very good, indeed. The danger of arousing romantic or sexual passion justifies restraint before marriage. Within marriage, maximizing physical affection keeps the passion growing. A couple's plan for ecstatic epithumia love should include the little touches as well as the main event. I Corinthians 7:1-4 warns against the dangers of sexually charged touching among the unmarried, but encourages husbands and wives to have, hold and possess each other's bodies. A one-flesh union is not a one-act play. Within the circle of epithumia, marriage is a contact sport. Every opportunity for affectionate contact is an opportunity to increase desire for each other.[102]

How do spouses love each other? They love each other as human beings who are unselfishly committed to doing good for each other. They love each other as community members who give each other a sense of belonging. They love each other as friends who share the joys and sorrows of life. They love each other as romantic lovers who are totally fascinated with each other. They love each other as sexual lovers who are fully satisfied and ecstatically ravished with each other. A one-flesh, one-mind union encompasses all five circles of love.

---

[102] Ed Wheat taught that non-sexual touching is essential to building the thrill of intimacy within marriage.

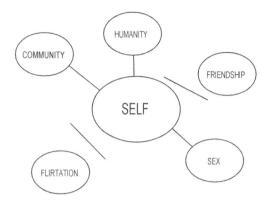

The self-centered autonomous personality makes social contacts according to individual values and preferences.

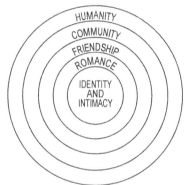

The centered self is a personality in relationships, recognizing all levels of social context as integral to purposeful life.

The Inner Circles

The one-flesh one-mind union of marriage is the innermost circle of human love. Husband and wife are united in their shared humanity, their membership in a community, their friendship and their exclusive romance and intimacy. Relating to each other within the inner circles of romance and intimacy brings oneness in relating to friends, family, community and the world. The inner circles of marriage are strengthened by a couple's connectedness to each other in the outer circles of love. Agape love, altruistic acceptance of fellow human beings and willingness to serve them, gives a couple oneness in their common humanity. Storge love, the sense of belonging to a community and sharing in its privileges and responsibilities, establishes a couple's oneness in shared beliefs and values. Philia love, the love of comfortable friendship, is at the heart of the covenant of companionship which binds husband and wife together through all of life's experiences. Eros, romantic love, mutual attraction nurtured by flirtation and courtship, is brought home after the wedding to focus only on the couple's continuing fascination with each other. Epithumia love, the love of strong desire to possess and enjoy, is reserved for the intimacy of the one-flesh union of husband and wife within marriage.

The inner circles of romance and intimacy are truly at the heart of marriage, forming emotional and physical unity which can never be found elsewhere are indeed radical. The one-flesh one-mind union of marriage is the most basic structure and yet the most complex experience of God's plan for human connectedness. Taking a spouse to have and to hold is conditioned on simultaneously giving oneself to be possessed and caressed by one's mate. Endowing a spouse with all of one's earthly goods includes transferring proprietary rights to one's own body over to one's mate (I Corinthians 7:4). Paradoxically, this elevates each spouse's sense of identity and value. Each is treasured by the other, and each is motivated to continually present his or her body as a worthy gift, pure, complete, and pleasing.[103] Good hygiene, good manners and good attitudes enrich the mutual giving of romance and intimacy.

Romance is usually associated with the pursuit phase of a relationship, and marriage is sometimes seen as giving up

---

[103] The parallels between marriage and the relationship of Christ and His Church are apparent. Ephesians 5:22-33 makes this explicit. The presentation of the body to God in holy, acceptable reasonable service (Romans 12:1) may also have implications for godly marriage.

the chase. Flirtation puts out bait and advertises availability. Courtship lures and persuades. Then comes marriage, and the game is over. Or so many people think. The pursuit goes on, either within marriage or elsewhere. The excitement, intrigue and humor of romantic love are addictive. The young man who said he was in love with love was admitting his addiction to the thrill of the hunt. The need for connectedness is not satisfied by superficial relationships or sexual conquests, nor is it content with a monotonous marriage in which conversations follow predictable scripts and even sex is reduced to perfunctory performance of marital duty. The pursuit must go on, with husband and wife keeping their romance thriving through continued flirtation and courtship, provoking each other's curiosity and pleasing each other creatively.

The fascination of flirtation and courtship is at the heart of romance. Catching each other's signals and pouring on the charm, a man and a woman enjoy anticipation of drawing each other closer. Marriage takes the uncertainty out of the mutual pursuit, but the romance should continue. Taking each other for granted physically leads to boredom in the bedroom. Sexuality involves more than predictable sex. Rather than stifling romance, marriage provides a context for heightened enjoyment of flirtation and courtship between husband and wife. Those looks in the eye, that special smile, a peck on the cheek, a particular kind of hug—couples can constantly remind each other of their mutual attraction and shared intimacy. Good-bye kisses, welcome home kisses, and just-because-you're-there kisses keep the home fires burning. Husbands and wives should flirt with each other, signaling their physical interest through playful gestures and words of affection. They should court each other through notes, meaningful gifts and courteous behavior.

188

Everything that single people do to attract mates married people should do to keep them.[104]

An obvious way to maintain the emotional energy of dating is to continue dating each other throughout the marriage. The honeymoon may be both a highly anticipated rendezvous and an anticlimactic letdown after the stress of preparing for the wedding. If the couple plans well, getting back home and back to work does not have to introduce a life of drudgery with no time for romance. During courtship, the couple planned dates, special days or evenings together which required careful preparation. They looked forward to these special events, and made sure they were at their best for each grand occasion. Their appearance, demeanor and conversation made it clear that each was the most important person in the other's life. People who saw them gazing into each other's eyes, holding hands or slipping their arms around each other commented, "Young people in love are so cute!"[105]

Within a few years of the wedding, things change dramatically. Hand-holding and hugs are less frequent when there is a baby, a diaper bag, a bottle, a blankie and all manner of infantile paraphernalia to transport. Gazing into each other's eyes is unwise when the twins are having a food fight with their Happy Meals. Pushing a stroller, changing diapers, baths, potty training, colic, the ... well, the list goes on for about eighteen years per child. By the end of a typical day, the bedtime story for the children is the only bedtime story the couple gets. Children are a heritage from the Lord (Psalm 127:3), but, oh, the humanity!

---

[104] Another reference to the relationship between Christ and the Church seems relevant. Revelation 2:4-5 can be applied to marriage: the way to maintain our first love is to do the first works, to change our mindset from being routine to being romantic, to maintain enthusiastic pursuit of each other.

[105] Puppy love can lead to a dog's life by two paths. If the puppies never grow up, they keep expecting the same immature amusement, and do not develop a richer relationship. If the puppies think that growing up means no more treats or toys, they become junkyard dogs, and are always at each other's throats.

Parenting is a high privilege and a sobering responsibility, but a couple's greatest gift to their children is parents who are deeply in love with each other.

A word to the wise: "babysitter." The goal of parenting is to facilitate the children's growth into responsible adults. The connectedness of marriage is a one-flesh one-mind union for a lifetime. The connectedness of parents and children is also life-long, but the utter dependence of infancy is left behind as children move towards becoming adult friends of their parents. To maintain the romance and intimacy of their marriage husband and wife need "couple time," just the two of them at ease together. To grow socially, children need time away from their parents, learning to relate to other people. The Puls children grew up with "other mothers," friends of their parents or parents of their friends, people who connected with them as confidantes and mentors throughout their early years. A carefully chosen babysitter can do far more than provide a few hours of child care. Again my friend Bob, father of seven, has sage-like advice: It takes a Christian village to rear children and we do not comprehend how desperately we need each other.

Even without children, there may be a severe letdown soon after the honeymoon as mundane concerns demand attention. Employment, shopping, meals, laundry, bills, and a shared bathroom bring a couple down to earth in a hurry. Before marriage, a couple's time together is carefully planned for maximum enjoyment. Dates are designed as pleasurable interludes for sharing good food, good entertainment and good manners. On a date, a man and a woman present themselves as positively as possible. Compliments and consideration fill their conversation. He opens doors for her, and she thanks him for every sign of courtesy. After marriage, disillusionment can set in as the daily routine chips away at the couple's romantic images of each other. Negative images creep in as impatience and disagreement displace good manners and unkempt hair and bad breath betray the knight in tarnished armor and his snoring beauty.

First love can be revived by first works. Courtesy and good hygiene are always in style, but the romance of dating should also be maintained. Planning special time together nourishes the inner circles of marital love. Whether it is dinner and a concert, a weekend getaway or just a leisurely scenic drive, a couple needs time to be a couple. Their couple time should be planned and anticipated as enthusiastically as their dates were before marriage. Three rules distinguish a date as something really special:

œ Choosing a place both spouses will enjoy. Husband and wife can take turns picking activities or destinations.

œ Going alone together: no double-dating or visiting friends or relatives.

œ No arguments: past, current and potential issues should be put on hold.

The idea is to reintroduce the magic, the mystique, the romance of early courtship. Being together with no distractions reminds a couple of what brought them together in the first place. Favorite places, favorite songs and simple activities can bring back memories and feelings which tend to get pulverized by the daily grind. New restaurants and new experiences together can freshen the atmosphere of joyful fascination which is at the heart of romance.

Dating couples are usually on their best behavior. Dating manners are among the first works which rekindle first love. General guidelines include acting as if each evening out were a first date.

œ Dressing for the occasion, as if trying to make a good impression.

œ Treating the spouse as a person whose affection must be won.

œ Using eye contact, physical closeness and charming conversation to make the evening romantic.

œ Staying out a little longer than parents might appreciate.

œ Treating a night (or day) out together as an eagerly anticipated privilege reminds spouses of how important they are to each other. Phoning each other to make arrangements for the date or even driving around the block and ringing the doorbell might be added touches to enhance the romance. When a husband and wife date each other, they are not escaping from reality. They are giving their undivided attention to the innermost reality of their marriage: their growing one-flesh one-mind union. Romance and intimacy are at the heart of a healthy marriage.[106]

Planning a night out can be romantic, but planning an intimate night in deserves at least as much attention. Marriage provides a context for a full range of sensual pleasure between husband and wife. Sexuality is much more than sex, and sexual intercourse is much more than a bodily function. Within marriage, a couple has the security and the time to develop expertise in bringing joy to each other in all the circles of love. Their exclusive one-flesh union gives them freedom to express and explore their desire for each other in an atmosphere of complete trust. The question is no longer, "How far can we go?" but, "How much fun can we have along the way?" Careful planning and preparation can increase the anticipation of a satisfying time together in bed. Sex within marriage is not a matter of seduction or conquest, but a lifetime of learning to bring pleasure to each other.

Bringing pleasure to each other means dwelling with each other according to specific knowledge of each other's needs

---

[106] One couple got a wake-up call when I gave them an assignment to start going out on weekly dates. After their "first date," the woman said, "Dow, if that had been our first date; it would have been our last." They had lost the romance of first love. Romance should grow as love matures.

and desires. Far from being strangers in the night, husband and wife should know each other extremely well. Knowing one's spouse is a knowledge gained from intimate experience (Genesis 4:1; Matthew 1:25). Adam and Eve did not learn about sex from parents, friends or the health teacher at school. Whatever instruction or intuition God gave them, they learned by experience how to bring pleasure to each other physically. Adam knew that Eve's life was bound up with his, and that she would be the mother of all future generations (Genesis 2:23; 3:20). At the heart of their shared life, "Adam knew his wife." The pleasures and purposes of sex are bound together at The heart of marriage.

Discovering and rediscovering each other physically in a permanent one-flesh relationship brings true sexual satisfaction. Spontaneity in physical affection, including sexual intercourse, is one of the greatest joys of marriage. Husband and wife should always be available to each other whenever physically possible. Neither of them should hold back sexual contact unilaterally (I Corinthians 7:5). While being reasonable about their responsibilities, they should be at least a bit playful about their desire for each other. Outside the protective covenant of marriage, sexual passion can be catastrophic — within marriage it can energize all levels of the relationship between husband and wife. Dwelling with each other according to knowledge means complete openness in both verbal and physical communication. Just as verbal communication is more satisfying when it follows accepted patterns of courtesy and logic, physical communication can be enhanced by thoughtful consideration. Marriage provides the only secure context for thinking through a life-long sexual relationship. A healthy couple will not have to make appointments with each other for sexual encounters, but carefully planning some extra-special nights in will enrich their knowledge and enjoyment of each other.

Counselors and couples should be thoroughly familiar with the facts of sex. Sound medical information, basic sexual technique and remedies for typical problems are presented in Dr. Wheat's *Intended for Pleasure*. The chapter entitled, "One Flesh," gives fairly detailed instruction for mutually satisfying sexual intercourse from arousal to afterglow.[107] In *Love Life*, Dr. Wheat describes the context of multi-faceted love which makes marriage the only context for full enjoyment of sexuality. In chapter six, "How to Love Your Partner Sexually," medical, biblical and personal aspects of sexuality are presented as fundamental to the lifelong love affair between husband and wife.[108] I have used these books extensively in my counseling practice, and highly recommend them for their timeless accuracy and sensitivity.

When conducting *Love Life* seminars, I assign an exercise called, "Practicing Physical Communication through Pleasuring." This is a two-phase format for exploring each other's bodies and discovering how to maximize each other's pleasure. The one-hour exercises are designed to establish or reestablish good physical communication between husband and wife. During the first phase, the hour together in bed is given to the satisfying feelings of caressing and being caressed as the partners take turns touching each other gently from head to toe. The sexual organs are not caressed in Phase One — the emphasis is on simple pleasures of physical contact, not necessarily leading to intercourse. In this phase, each communicates what feels good, where to touch and how to touch to bring optimal pleasure. Each will discover patterns of responsiveness as they learn to build sexual love through physical communication. These sessions may quite naturally lead to sexual intercourse, but the primary purpose is to learn to converse physically, to enjoy tender touching for its own sake as a way of sharing intimate affection. In the second phase, what they have learned

[107] Ed Wheat M.D., *Intended for Pleasure*, Fleming H. Revell, 1977, pp.79-90. (Revised 2010)

[108] Wheat, *Love Life*, Zondervan, 1980, pp.67-83).

about each other's bodies helps them move on to systematic stimulation, including attention to the genitals and to the wife's breasts and nipples. Both husband and wife concentrate on their own sensations of pleasure, which are increased by all they have discovered about giving each other pleasure. The whole purpose of these exercises is to learn to pleasure and be pleasured by one's marriage partner, to find together the sexual fulfillment and loving intimacy which builds, heals, renews, refreshes, restores and sustains their marriage relationship.

Romance and intimacy are at the heart of the one-flesh union between husband and wife. Giving each other the full attention of first love by doing the first works which brought them together, couples forge bonds of emotional and physical attachment which cannot be broken by trials or distractions. A woman considering whether to repair or replace a major appliance said, "Well, I guess if I take care of what I already have, I won't be looking for a new one." This principle is even more applicable to marriage. Any item of value requires attentive care. A cherished spouse, God's gift of intimate companionship, deserves more concentrated attention than any mere possession.

Relating to Family and Friends

When the preacher says, "I now pronounce you husband and wife," the couple has a new middle name: "and." No longer seeking to be autonomous individuals, they are connected in the most intimate and permanent human union. Their union in marriage becomes the core of their identity and the foundation of all of their other relationships. Relating to each other as husband and wife becomes the basis for relating to everyone else. Couples must realize this or risk grave dangers. Separate ways of relating to friends and family members put a division at the center of the couple's relationship with each other. Seeds of jealousy are planted whenever there is defensiveness or competition over "his" and "her" friends and family. The "and" of the marriage union redefines all other relationships.

The one-flesh one-mind union of marriage redefines all other relationships, but does not destroy them. Leaving father and mother to establish a new home requires a clean break from the dependency of childhood. Honoring Christian fathers and mothers includes respect for their positions as parents, and the appreciation and affection they have earned if they have done their job well. Friends of either spouse must never interfere with the primary friendship between husband and wife. Especially during the early years of marriage, many people find it hard to understand that nights out with the crowd have to give way to nights at home with a spouse. Friends of both spouses can nourish the friendship between husband and wife if everybody realizes that the best friends of the couple will be those who relate to them as a couple, rather than as separate individuals. The romance and intimacy which are exclusive to the marriage relationship thrive best when the circles of belonging and friendship are strong and supportive.

The King James Version calls love "charity" in I Corinthians 13. Charity begins at home. The circle of belonging, the love which establishes basic trust and identity, begins with those who share the same household. A couple whose love for each other is secure are prepared to be loving parents to their children. In child-training, a united front as parents grows out of a deep union as husband and wife. The security of a strong marriage builds the security of a stable home. Having a creative and dynamic relationship with their children is essential if parents are to have the maximum positive impact on their lives.[109] The key to any significant relationship is spending meaningful time together. Popular usage of the term, "quality time," includes purposeful activity in which one-on-one interaction is prominent. Meaningful interaction between parents and children at all times builds trust (Deuteronomy 6:1-9). There should be no meaningless non-quality time in any relationship, but there should be special times to focus on each other without distractions.

A family's long-term recreational plan should leave room for routine whole-family activities. Weekends usually provide long blocks of time that families can spend together. Planning a picnic or a bike ride can create a memorable event. Choosing and preparing food to eat at a favorite park might be a family project in itself. Mapping out a bike ride prepares the family to enjoy points of interest, as well as noting landmarks to check progress along the way.[110] Involving children in planning stirs interest in the event and builds a team spirit in the family. Children learn that their input is welcomed, and

---

[109] Honoring parents, while a commandment for both Christians and non Christians, does not always include respect. A non Christian parent may deserve respect, most do. However if your father is a drunk and your mother is a prostitute they deserve neither respect nor are they ones whose counsel would be wise. Therefore the idea of honoring one's parents Biblically has two components that are absolute commands; do not do anything to bring your parents to public shame eg., going to jail for wrong doing. Secondly when your parents are elderly you are required to help them financially to the best of your ability when they have a need. Therefore both Christian and non Christian parents can be honored regardless of their behavior, but here the son or daughter of Christian parents should have the advantage of a bonus, of good biblical counsel and feelings of genuine respect.
Although it is impossible to prevent the tragic consequences of brief lapses of judgment, the element of neglect in some accidental deaths of children suggests that bonding between parent and child has not made "out of sight, out of mind" impossible.

[110] The Puls family logged their bike treks on a Grand Rapids street map. A few weeks after wearing off her training wheels on one of those trips, Lisa Puls pedaled twenty miles with her "Dodie," Gordon. Later, somebody pointed out that pedaling a twenty-inch bike twenty miles takes more revolutions of the pedals and wheels than pedaling a twenty-seven inch bike in high gear the same distance. Lisa was a healthy little girl.

catch the enthusiasm their parents have for shared activities. Conversations before and after simple activities magnify their significance and strengthen bonds of shared experience.

Throughout all aspects of planning a marriage, a couple's first responsibility beyond their relationship with each other is their relationship with their children. The sense of belonging, with its comforting acceptance and challenging expectations, gives children a nurturing environment in which to grow into confident, responsible adults. Parents who model a loving relationship enable their children to love. Good parenting prepares the next generation to be good husbands, wives and parents.

Ideally, everyone would have this legacy, and adult friendships between parents and their offspring would be perfectly healthy. In the real world, the complexities of a couple's relationships with their parents and siblings can bring discord into their marriage. As a son or daughter leaves the parental home, bonds of affection and tradition remain. A mother's concern or a father's advice may be well-intended and graciously received but a couple's decisions must be their own, worked out in their own purposeful conversations. Holiday celebrations, vacations and family customs must also be planned by husband and wife to suit their own needs and tastes. Brothers, sisters, aunts, uncles and cousins do not lose their legitimate ties to the couple, and these relationships will also require adjustment. In a very real sense, husband and wife marry into each other's families, and will have to find ways to get along with their new relatives. Members of their extended families will also have to get used to the fact that the boy or girl who grew up before their very eyes is, indeed, grown up and is now primarily and permanently attached to a spouse who must be accepted and reckoned with in all family relationships.

Nobody grows up in a perfect family. The blanket term "dysfunctional" covers a multitude of distortions in family relationships. Alcoholism, verbal and physical abuse, promiscuity, and codependency within the childhood home of a spouse require coping strategies which carry over into marriage. Idiosyncrasies in perceptions and behaviors are also family baggage which needs to be unpacked. Marriage changes a couple's identity. They are no longer a man with his presuppositions and a woman with her separate presuppositions. They are husband and wife, and their primary responsibility is to integrate their past experience into their unified life together.

Advising newlyweds to live fifteen hundred miles from either set of parents is one way to emphasize the extreme importance of establishing their new identity. Dad's wallet and Mom's apron strings cannot be at the heart of healthy adult relationships between parents and their sons or daughters. "No, we are not coming over for dinner every Friday night." "Yes, we're in a tight spot, but we have to learn to handle these things ourselves." If a couple decides together that an occasional dinner with parents fits into their marriage plan, they can choose whatever night works best for them. If a couple decides together that a carefully documented and promptly repaid loan from a willing and able family member will not have unwanted side effects that is their business.[111] The new home which the newlyweds are establishing must be their own, whatever their parents and other relatives might expect of them. Whether they actually move fifteen hundred miles away or not, they must distance themselves from the "givens" of relationships with their respective families. Things will not continue as they were

---

[111]   Business is precisely what it must be. Indebtedness to a friend or family member, if not kept "strictly business," can deteriorate into crippling emotional as well as financial bondage. The attraction of a no-interest or low-interest loan obscures the risk of long-term obligation. "He who goes a-borrowing goes a-sorrowing" because indebtedness affects relationships as well as finances. There is also the adage, "The best way to make a distant relative is to loan money to a close one." And finally, "Debt is not an inconvenience it is a calamity".

from the Creation. Marriage is a new creation, a new household which will have its own identity, its own customs and traditions, and its own future. If the bride and groom are going to build a home for their own children, they will have to quit relating to their parents as dependent children and start relating to them as adult friends.

Adult friendship with parents bears the same weight as other adult friendships. Privileges and responsibilities of a healthy relationship include time spent together, shared interests and mutual trust and consideration. Workable adjustments of family traditions are vitally important in a marriage plan. Holiday meals, casual visits and even whole days with parents must be negotiated by husband and wife, not dictated by previous habits. Newlyweds should already have a plan in place for how they will spend the holidays during their first year of marriage. In later years they will be concerned with making their own home the center of traditions shared with their own children. Depending on geography and lifestyle, alternating activities between his parents and hers is a good place to start a sensible plan.

Whatever the occasion or frequency, meals together are usually helpful in maintaining legitimate ties to each other's homes. Everybody eats, so a shared meal requires no special skills other than food preparation,[112] and brings family members together in an activity they can all enjoy. Small talk around the dinner table keeps communication open. "Pass the peas, please," and comments about the delicious main course mingle with anecdotes from the past and questions about plans for the future. Some of the stories about "the time when…" become

---

[112] Food preparation is an art which has its own value in intergenerational bonding and adult friendship. As women warm a kitchen with the aromas of Grandma's recipes, they warm each other with friendly conversation. Men gathering at the barbecue grill with tongs and fire extinguisher share the primeval bonding of successful hunters. In either case, food preparation unites people in purposeful shared activity, which is at the heart of lasting friendships.

familiar even to the youngest children, and lay the foundation for a sense of family history and rootedness. Personalities shine forth as family members build their identities through telling the tales of their triumphs and challenges, as well as their hopes and disappointments. If the family that prays together stays together, there is also some truth in saying that the family that dines together binds together.[113]

Of course, in families whose conversations are heavily laced with criticism, sarcasm, and ultimatums, mealtimes are cruelly and unusually punishing. "Hey, meathead, pass the peas, before I toss this fork at ya!" is not an invitation to conversation. If verbal abuse is put on hold while mouths are busy eating, angry eyes still glare at each other. If this is characteristic of a family's meals together, children will look forward to growing up and getting out of the house. Traditions poisoned by acid tongues are not worth perpetuating. Holidays or reunions bring temporary truces punctuated by stabs at old wounds.[114] Grilling the burgers and then grilling the children about their sins of omission and commission does not aid digestion.

Newlyweds need to make a clean break from their childhood homes in order to establish their own home. Careful consideration of their relationships with extended family members will help them decide the degree and frequency of their involvement in existing family traditions. If contacts with parents and other relatives are comfortable for both husband and wife, frequently shared activities build bonds of real

---

[113] Some parents carefully plan family discussions as the children reach their teens. These choreographed conversations can present a wealth of well-timed information and recommended reading. In the Middle East, meal times are family times where conversation and humor fill the home. Even friends meeting at a restaurant spend literally hours in conversation with many teas after dinner. We in America miss the fellowship of a meal through addiction to fast food and fast eating. In other cultures, a happy meal is both physically and socially nutritious. What we call a happy meal is neither.

[114] A family with several daughters eventually quit visiting a relative who asked, "Where's the pretty one?" too many times.

friendship. If either spouse feels left out or must be on guard against negative treatment, the couple must plan more carefully. Limiting the frequency and length of visits minimizes potential conflict. Going into each visit with a game plan helps with damage control if either spouse is offended by thoughtless or malicious in-laws. A couple's united front in dealing with their parents is as important as their united front in dealing with their children. The deep union of a marriage is nourished by being of one mind in adjusting all other relationships to a couple's primary responsibility to each other.

A covenant marriage entered by vow assures a couple that they will always be each other's best friends. Friendship is a lifelong conversation, and they have committed themselves to lifelong companionship. Other friends may enter or leave the discussion, but husband and wife will always be there for each other. Their lifelong conversation, their pursuit of a one-mind union, is their primary responsibility, encompassing all the circles of love. Other people may enrich their circles of service, belonging and friendship in various ways, but the "and" of husband and wife is an exclusively intimate and permanent union. Since they are personalities in relationship at the heart of their identity, a married couple must view all other relationships from within this sacred oneness.

Long-term friends of either spouse will recognize the primacy of the marital bond, and learn to relate to both husband and wife. Friends who try to relate to husband or wife inject undue stress into the marriage as well as into the friendship. Even when planning an evening's activity, there should never be a winner-take-all choice between a spouse and a friend. That choice was made once-for-all at the wedding. Husband and wife have determined that they plan to spend their lives together. All other plans and all other friends are secondary to their commitment to each other. Since the marital conversation will go on for a lifetime, wise friends will adjust to this. Same-sex friends may share interests and activities which do not involve both spouses and couples may relate well to men and women who were closer to either one of them before the wedding. Friendships which tend to pull husband and wife away from each other will be overpowered by the powerful union of a strong marriage or will bring alienation of affection and possible destruction to a weak one.

In weak marriages, friends of each spouse give advice on how to get along with a problematic husband or wife. In strong marriages husband and wife take counsel together about how to get along with their problematic friends. Any friendship becomes problematic when it disturbs the unity of husband and wife. As with family activities, time spent with friends should be planned carefully to enrich the marriage rather than to escape from it for a few hours. Respect for each other's friends must be balanced by their respect for the marriage. A wife who wants to continue bar-hopping with girlfriends or a husband whose nights out with the boys include strip clubs is not strengthening a marriage. This seems unnecessary to point out, but it is precisely the kind of situation that appears regularly on the pop-psychology shows on radio and television. Describing the radical heart-radical marriage from a biblical viewpoint does not mean being blind to the low views of marriage prevalent in the world.

True friendship between husband and wife creates room for full enjoyment of other friendships. The exclusive circles of romance and intimacy are restricted to marriage, but the wider circle of friendship includes family members and acquaintances of both. From their secure inner bond of oneness the couple reaches out together to maintain and nourish healthy relationships with people whose lives are interwoven with their own. Planning how to relate to friends and family as a married couple does not require artificiality or manipulation. There is no need for rigidity or regimentation. True friendship is not based on micro-managed "quality time" together, but grows with shared experience. Specialized interests related to work or hobbies might not be shared by a spouse, but can be the basis of productive friendship. Family members have a reservoir of unspoken memories which only gradually flow into the life-long conversation between husband and wife.

Planning relationships with friends and family is not setting unnecessary boundaries. It is a determination to let charity begin at home in the new home being established by husband and wife. At no time will either spouse let the other be "out of sight, out of mind:" both will relate to other people from their primary identity as a married couple. Women who meet for breakfast and men who go fishing together are not threatening their marriages. Men who go fishing all weekend every weekend and women who never have breakfast with their husbands may have to reconsider their priorities.[115]

Remembering that oneness as husband and wife is their highest relational priority; a couple should adjust other relationships gently, integrating friends and family into a circle of mutually supportive allies. Since the image of God includes personality in relationship, His children should be living out that image as richly as possible, demonstrating His love helpfully by relating to as many people as possible as helpfully as possible. Beginning at home with their love for each other and for their children, husband and wife can spread God's love to their family and friends through purposeful shared experiences.

Regulating Finances

Spend less than you make. "And that's all I have to say about that." Anybody can agree to the general principle. If it were impossible to spend money we did not have, most people

---

[115] "Give a man a fish and he eats for the day; teach a man to fish and he's gone every weekend." It's a current joke, but it isn't funny when you consider how much time in a lifetime might be spent on a boat or pier (or on a golf course).

would be forced to live more simply and marriage counselors would have a drastically reduced workload. It has been said that more than seventy-five percent of all arguments in the home are about money. "How do we handle expenses?" "Who is in charge of family finances?" "Did we really need to buy that?" Ed Wheat said it seemed that many couples mispronounced part of their wedding vows, and said, "until debt do us part." Many couples fall into a debt trap within the first few years of marriage. Unless there is exceptional wealth to begin with, newlyweds need time to establish a financial base before they can afford the lifestyle to which they would like to become accustomed. The relative financial stability of their parents and older friends makes young couples want to get all the bells and whistles of a comfortable life as soon as possible.

One problem lies in getting the bells and whistles sooner than possible. Creditors have even changed the meaning of the word "possible" in financial matters. People no longer say "We don't have money for that." They say, "We can charge it."[116] There is no such thing as "easy credit;" the term should be "quick debt." It has become fashionable to spend more than we make, irrationally expecting to catch up on indebtedness at some undefined point in the future. Fashionable spending provides the illusion of a fashionable lifestyle. Most of the accoutrements of keeping up with the people on television are throw-away baubles destined for the trash heap. The latest car, the newest high-tech entertainment, the trendy clothes, the gizmos, gadgets and toys—everything will have to be replaced next year, if not sooner. Shopping malls are not places to purchase basic

---

[116] At one of many times when Gordon and Joyce Puls said, "We don't have money," four-year-old Michele cheerily said, "We've got checks!" Fortunately, she outgrew that philosophy. Too many couples do not.

needs, but places to feel a false sense of community in corporate worship at the altars of consumerism.[117]

The logical corrective to spending more than we make is to quit spending so much, but that might mean not having things which we think we deserve. Many people are deluded into thinking they can easily increase their incomes until they make more than they spend. Regrettably, while credit institutions invite people into a downward spiral of debt, financial gurus keep inventing get-rich-quick schemes as an antidote. The late night commercial about debt consolidation is matched by an offer of an exclusive franchise to sell celery de-veiners. One representative of a pyramid sales group told a former missionary, "After a few years with us, you'll have enough money to get the Lord's work done the way it ought to be done." Professions of faith, sincere or not, lure believers into some of the most preposterous scams the Better Business Bureau has encountered. The "health and wealth gospel" makes evangelists entrepreneurial and entrepreneurs evangelistic in calling people to faith in their programs.

There is no inherent sin in being an entrepreneur. When I was a head resident at the University of Arkansas my two daughters asked for an allowance. I told them that there were over 17,000 students at this university, and if they couldn't get some of the students' money in their pockets, they didn't understand the free enterprise system! Melissa, the oldest, built up a clientele of students who bought cookies from her during their study breaks. She slaved over a hot stove for hours to create

---

[117] The new vocabulary of consumerism is revealing. The obsolescent word "store" suggests a place where things are stored, where necessary items can be replaced from time to time. A "shop" clearly identifies itself as a place to shop, where the urge to spend money can be vented. Calling a business a "boutique" gives it a charming, exotic aura which somehow justifies higher prices. Even Christian children are being indoctrinated in consumerism. I once asked my 16 year-old grandson how his high school career was going, and he replied, "Oh, they're teaching us how to be so-called name it and claim it good little consumers."

her products until her little sister Sarah's business blossomed. Sarah simply marked some boxes, "Sarah's Cans" and put some on each dormitory floor for collection of beverage cans. Twice a month, she emptied the boxes into plastic trash bags and took them to the recycling center. Her income surpassed Melissa's profits with much lower demands on time and effort. Sarah cut Melissa into her business as a forty-percent partner, and assigned her to the upper floors. Unfortunately, the get-rich-quick schemes of the late night commercials and the pyramid plans are far less practical than the imaginations of two little girls.

The fallacy of the get-rich-quick attitude is double-edged. Getting rich is not a big enough goal to satisfy human needs for identity and relationship, and those who get rich seldom do it quickly. My son Jacob was eleven years old when he wanted to open a skateboard shop. After discussing child labor laws, inventory requirements and overhead expenses for about an hour he agreed that his skateboard shop would not be profitable. He decided to become a blueberry farmer on some land we owned. A good friend was knowledgeable and successful in raising blueberries, and counseled us concerning water systems, weeding, fertilizer, bird problems and other considerations. We took a university extension course on pruning and plant care, and decided the project required time and hard work which we were willing to invest. There was plenty of hard labor in preparing the land and transplanting two acres of full-grown plants. When his first crop came in, Jacob repaid the loan I had given him for the plants, and gave the rest of his money to missions. This was one young man who learned that get-to-work-quick-and-keep-working was the only sure way to financial success.[118] His giving to missions showed his commitment to use his resources unselfishly. Those whose main

---

[118] The blueberry crop ripened early, giving Jacob a jump-start in selling his berries to local restaurants at top prices.

goal in life is to get rich just for the sake of being rich fall into a trap where financial problems are only the beginning of sorrows (I Timothy 6:9).

Financial problems are a factor in almost all divorces. Misunderstandings about income and disagreements over spending are common if couples have not communicated clearly about their strategies for handling money. Couples who do not discuss finances are headed for financial failure. The word "economy" comes from a Greek word for household. The household created by their marriage is an economic partnership which husband and wife manage together. A clear understanding of sources and limitations of income should be the basis of agreement about spending. Counselors often deal with people who have made unwise financial decisions because they did not clearly understand their resources or carefully consider an estimate of their real needs.

Many unwise financial decisions are made unilaterally, without even consulting one's spouse. Credit card purchases and investments should be matters of discussion and mutual agreement between husbands and wives. The amount is not the issue. Except for money budgeted to each spouse for discretionary spending, no money should be spent without total wholehearted agreement. If one spouse questions the wisdom of an expenditure, reservations should be openly discussed and the purchase should be postponed until prayer, fasting and careful consideration of consequences and alternatives bring a unified decision of compromise. Impulse buying, selfish buying and secret buying create patterns of financial disorder which bring many couples into counseling offices and divorce courts.

Sometimes the problem is compounded by competition in earning and spending. The image of the husband as the breadwinner who gives the wife an allowance is no longer valid in most marriages. The wife may earn more and be better qualified to manage money. In two-income marriages the concept of a division between "his money" and "her money" often creates deeper divisions. It seems more appropriate for a one-flesh, one-mind union to have a unified financial plan. No matter who brings in the money, both husband and wife need to know where it comes from and where it goes. Unilateral financial decisions can bring disastrous results. At any income level, survival depends on spending less than comes in. If one spouse makes major purchases or indulges in impulse buying without consulting the other, spending quickly exceeds reasonable limits. If both spouses are spending independently, the left hand may not know that the right hand has spent the last dollar. Illusions about unlimited resources lead to illusions about unlimited needs. The spiral of spending quickly drains the bank account.[119]

Instead of charging into the valley of debt with creditors to the right and con artists to the left, couples need to be meticulously reasonable about finances. A clear view of their income and expenditures is an absolute necessity. Putting a paycheck into the bank and then spending freely for a few days guarantees disaster. Impulsive use of a credit card with the intention of catching up next month can loosen an avalanche of high-interest debt. Actual earnings and expenses should be recorded and analyzed in order to establish a realistic budget. Savings or reserve funds should not be considered available for anything but their planned use. What actually comes in each week or month must be more than what goes out. Checking exact figures can be sobering. A serious imbalance does not indicate the need to get a second job or buy a lottery ticket.[120] Looking for ways to increase income is not as realistic

---

[119] "Their marriage was perfect except for one flaw: he was quick on deposit; she was faster on withdrawal."

[120] I have personally counseled with three families who "won" the lottery. Their "luck" ruined every family relationship and close friendship they collectively had, because everyone felt entitled to a share of the "winnings."

as looking for ways to decrease expenses. I Timothy 6:6-10 warns against obsession with wealth. Accumulating money or things is a sign of covetousness. Believers should be content with "food and raiment," basic sustenance and covering. In current terms, basic needs include housing, clothing, food and transportation (personal vehicle or mass transit). The first place to regulate finances is in the "miscellaneous" category; so-called discretionary spending which often shows severe lack of discretion.[121] Next on the chopping block might be some of the perceived basics; adequate quality of life can be maintained without having the newest and best of everything we need. A one year budget should be established based on actual foreseeable income and realistically planned necessary expenses.

Spending less than what comes in requires doing the math. Exactly how much comes in? What are the sources of income? What is the total net income after tithing and taxes? What is the exact amount available for expenditures? In many homes, it is crucial to know exactly when income is available; the money has to be in the account before the bills can be paid. Exactly how much is needed to pay those bills, to cover fixed expenses for food and shelter? Clothing, transportation, and household necessities should also be calculated. How much of the average monthly income must go to the average monthly cost of basic needs? After all bills and other obligations have been paid, how much is left? Most couples in financial trouble have overestimated their discretionary spending limit because they underestimated their fixed expenses. Fixed expenses should include money earmarked for savings and giving as well as money needed for regular bills. The first step in financial planning is to establish a basic budget: the first step

---

[121] The "Miscellaneous" category in an average-income budget should be between two and five percent. Unfortunately, for most families in debt it hovers between eight and twelve percent.

in establishing a budget is to document actual income and expenses.

Strict budgeting can have dramatic effects. A couple who came to the United States as boat people ate rice, slept on flower sacks and washed up in the sink as they worked for meager wages in an uncle's bakery. For three years they saved almost all of their income while living in the bakery with its cement floor, running water and its freedom from insects, snakes and other hazards of their home in Vietnam. They bought the bakery for cash and eventually built their business into a chain of shops. A woman I counseled had inherited half a million dollars, a modest home and a used car from her mother — a single parent who had always worked for a minimum wage but lived frugally and invested wisely.

A budget is a beginning. Financial planning goes beyond number-crunching to consideration of values and goals. If there is no clear purpose in earning and spending, a couple is still caught up in a cycle of blind consumerism. Buying a donut shop or building up an estate is a target which justifies sacrifice. A five-year plan sets goals which will motivate husband and wife to think twice about impulse buying.[122] Choosing a modest lifestyle may give them room to choose work they enjoy, even if it means foregoing some toys. Being of one mind about finances starts when money and possessions are put in their places as tools to be used to accomplish worthy purposes, rather than as ends in themselves.

For believers, giving to the Lord's work should be a priority. The instruction in I Corinthians 16:2 to give "as the Lord has prospered you" indicates that giving should be systematic and proportional. Christians agree that the tithe is a reasonable expectation, whether considered as a command, a guideline

---

[122] Many couples use a ninety-day chart to stop impulse buying. They write the item down when the temptation for impulse buying is present, and if they still feel the need after the ninety-day period is up, the next question is, "Is the money available in our budget?"

or a starting point. I believe the tithe represents our solemn obligation to give a token of our earnings back to the Lord's work. Except for those in abject poverty, systematic proportional giving is possible at any income level. What we do with our resources is important to God. He wants us to understand the principle of ownership: He owns everything and we are merely stewards of His wealth. Since God owns everything, what He entrusts to us must be used under His direction. The tithe was established long before Israel was founded and is strictly an acknowledgement of God's ownership of everything we have.

Regular giving to the local church whose ministry we share is a basic responsibility. Beyond that, wisely apportioned giving to other legitimate causes increases our ministry and blessing. Some well-meaning Christians think nothing of giving to various appeals, whether these are secular or nominally Christian. Giving is to be commended; "thinking nothing" is foolish. Proverbs 20:16 warns against making loans to strangers. If we are careful about purchasing a used car, we should show at least equal diligence in checking out an organization to which we entrust the Lord's money.

A man in his early forties owned his own home, including a ten-acre lot with a racquetball court, a go-cart track and three rental properties. He also owned a gas station in our town. I asked him how he managed it all. He said that he had enjoyed working at the station when he was in high school, and chose to stay at the job when most of his friends went off to college. Soon he was able to buy the station. He said he was not a financial expert, but that his Christian faith taught him to give and his dad taught him to save. He decided that since he gave ten percent to the Lord's work, he should also save ten percent of his income. His financial plan was not sophisticated, but it was very effective. He owns all his property outright because he followed the simple plan: give ten percent, save ten percent.[123]

A one-year budget is just the beginning of an overall plan to regulate finances. A savings account, no matter how small, builds financial discipline as well as financial stability (Proverbs 21:20). A couple should plan to own their own home in a short period of time, preferably ten years.[124] Other indebtedness should be taken care of within five to seven years so that the couple can live debt-free. The goal is to have unencumbered land, investments and other assets to pass on to godly children who will use them as resources for ministry to a new generation. The Bible says that a godly man leaves an inheritance to his grandchildren and that fathers can leave homes and riches to their children (Proverbs 13:22; 19:14).

I once counseled with a couple who had accumulated a large amount of wealth through hard work, wise investments and God's blessing. They wondered whether they were obliged to leave an equal amount of money to each of three grown children. I told them that they had no biblical obligation to leave equal shares, but should leave the bulk of their estate to the godliest of their children. I suggested that they test their children by giving each of them a larger sum of money than he or she had ever handled before and watching to see what each child did with it. The oldest bought a sports car. The middle child spent the money redecorating a condo. Two weeks after the gift was given, the youngest child called his parents with a question. He and his wife wanted to give all of the money to missions, but wanted to ask for permission to give it away. This young couple had no idea how wise their decision was.

---

[123] One godly Christian businessman gave 90% and lived on 10%. He followed this policy when he first started his business as well as when he was a multi-millionaire. He was used of God to help missions worldwide.

[124] Outright ownership of the home provides the security and freedom to give and invest joyfully. The home should not be jeopardized by speculative mortgage options, but should be paid off completely as soon as possible.

Ultimately, all of our resources come from God, and we should seek His approval for how we use them.

Reinforcing Knowledge

True wealth is more than material possessions. "The man who knows right from wrong and has good judgment and common sense is happier than the man who is immensely rich (Proverbs 3:13, Living Bible)." Knowing how to make one's way through life with maximum effectiveness is a rare treasure. Such wisdom begins with obedient faith in God (Proverbs 1:7; 2:6-10). Asking God for wisdom clarifies decisions for those who approach Him in simple faith (James 1:5-8). Biblical wisdom is timeless.

Besides revealing the character of God, the Bible teaches principles of life which work in any time period or culture. The first four of the Ten Commandments speak of relating to God, the last six speak of relating to other human beings. Since the essence of the Trinity includes personality in relationship, God's image-bearers are designed to be personalities in relationships. The Bible tells how that is supposed to work.

The Bible also tells believers to be as wise as serpents and as harmless as doves (Matthew 10:16). Watching out for personal interests without exploiting or manipulating others seems a paradoxical impossibility to most people. The Golden Rule does not say, "do unto others before they do unto you" any more than it says that "those who have the gold make the rules." Personalities in relationships can be shrewd without being evil. Believers are to be wise about their dealings with the world, but innocent of any malice. To function in a fallen world where relationships are tainted with sinful actions and motives, believers must be street-smart without becoming cynical. The book of Proverbs is full of common-sense principles for governing every aspect of life in any culture at any time.[125] Believers are not of the world in their fellowship with God, but they are very much in the world in their interaction with fellow human beings. Fullness of grace in the heart is no excuse for empty space in the head. Wise as serpents — alert, informed and supremely prudent in pursuing and protecting legitimate interests. Harmless as doves — with no ill intentions or unnecessary offense to others. The balanced life of a believer will reflect the image of the God of truth and love, the image displayed perfectly only in Jesus Christ.

How does the character of Jesus Christ work into the complexities of the lives of believers as personalities in relationship in a fallen world? All relationships, all decisions and transactions, all thoughts will be captive to Christ, controlled by a mind set compatible with His (II Corinthians 10:3-5; Philippians 2:1-15). Approaching all aspects of life as opportunities for ministry, believers are on earth to further the reconciliation of the world to God (II Corinthians 5:18-21). Choosing a life of service is far different from resigning oneself to a life of slavery. Christians will face opposition as they aggressively pursue God's purposes, but we are not here to be victimized because of our ignorance and passivity. The gospel does not enslave; it liberates. The choice to identify with Jesus in a life of ministry is not a choice to abandon all earthly responsibilities and privileges.

Old Testament prophets are often stereotyped as loners who disconnected themselves from the world to identify with God, speaking into the culture from the outside. This image owes much to the histories of Elijah and John the Baptist, who were dramatically isolated from the mainstream society of their times. Speaking into the culture from the outside remains an apt

---

[125] Our book, *Finances: Biblical Wisdom/Radical Action* (revised 2008, 2011, 2016), is a first effort to tap some of this wisdom for contemporary use. Available at: combatkarate@aol.com. (Now in Spanish)

description of Christian witness. Yet in spite of eccentricities and idiosyncrasies, God's representatives do not escape mundane concerns. When Elisha and his protégés were cutting trees into timber for a shelter, work stopped to deal with the loss of a borrowed axe head (II Kings 6:1-7). Ecclesiastes 10:10 speaks of the value of keeping tools in good shape: using a blunt edge requires more strength. Even prophets found it necessary to equip themselves to take care of earthly business.

Blunt tools require more force. A praiseworthy craftsman takes care of his tools. Anyone who attempts home projects or repairs eventually learns the value of having the right tool for the job, knowing where it is, and keeping it in good working order. The metaphor has broad application to the art of living. The way people handle the tools of life will vary with their differences in character and purpose, but everybody faces the same basic projects and repairs while trying to build a life. Making a life includes some way of making a living. We all have to do something which gives others some product or service which will make them want to supply our needs in return. Whether we are surgeons or taxidermists, teachers or telemarketers, we need to hone the tools of the trade and know how to use them effectively. Beyond our trades and professions, we need to develop knowledge and skills which enrich us as human beings.

In marriage, the husband and wife share a partnership in building and maintaining a life together. No matter how much ability and intelligence each brings to the partnership, life will demand continuing education. For professional advancement and personal enrichment, lifelong learning is part of a good marriage plan. Professionally, continuing education is part of the job. It is a necessity for staying current in career fields, upgrading skills, addressing weaknesses and keeping licenses and certifications up to date. Life in the information age demands adjustments as dramatic as those demanded generations ago by industrialization—people who do not learn to use the best available resources, tools and techniques will be left behind. Personally, as careers become more high-tech, people need to be reminded to relate to each other as complete human beings rather than letting their identities be absorbed in their job titles. As jobs require maintaining expertise in increasingly narrow specializations, people must learn to broaden their interests just to be able to have meaningful conversations away from work.

Life is an ongoing education. Setting time aside for formal workshops, college course work, seminars and training sessions shows the diligence God requires of approved workers. II Timothy 2:15 speaks directly of the need for concentrated application of Scripture to life (I Timothy 4:16), but believers are expected to be diligent in everything they do. Everything should be done from the heart, as a service to God (Colossians 3:23). Everything should be done vigorously, with one's full strength and commitment (Ecclesiastes 9:10). Besides formal education, diligent workers will keep up with journals and other publications relevant to their fields, and pursue every opportunity to sharpen their knowledge and skills.

On the home front, lifelong education may take many directions. Relating to God involves meeting with Him in His Word and searching the Scriptures which reveal His character and purposes. Relating to each other as husband and wife means sharing interests and desires at all levels and learning to build each other up as complete persons. Relating to family, friends, community and the world takes constant alertness and a conscious effort to make all relationships purposeful and productive. Since God's character and purposes focus on personalities in relationships, learning must not be for self-aggrandizement, but for getting connected with other human beings in helpful ways. The traditional liberal arts curriculum of earlier generations placed great value on core courses in the humanities, fields of study particularly concerned with what it means to be human, to be humane. History, literature and the arts were considered essential to the education of civilized human beings. Revisionist history and deconstructionist approaches to literature and the arts have eaten away any foundational consensus which may have existed in the humanities, but most people still feel a need to be more than a name in a box on an organizational chart. Hobbies, sports, travel and other personal interests give people a sense of worth, a feeling of being uniquely valuable personalities.

Whether for career advancement or personal enrichment, couples should plan to keep learning throughout their lifetime together. The possibilities for furthering one's education are virtually limitless in an age when everyone has access to almost all the information in the world. Everything from the weather in Bangladesh to degree-granting courses of study is just a click away from any computer. Colleges and public school systems open their doors for community education. The "knowledge explosion" has created an expanding universe of opportunities for learning. Knowing only what one needs to know to survive does not fulfill the potential of a personality built for relationships. All work-related training and no playful learning makes Jack a dull boy and Jill a dull girl.[126]

Any interest can become a lifelong field of study. Interest in history evolves into role playing and reenactment based on eyewitness accounts and diaries. A controversial public issue provokes extensive research and active involvement. Family needs suggest new areas of study.[127] Hobbies turn into serious intellectual pursuits. Special training is necessary to complete

---

[126] My wife is multilingual, a definite asset in her work as a flight attendant. We have had fun with this on some of our date nights when Joanne has tried to converse with me entirely in one of her acquired languages while I use a phrase book.

[127] Gordon's graduate studies in teaching the gifted and talented were a response to his children's educational needs, not a career move.

projects. The best cooks, golfers, do-it-yourselfers, money managers and conversationalists have learned all they can about what they love to do. Whatever captures the heart soon captures the mind. A person's attention is worth the time and effort of continuing education.

Many adults find enjoyment and enrichment pursuing interests which began in childhood. Somebody gave a toy train to a little boy — decades later the layout includes scale-model buildings constructed from the original architect's plans. A little girl watched while an elderly woman sewed — now a new generation is warmed by intricately detailed quilts. A plastic trumpet at Christmas introduced a lifetime involvement with music. A family trip stirred the imagination of a future explorer. Parents whose childhood interests have grown into satisfying adult pastimes will look for ways to spark their children's curiosity about diverse fields of learning.

In fact, involvement in the education of children is a primary responsibility of parents. In traditional cultures, parents teach children everything they need to know to become responsible members of the family and community. When each home was self-sufficient, every family member was fully engaged in learning to meet the needs of others. As technology progressed, parents would apprentice children to craftsmen to learn specialized skills. The increasing value of literacy led to more formalized and prolonged education and the development of schools. Accepting parental responsibility for educating children does not mean turning back the clock, but it does mean being proactive in choosing what, where, how and by whom children will be taught.

Christians have a particularly acute need to be active in their children's education. The family is being discredited as a learning institution precisely because most individuals trivialize or reject biblical ideals for husbands, wives, mothers and fathers. If parents do not devote themselves to training their children up in the way they should go, the schools take possession of the children by default. The old Soviet Union frequently took talented children from satellite states back to Russia for extensive education, knowing that whoever molds the mind of the child holds the loyalty of the adult he or she becomes. Blindly surrendering children to a school system risks their indoctrination into whatever world-view their educators teach. As one county school superintendent once said, "The children belong to us." The biblical view of marriage and family emphatically declares that children are God's gifts to parents, and that the instruction of godly parents is to be treasured by children (Psalm 127:3; Proverbs 1:8).

Public school, private school or home school? Parents who are committed to biblical principles of child-training must decide which context best suits the needs of their children. Public schools offer the best resources of the mainstream culture but expose children to cultural values which neglect or contradict biblical teaching. Private schools attempt to provide sound moral guidance but may have limited curricula. Home schooling provides maximum parental influence but minimizes interaction with conflicting world-views. Each educational milieu tends to become ingrown, disparaging the strengths of the others.

Public schools have taken possession of children by default as parents have transferred responsibility for child-training to professional educators. The strength of the public school system is also its weakness. Government support underwrites the broadest spectrum of educational opportunities, but also brings concerns about political correctness. Schools paid for by everybody can ill-afford to offend anybody. The fully equipped chemistry lab, the comprehensive advanced placement curriculum and the state-of-the-art football stadium are offset by the lawsuits over prayer and Bible-reading and the laissez-faire atmosphere of the sex education courses. Many Christians and moral conservatives are uncomfortable on the tightrope and opt out of the public schools to regain their balance.

Private schools operate *in loco parentis*, drawing students from families who share a consensus of core values and academic expectations. Applications often include extensive coverage of beliefs and behaviors which must characterize students, parents and staff members. The weakness on the reverse side of this strength is that a list of dos and don'ts is most efficiently enforced through legalism, and children learn to conform to the standards only when external pressure is present. Among Christian schools there is another piece of ragged laundry – the most exemplary Christian is not always the best teacher or administrator. Idiosyncrasies, ignorance and outright incompetence in front of a class or in the front office justify the stereotyping of Christian schools as less than second-rate educational institutions. Parents whose children have been burned by legalism or bored by mediocrity become disillusioned with private schools.

Home schoolers believe scholarship begins at home and make learning a natural outgrowth of family relationships. The quintessential "mom-and-pop" operation is two parents training their own children. Parents act as personal learning coaches, sometimes teaching formal lessons, always ready to respond at teachable moments throughout each day. What Mom and Pop do not know can be learned from other sources. Publishers catering to home-schoolers offer fairly extensive curricular materials and home-schooling organizations provide a network for mutual support and group activities. As in other educational contexts, the strength of home schooling is also its greatest weakness. When parents take almost complete control of what, where, how and by whom their children are taught, there is limited opportunity for the children to interact with the broader circles of community, culture and global humanity.

In training children to take a biblical stance in a sinful world parents should think of working from the inner circles of home and community toward the outer circles of national and international society. Family and like-minded friends constitute the inner circle which home-schoolers correctly emphasize as the foundation of character and values: the organic root of society. Church and community have standards and traditions which private schools correctly represent as essential to productive corporate interaction: the functional machinery of society. Governmental institutions establish rights and responsibilities which public schools correctly propound as necessary to maintain the general welfare: the organizational structure of society. Education at each of these levels is vital to the training of fully connected human beings. Just as the biblical principles of Christian families must not be trampled upon by educators who reject all absolute values, Mom and Pop must realize that their children will have to move out of the home and reach out to the world, and private schools must beware of growing hothouse plants which thrive only under extremely controlled conditions.

Christian parents have primary responsibility for training their own children. A plan for a marriage must include the careful thought and difficult decisions involved in planning the children's education. Every possible opportunity for learning should be built into the home. Private schools should be held to the highest standards of academic excellence, and public schools should be monitored closely by parents concerned about matters of faith and conscience. A lifelong love of learning begins at home.

Relaxing

Families need to spend time together. The term, "quality time," has been used and abused almost beyond recognition.

It is true that time should be set aside to focus on the quality of relationships. Husbands and wives, parents and children should not be strangers whose paths cross at the refrigerator or the bathroom door. When jobs, school and other obligations outside the home pull family members in different directions, scheduling time together becomes necessary. A block of time set aside for shared activity with no distractions is, indeed, quality time. A tightly structured Tuesday night appointment from 8:32 to 9:17 might not be quality time. The amount of time is less important than the amount of undivided attention — taking a cell phone or a laptop on a bike ride with the family is not a good sign. Businesses which cultivate a "family atmosphere" try to make employees feel at home, accepted and respected as complete human beings. A family which functions with a business atmosphere makes it hard work to find acceptance and respect at home.

True relaxation is a disappearing art. When they were agitated over the execution of John the Baptist, Jesus told the apostles to "come apart and rest awhile." Preachers have used the clever expression, "Come apart or you'll come apart." Life is stressful, and unless tension is relieved; people snap. Temporarily stepping aside from the conflict refreshes mind and body. Jesus did not invite the apostles to give up the fight because the stakes were too high. Their time of rest was to prepare them for even harsher battles. They needed to be at ease for awhile, to clear their thoughts in the presence of Jesus. Matthew 6:31 could be paraphrased, "find a place of your own to spend time away from motion, business or labor." That should be the definition of a Christian home — a place of secure rest from the pressures of public life. "Quiet time" should be more than a few minutes of closely guarded devotional exercises. Psalm 131:2 speaks of calming oneself, of smoothing one's thoughts, of being still and silencing oneself like a contented weaned infant. Believers should know how to enjoy true rest.

Spiritual rest in fellowship with Jesus (Matthew 11:28-29) should be matched by physical and mental contentment.

Relaxation is rare because true contentment is even rarer. Since nothing can separate believers from the love of God (Romans 8:28-39), lives of unfailing strength and independence from external circumstances are possible (Philippians 4:11; I Timothy 6:6-8; Hebrews 13:5). The contentment expected of believers is not smug self-sufficiency but active trust in the sovereign love of God. Jesus did not grasp at the recognition due Him as a member of the Trinity, but was content to live and die according to the divine plan. Believers do not need to compete for recognition or grasp at the world's prizes, but can have minds set on fulfilling God's purposes (Philippians 2:1-16). Life is not a race with death for worldly rewards — it is a race for the prize of God's heavenly call (Philippians 3:13-14). Believers can "run with patience," following the example of Jesus in confident endurance in pursuing God's will (Hebrews 12:1). Impatience, frustration, fear and unbelief can be set aside while dealing with the affairs of this world because the affairs of the world to come are securely settled. Paul says, "I have learned, in whatsoever state I am, therewith to be content (Philippians 4:11)." Jeremiah Burroughs paraphrases, "I find a sufficiency of satisfaction in my own heart, through the grace of Christ that is in me. Though I have not outward comforts and worldly conveniences to supply my necessities, yet I have a sufficient portion between Christ and my soul to satisfy me in every condition.[128]

Contentment makes relaxation possible. A person who is grasping for everything has trouble holding onto anything and fully enjoys nothing. Those who can rest from their labor in calm security appreciate and enjoy what they have. For a contented person, relaxation is freedom from tension, freedom to savor the joys of life. Discontented people carry their internal

---

[128] Jeremiah Burroughs, *The Rare Jewel of Christian Contentment*, Banner of Truth, 1984 (1648), p.18.

tension into everything they do. They may have avocations, amusements and recreation, but they do not know how to truly relax. Their avocations, the hobbies they pursue away from their jobs, become hard work as they seek elusive ideals of perfection. Their amusements, what they do to stop "musing," also escalate as it takes newer and bigger thrills to get them to stop thinking about their worries for even a few minutes. Recreation, their effort to rebuild themselves through low-intensity activity, turns into obsession with fitness and competition. They are so goal-oriented that they can hardly conceive of doing anything simply for its own sake. Truly contented people can find the joy in simply being — everything they do, including their primary occupations, is permeated with relaxed confidence.

Contentment and relaxation mean more than eating a good meal and then taking a nap. The positive value of avocations, amusements and recreation is in interrupting the work-eat-and-sleep schedule with reminders of the joys of being complex personalities in satisfying relationships. Getting away from the mundane routine puts life into perspective. An artist working meticulously to create a precise impression of the light reflected from a dew drop on a flower petal needs to step back occasionally to get the big picture of the landscape she is painting. The inchworm measuring the marigolds needs to stop to smell the flowers and enjoy their beauty. A person's identity as a human being needs to grow beyond a job title, and a family's relationships need to grow beyond perfunctory performance of household roles. Contentment does not mean having the same scripted conversations every day. Relaxation does not mean falling asleep in front of the television every night. Avocations, amusements and recreation are imaginative ways to relax from workaday stress without losing consciousness.

The word "vocation" has lost much of the richness of its earlier connotations. A vocation was a calling, a life mission laid upon a person by God Himself. In the broadest sense it included the effective use of every ability and opportunity for useful activity. In more recent popular usage, "vocation" is synonymous with "career" or "job." Given this limited definition, another word was needed to describe what a person did with life "off clock." An avocation is something a person does "away from a vocation," an off-duty activity. Amateur musicians, artists, chefs, craftsmen and seamstresses turn what is a vocation for others into an avocation for themselves because they are lovers (Fr. amateurs) of the field. Occasionally a truly devoted amateur turns into a professional, but usually the avocation is a satisfying departure from required work. Tom Sawyer was able to recruit amateurs to whitewash a fence by convincing them that what looked like work was really play. That is the secret of an avocation: it may look like work, but the amateur finds as much joy in the process as in the product. Even those who say they love their work can be enriched by doing something just for the fun of it.

Amusements are most emphatically just for fun. Traditionally, mindless folly has been grossly underrated. Hedonism aside, there is a lot to be said for switching the brain into neutral for awhile and coasting through some preposterously meaningless activity. For one thing, almost everybody but the most rigid rationalist can do it. And it is very relaxing. People concerned about their images make silliness a secret pleasure, but self-conscious stupidity is an oxymoron. Once in awhile fun can be its own excuse: ludens gratis ludens, laughing for the sake of laughing. A healthy sense of humor can find fun anywhere, [129] but some people get so overheated by stress that they have to learn to stop, drop and roll in laughter to

[129] Malcolm Cronk, respected Bible teacher of another generation, was bald enough to radiate a halo in a well-lit room. A youth group at a Bible conference taped together tufts of their own hair to make a toupee which he tried on when he rose to give his last sermon of the week. He was deep in conversation with a crowd of guests in one of the cottages after the service when refreshments were served. The hostess said, "Cronk, will you say grace?" He looked up impishly and said, "Grace."

avoid burning themselves out. Just because the culture has lost its sense of true humor and amuses itself with gutter comedy, believers do not have to curb their enthusiasm for a good laugh. Just because a drunkard thinks getting a red nose is a side-effect of having fun, believers do not have to be blue-nosed Pharisees about simple pleasure. The romance between husband and wife and the joy shared by parents and children thrive on the ability to share the humor in life. Even an infant can "know the joke," sensing the relaxed acceptance permeating family relationships. At 91, Gordon's mother interrupted a laughter-filled conversation to say, "I don't know what you're laughing about, but I'm just tickled that you're having such a good time."

Recreation is a form of relaxation somewhere between the complete release of amusement and the purposeful pursuit of an avocation. Vacations, bike rides and picnics in the park get families away from hum-drum care to rebuild their bodies and their relationships. Activities which separate them are set aside in favor of activities which bring them together. Each family member can shine as everyone's skills and knowledge are needed to set up a tent or to find a way to drive through Atlanta. The son who can outrun Dad and the daughter who can ride a horse better than Mom know something good about themselves. Revealing conversations can develop out of trying to decide where to go for dinner. Making decisions while reading a menu or a roadmap can bring out the best or the worst in people (and who dares try to refold the map?). When young children play, they often act out adult roles and relationships. Family recreation should have similar play value, giving family members insight into ways to act and relate in more challenging situations.

Breaking the routine to enjoy personal interests and family relationships nurtures physical and mental health. Every family needs to get away together for a week or so each year, if at all possible. Weekend getaways dispersed throughout the year are also very effective. The idea is to plan a family vacation together, taking into account each family member's input. It does not have to be a budget-busting tour of theme parks or exotic resorts. The cost is not as important as the priceless opportunity to build memories of a godly family having fun together. Camping, fishing, sightseeing, swimming or bike-riding can fill hours and days with family togetherness. Sometimes just getting mom, dad and the kids into the car and onto the highway reminds them how much they really like each other.

"Take me out to the ball game" may be a good suggestion. If fans do not become fanatics, there is a healthy bonding in rooting for the home team, whether Little League or professional. School and community sports programs can bring neighborhoods and families together — or tear them apart. The obsessively competitive spirit of intense rivalries can bring out the worst in parents and children. Organized sports originated in more or less friendly games between communities but have grown into what amounts to serious warfare among some fans. As long as participants and spectators maintain high standards of good sportsmanship, the camaraderie and teamwork of sports build character and healthy relationships.[130] In most school systems the athletic department is the most visible and popular program at least in part because it can be understood and enjoyed by the whole community. Coaching, playing and cheering can unite family members in a common cause and bring them into productive relationships with neighbors who share their interest in sports.

---

[130] My father coached my team to a Little League World Series championship when I was twelve years old. He also coached my sister's fast pitch softball teams to two national championships. He was also my football, basketball and boxing coach, and my scoutmaster. He did all this to build confidence and character in his sons and daughters. The voracious competitiveness of some parents and coaches shows that even youth sports are affected by the society's shift in values. The lifestyles and drug use of many professional athletes further taint what could be healthy enjoyment of teamwork and physical prowess. The roles some athlete's model are neither attractive nor healthy.

Families can enjoy sports without season tickets for every team in town. Jogging, swimming walks, bike rides and aerobics are healthy non-competitive activities within the range of every family member. Following the trails in local parks on foot, skates or bikes provides a scenic closed-course trip which may include a swim or a picnic. Young children enjoy playground-hopping, exploring the equipment at various sites. A ride, walk or run may have a destination such as a zoo, museum or library. Airports and area landmarks are also good places to visit. Swimming in a pool or spending a day at the beach almost always includes gentle horseplay which builds cherished memories. Fitness programs in the home or at a gym strengthen bodies and relationships. In as many ways as possible, families should play together, rather than splitting up for individual activities.

Some sports require special equipment and skills. Tennis, racquetball and golf may be enjoyed by anyone with moderate ability. Scuba diving and horseback riding are very satisfying to those who invest the time and effort to do them well. Backpacking and mountain climbing richly reward careful preparation. These activities are more appropriate to particular age and skill levels, but the whole family can share the joy of each member's special sport.

Back home, the family can be drawn together in special projects. Couples and families can establish better communication and mutual respect over a joint work project. Rather than going their separate ways to pursue divergent interests, they can be united in doing something to improve or enrich their home. Redecorating a room, landscaping the yard, planting a garden or refinishing furniture can be hard work, but doing it together can relax tensions as family members set aside distractions and focus on a common goal.

My involvement in my son's blueberry venture involved what can only be described as downright drudgery, but learning and working together forged strong bonds of understanding and affection.[131] Seeing something that needs to be done and doing it together is one of the best ways to build lasting friendships, especially within the family.

For believers, shared projects motivated by shared faith put Ephesians 4:15-16 into practice at home as well as at church. Preparing Sunday school lessons, supporting and visiting missionaries, inviting other families to Sunday dinner or having the youth group or the neighbors over for special events will make the home a place of ministry. The strongest churches are built on the strongest homes. The cultural shift away from God has led many church growth advocates to think that strong churches must bolster or bypass weak families to build strong church members. When godly families are bound together and nourished by the diverse gifts and ministries of godly fathers, mothers and children, the Spirit of power, love and a sound mind breaks through more dynamically than in church programs which try to motivate family members individually.

Strong families and strong churches do not circle the wagons and wait for the Millennium; they multiply their blessings by going forth to subdue the earth, bringing every human concern under the Lordship of Christ. P.T.A. and school boards, service clubs and local government must not be abandoned to the pagans. Paradoxically, vigorous activism relaxes the spiritual burden of believers as they pay the debt of gospel proclamation and application to their communities. The whole family can get involved in getting out the message of God's judgment against pornography, homosexuality, abortion, injustice and bigotry. Less confrontationally, godly families

---

[131] My wife spent one day a week with Jacob's blueberries at the farmers market as part of his home schooling experience. Doing karate together and teaching self-defense clinics together has also forged a powerful relationship of affection and mutual respect for Jacob and me (Joe Burress Martial Arts Association, Integrated Fighting and Combat Karate.).

can exert their influence by simply being good neighbors, participating in meetings and celebrations related to common human cares and joys.

The home can minister to the neighborhood in imaginative ways. Cultivating an "open house," a home where any guest feels welcome and safe is implied in the gospel mandate. The Greek word for fellowship (koinoinia) includes sharing in communion, communication and community. The New Testament church grew through fellowship in homes — a prominent person's coming to Christ would affect the whole household (oikonomia). The principle of strong homes building strong churches is rooted in the literal historical experience described in the book of Acts. Home Bible studies, prayer sessions, and children's Bible clubs and vacation Bible schools are logical extensions of the home-based ministry of the New Testament.

Coming apart to rest does not mean vegetating irresponsibly. It means tapping into the real sources of personal and family strength. God connects with His people and builds connections among them as they learn that they most accurately reflect His image when they live as personalities in relationships. Relaxing the artificial tensions of finding identity only in job descriptions and social roles may require carefully considered effort. Avocations, amusements and recreation have their legitimate places in godly, productive lives.

Catalogue of Catastrophe

Failure to follow God's plan for marriage brings tragic consequences. If there is no divinely supported covenant of companionship, every trial or temptation threatens the couple's unity. If there is no plan for the balance and growth of the marriage, every new problem threatens the couple's stability. The course of life includes many foreseeable hazards which challenge even the most committed and best prepared couples. Without a clear claim to God's blessing and a clear plan for action, the road can get very bumpy, and the marriage is always at risk. God's Word provides a reliable map for the marriage journey. If God's roadmap is not followed, a wrong turn can quickly put a couple on the path to divorce. However, healing and restoration are possible through a return to God's plan. The responsibility of churches and Christian counselors is to proclaim and maintain God's plan for marriage while giving couples loving discipline and direction.

Mile Markers

Martin Luther called marriage a "training ground for spirituality." He considered disagreements, arguments and disputes "opportunities for expressing godliness and love."[132] Someone has said that if two people are in perfect agreement, one of them is not thinking. When two people are committed to being completely open with each other, they will discover that being of one mind takes hard work.[131]

Being of one mind does not, in fact, mean absolute agreement in every detail of every decision. It does mean seeking thorough understanding rather than agreeing to disagree. If a couple agrees to agree they will see that most of their differences are relatively inconsequential and they will

---

[132] Martin Luther, *By Faith Alone*, James Galvin, general editor, World Bible Publishers, 1998, reading for February 20.

[133] Field Marshal General Montgomery during World War II told his

troops not even to think of marriage until they had mastered the art of battle.

work hard to resolve the major issues of their marriage. Again, it is crucial to recognize that the marriage itself, their one-flesh one-mind union, is their essential identity and that they do not confront each other as separate, independent individuals.

Just as young children go through critical periods during which life skills are learned, married couples face challenges specific to various stages of their life together. A child is not expected to walk before bones, muscles and coordination are adequately developed. Even then, it is not a matter of suddenly leaping from Mother's arms, landing on two feet and scampering off. There are milestones such as rolling over, crawling, sitting up, standing with support, then standing unaided followed by a period of one-two-three stepping and falling. Similarly, most marriages progress from baby steps to a confident walk together through the challenges of life.

In the game "Milles Bournes," players try to accumulate mileage cards while avoiding road hazards. For each hazard card there is a corresponding remedy card. There are also highly valued cards which eliminate particular hazards for those who hold them. Marriage is not a game, but it can be compared with the journey depicted in "Milles Bournes." Like a road trip on the interstate, it involves going the distance in the right direction and being prepared to deal with the dangers of the road. Although hazards may pop up at any time, some of them are most likely to appear at specific mile markers. Each of the hazards can be remedied and thoughtful planning can diminish their impact.

While each of us is conscious of being basically the same person throughout life, age and experience affect our perceptions and responses. In marriage, our shock absorbers will be tested early when we discover that the goddess snores or that Prince Charming does not pick up his socks. Those who marry youngest may be surprised at the immaturity of their spouses. If education or a career delays marriage, husband

234

and wife may be set in their ways and have difficulty making the transition from the habits of single life. Most of these early adjustments are so commonly expected that many couples work through them with relatively good humor.

Once the wedding pictures have been put away and the extra toasters have been disposed of, the couple settles in to live more or less "happily ever after." And many succeed surprisingly well. When divorce was more unacceptable and less convenient, couples were encouraged by friends and family to "work it out," to find some way to find contentment, if not joy, in their marriages. As society's expectations have lowered and the support of extended families has diminished, troubled couples see escape as a more viable option than endurance.

Christian counselors may be the only people that a couple know who maintain a high view of marriage and offer guidance through the hazards of the marriage journey. If we are to provide profitable roadside assistance we need to familiarize ourselves with the roadmap, and with the tools and skills needed to make emergency repairs. Recognizing the dangers associated with certain mile markers is vitally important. Learning from the mistakes of others can keep couples from repeating them. Learning that others have made mistakes can keep couples from despairing over their own.

The first of four especially hazardous stretches of the road comes around the five-year mark. Couples are beginning to question their choice of each other as mates. They have started to neglect each other as romance gives way to routine. Sometimes the focus of the marriage shifts from the things they like about each other to an intense look at each other's shortcomings and faults. At the five-year mark a spouse who still feels marketable on the dating scene may feel trapped with an unworthy partner. Benjamin Franklin wisely stated, "Go into marriage with your eyes wide open, and then close them halfway." The idealism of courtship turns into perfectionism and erosive criticism if the couple does not realistically accept the fact that they are only human, with idiosyncrasies and limitations which may sometimes seem offensive. Differences which cannot be overlooked must be looked over lovingly and reasonably.

Being loving and reasonable about each other's humanity is difficult at the five-year mark because of increasing responsibilities. There may be several small children whose needs cut into the couple's time for each other or eliminate it altogether. This is often a time of increased financial burdens, including accumulation of high debt. The cost of baby furnishings, diapers and formula may put payments on a sports car or boat beyond the budget. Couples who choose bankruptcy further complicate their lives and add stress to an already fragile relationship. "Debt leads to despair... If you can't buy it for cash you don't need it."[134] The weight of indebtedness increases the burden of added responsibilities just a few years into the marriage.

Being reasonable at the five-year mark will be much easier for a couple who have been reasonable from the start. Rushing to have all that others have, many couples amass insurmountable debt and accustom themselves to a lifestyle they cannot afford. Staying debt-free requires meticulous planning and strict self-discipline, but it will provide the freedom the couple needs to build a good foundation for their marriage. Knowing the difference between necessities and luxuries is a lesson many learn painfully late. Arguing over whether to buy a motorcycle or a minivan typifies the conflicts which cluster near the fifth year of marriage

---

[134] Our book, *Finances: Biblical Wisdom/Radical Action*, Alethia Publishing, 2003, p. 39 (revised 2008, 2011, 2016). Going into bankruptcy is becoming easier— getting out is extremely difficult. Only a small percentage of bankruptcies are business-related. Personal bankruptcy is being used as a cure-all for financial irresponsibility. Almost invariably it only makes the disease worse. The old saying is still true: "Better to go to bed supper-less than to rise in debt."

To be loving at this marriage milestone involves keeping couple time regular and planning activities which include fun time with the kids. For the family's sake Mom, Dad and the kids need time to enjoy being together. Planning family activities and recording them in scrapbooks, journals, or technology provides a heritage of love for one another and growth together. For the couple, regular just-the-two-of-us time together is essential. Quiet
talks after the kids are in bed and occasional date nights will maintain communication and strengthen the feeling of being in this adventure together. Marriage, like any true friendship, is a lifelong conversation. If one spouse says ominously, "We need to talk," the conversation has been neglected too long.

Premarital instruction in planning and communication can steer a couple in the right direction to bypass the worst effects of these early marriage challenges. Couples who are struggling with them can be shown the way back to their first love through clear identification of issues which disturb their marriage and patient guidance in working through possible solutions. Working from God's plan for marriage has immeasurable advantages over working from each spouse's mistaken expectations. At the five year mark the biblical principles of the oneness and the permanence of marriage form the basis for negotiating and correcting issues which threaten to divide and break the couple's relationship.

Marriage is not static. In some respects, it is like an ever-changing mobile of experiences and emotions, relationships and responses. As the years go by, day-to-day concerns can stifle communion between husband and wife, just as the cares of this world can stifle communion with the Lord (Matthew 13:22; II Timothy 4:10). As responsibilities and circumstances change, maintaining oneness takes planning and hard work. A building contractor has said, "What's decided gets built; what isn't decided gets built." With or without wise decisions and careful planning, what goes into a marriage day by day gets built into the marriage. Counselors can encourage couples to plan for particularly bumpy stretches of the road and can help them navigate through the most hazardous spots.

The second hazard sign on the marriage journey is near the ten-year mark.

Couples are not only facing substantial debt, but they are also discovering that material possessions do not bring satisfaction. Jesus warned that our lives do not consist in the abundance of the things we possess (Luke 12:15). The warning is double-edged if the things we possess enslave us to debt. We should be content with having basic food and shelter (I Timothy 6:8), but most of us are not. Contentment must be learned, and a materialistic society does not teach it. After ten years of trying to keep ahead of the Joneses,[135] many couples hit the wall and feel unable to go on. The dream house has become a nightmare mortgage, and much that glitters was purchased with credit cards. And the so-called Joneses who they tried to keep up with divorced shortly after declaring bankruptcy.

Besides financial concerns, other hazards are encountered near the ten-year mile marker. The children are increasingly involved in numerous activities, lessons and events, and somebody has to drive the shuttle bus to get them everywhere they go. Parents see less and less of each other as the time demands of careers and children create merciless schedule conflicts and painful conflicts over schedules. The career man or woman talks more with associates or employees at work than with the spouse at home. A stay-at-home wife experiences alienation and lacks outlets for her emotions. This is when women often begin to attach themselves to phantom

---

[135] In northwestern Arkansas, that was next to impossible. The owner of Jones Trucking Lines built schools and communities, put computers in every classroom in the Springdale school district, and built a recreation center with basketball gym, ice rink, Olympic size swimming pool, learning center, fitness center, reception area, and movie theater with free refreshments. These Joneses really had the goods, and used what they had to do good for their neighbors.

lovers on the Internet or to become addicted to the pseudo-society of talk shows, the latest internet fads, soap operas, and romance novels. Men may drift into confiding in female co-workers or bury themselves in a workaholic lifestyle. Contacts between husband and wife become infrequent and perfunctory.

Again, the way to head off this crisis is also the way to endure it if it comes. The couple needs to remember that they are committed to a one-flesh one-mind covenant. If they have planned their marriage, they need to keep their long-range goals in mind and encourage each other daily to live out their commitment. If they have no plan or if new circumstances have sent them on a detour, they need to outline steps they need to take towards a stronger marriage. Often, slowing down and paying more attention to each other renews confidence and affection. Cutting activities to a reasonable level will leave more time for daily intimate talks and discussions about the future. Spontaneous touches, hugs and kisses give assurance that the romance has not been lost in the rat race. The ten-year mark is a crucial time to reinforce the romance. If couple time has been neglected, regular uninterrupted talks need to be scheduled and date nights need to be reinstituted.

As the couple continues the marriage journey, the next major challenge is likely to come near the twenty year mark. By this time the children are in their teens and there have been disagreements about how to handle the increasingly complex issues of guiding them into adulthood. If communication between husband and wife has been neglected, years of blaming each other for problems have taken a heavy toll on mutual respect. The tenderness and emotional closeness which are the heart of love have been bruised. By this time dissatisfaction with career, lifestyle and personal achievement may be building towards a crisis. Life may seem to have lost its joy, direction and meaning, and one or both spouses may have lost hope of any significant change for the better.

It is at this point that the so-called "mid-life crisis" occurs. When life with a mate seems pointless and hopes for redirection have been abandoned, the couple gets into an adversarial syndrome. Each conversation becomes a battle to win against an enemy who must be conquered. The couple repeats old scripts over and over in dead-end debates over the fine mess they've gotten themselves into. Starting over with someone with whom there is no history, who laughs at old jokes and shares the excitement and wonder of a new relationship, becomes a temptation and a snare for many discontented spouses. If the partner will not change, they decide to change partners.

The idea that people cannot change is one of the most dangerous lies taught today. Statements such as "Once an adulterer, always an adulterer," are believed too easily. One of the greatest truths of the Bible is that we can become more than we are. Paul says, "I can do all things through Christ who is my strength (Philippians 4:13)." And again, "If any man be in Christ, he is a new creation; old things are passed away; behold, all things have become new (II Corinthians 5:17)." In I Corinthians 6:9-11, Paul lists fornicators, adulterers and homosexuals among those excluded from the kingdom of God, but goes on to say, "And such were some of you." Such were some of us before God washed, sanctified and justified us.

Closely related to the "nobody can change" lie is the lie that we cannot change anybody but ourselves. A Christian counselor who believed that would have to look for another occupation. To this lie the apostle replies, "Follow me as I follow Christ (I Corinthians 11:1)." And again, "You hath he made alive, who were dead in trespasses and sins (Ephesians 2:1)." We can see that people can be changed through the power of God and through following good examples. Discipline can also bring change. Paul says of a repentant fornicator, "Sufficient to such a man is this punishment, which was inflicted by many

240

(II Corinthians 2:6)." This instance of effective church discipline shows that people can take action, which will effect change in others.[130]*

To prevent a disaster or to rebuild after one, counselors can remind couples that change can transpire at any juncture. Wherever they are on the road (or off it), they can minimize damage and get their marriage going in the right direction. Sometimes all it takes is a little pointed instruction in communication skills. Once they know how to discuss an issue with some degree of civility, many couples can talk their way through to a solution. Some couples will need more help than others in discovering logical steps to bring about needed change. Counselors, pastors and Christian friends can come alongside to make sure plans for improvement are implemented consistently.

One change which could help many middle-aged couples is a return to their one-flesh one-mind covenant.[136] Whether they renew their vows publicly or quietly take stock of the state of their union, they need to bring their self-doubt and fear into the open and face their problems together. Their oneness in sharing internal struggles will give them oneness in meeting external challenges. For example, the "ask your mom" "ask your dad" merry-go-round that many teenagers ride can be stopped. Teens can be told that both parents will discuss their requests, and that they will come back with the answer they agree on, including whatever warnings or conditions they consider necessary. This example, in fact, is pivotal; disagreement regarding the children is often where spouses begin to go their separate ways. If the oneness of knowing and accepting each other has grown throughout the marriage, it will

---

[136] *Here again we find the federal government trying to impinge on the Christian counselors right and obligation to live out their Christian belief's and conscience, forbidding conversion therapies helping the homosexuals et al to move from aberrant lifestyles and to healthy Christian living.

Through the years I have seen hundreds of couples renew their vows after working out significant struggles through the Love Life seminars, at the Wheat Medical Clinic and currently at the Love-Life Marriage and Counseling Center. Students who have done supervised counseling at our training center have been privileged to see many couples re-marry each other after a divorce was "final."

enable the couple at the twenty-year marker to stay the course. If oneness has been neglected, steps must be taken to nurture it. If mid-life is welcomed as a time for reflection and adjustment as a couple, it will unite them, not divide them.

Further down the road, disputes about raising children are no longer at issue. Older couples face the opposite problem, what has been termed the empty-nest syndrome. The children have been the center of life in the home. Decisions, discipline and day-to-day interaction have given the couple a sense of belonging to a group. Their involvement in the children's activities has been given more time and effort than their relationship as husband and wife. Some couples have been so child-focused, so identified with their roles as parents that the empty nest reveals the shallowness of their relationship with each other. Once the children are out of the house, husband and wife seem to have no shared interests left.

Ideally, couples would continue to develop a growing, exciting relationship throughout their lifetime together. Laziness does not build meaningful relationships. A quality relationship requires focus and energy. If a couple is not constantly planning for the future, their future will catch them unprepared for its challenges. Two things need to be kept in mind. First, the husband-wife relationship is the primary bond of the family, and must be defended and nourished. One effective way is to keep dating each other through the years, planning just-the-two-of-us outings with the same enthusiasm and attention as during courtship. Secondly, it must be remembered that the family (parents and children) is the primary bond of society, and needs strength for the long haul. While rearing children, the joy of each moment must be savored and cherished without losing sight of the goal: adult siblings whose best friends are each other and their parents. Planning for these lifetime friendships will include creating memories through family activities and trips, and establishing family traditions such as reunions, celebrations and shared hobbies. Shared interests can be enjoyed even after

242

the children are grown, and get-togethers for meals or special events can maintain the warmth of the family's life.

The empty-nest is not a place of desolation or depression for parents who have done their work well. Taking the term literally, the empty-nest is a sign that there is a new generation of eagles flying to new heights. When our fledglings leave the nest we can let them soar on the wings we taught them to use. Back at home, we can revive the nesting behavior of our newlywed years, adapting our surroundings, our activities and ourselves to this new dimension of marriage.[137]

Since the marriage journey is a long trip on a hazardous road, attention to mile markers is extremely helpful. Planning and preparing for critical periods builds confidence that they not only can be endured, but they can be times of deepening and strengthening of a one-mind approach to life's challenges. Newlyweds who think love means never having a problem may think they are no longer in love when problems arise. Biblically, love means a commitment to go through each problem together and to come out on the other side with richer appreciation of each other. Those who have been married many years learn that love is the awe felt in the presence of one who has been a trusting and trustworthy companion through the storms of life, who has seen us at our worst but is still there understanding, accepting, encouraging—a one-flesh one-mind companion who knows all about us but loves us anyway. Much of The heart of marriage counseling is correcting misconceptions about love and helping couples discover and enjoy the real thing.

---

[137] Many of the hippies of my generation, now geriatric hippies, have produced non-launching children who never leave the nest, or return to it repeatedly. The sins of parents are being visited on their children. Sinful experimentation with drugs and sex accentuated the selfishness and unreliability of people whose children now lack direction and purpose. Ironically, some of these young people find help in the legacy of their hardworking grandparents—the very "establishment" against which the hippies rebelled. Healthy parents of the same generation do help their children, but most of the late bloomers are out of the home by the mid-twenties, rarely staying through the early thirties. "Home Sweet Home", *Newsweek*, March 28 and April 4, 2011, p. 29.

Any stage of the marriage journey can be hazardous. I once read in a Sunday newspaper about a couple celebrating their fiftieth wedding anniversary. As I looked at their picture I wondered what it would be like to have been married to Joanne for fifty years. I was rather rudely awakened from my reverie when I entered my office on Monday morning. I recognized the couple from the article there in the waiting room, in need of counseling. There had been a major blow-up at their anniversary celebration, with the seething anger of many years exploding in front of all their children, relatives and friends.

Many people can survive years of a bad marriage, but mere survival is not what we are about as Christians. Our relationships should thrive in Christ-like love. People who learn to swim by being thrown into the middle of a lake quickly learn to merely survive in the water. World-class swimmers thrive at the highest levels of challenge because they endure meticulous, persistent training. Most newlyweds have been thrown into the lake, and only dogpaddle through their marriages. Christian marriage counseling, in effect, takes people to the safe end of the pool and helps them work on basic skills needed to keep them on course through deep and troubled waters.

The Road to Destruction

Warning signs are plentiful on the road to divorce. In premarital counseling, we offer the couple a roadmap of biblical instruction, which if followed, will keep them on the right road. When counseling couples in distress we point out "wrong way" and "dead end" signs, biblical warnings, which if heeded, will get them off the wrong road. The profitable application of biblical principles includes:

Doctrine—clear presentation of God's truth as the standard for our lives.

244

Reproof — insightful exposure of points where our lives fall short of God's truth.

Rebuke — bold confrontation of willful departure from the truth.

Correction — patient assistance in making things right.

Instruction in righteousness — encouragement and guidance towards conforming to truth.

This is the biblical pattern for proclaiming and applying the truth of God's Word (II Timothy 3:16). Marriage problems arise through lack of planning, lack of commitment to work hard on areas of difficulty and discomfort, and lack of God's blessing through neglect of spiritual principles and resources.

A couple depending on good intentions and high hopes risks catastrophic disillusionment. The road to divorce is often paved with good intentions. If both husband and wife do not concentrate on building their marriage, distractions can break it down. The New Testament word often translated "temptation" can also be translated "trial;" something which breaks the pattern, distracts, disrupts. In a neutral sense, this could be anything which tests one's character, commitment or faith. James 1:2-5 says that such tests can be occasions of joy as God gives us wisdom to grow through patient endurance. Moral distractions, according to James 1:13-15, can be disastrous as common human desire turns to lust which seeks illegitimate fulfillment, leading to destruction. Trials and temptations easily distract couples. Too frequently they destroy marriages which are not securely grounded in God's truth.

The severest sin against marriage, adultery, illustrates the pattern of temptation, hesitation and participation which is a sinner's road to ruin. Temptation distracts a person from the purpose and value of the marriage commitment. During a period of hesitation, attention is focused on the temptation and options are weighed. Can I resist? Should I do it? What will happen if I do? Is it worth the possible consequences? The difference between noticing an attractive person and looking upon to lust after is a decision made in a split-second of hesitation.[138]

Adultery is seldom a split-second decision. Most often, it follows a period of double-mindedness, a hesitation phase in which faithfulness to a spouse becomes just one of the options to be considered. In fact, the words "unfaithfulness" and "adultery" are not identical in meaning, although they are often used interchangeably. More precisely, adultery is an act or repeated acts of extramarital sex. Unfaithfulness, more broadly, is an attitude of indifference towards the marriage covenant. Unfaithfulness describes a multitude of sins, which break faith, and may or may not include physical adultery.

Perhaps most married people think they could never fall into adultery. They cannot believe that they would ever be physically unfaithful. But unfaithfulness does not always lead to a physical relationship with a real partner. Chat-room fantasies, cyber-space lovers, sexting, and email prostitutes have added new twists to the temptations of phone sex and hard-copy pornography.

The problem is real but the partners are fake. Homosexuals, bisexuals, and transgenders go online posing as something they are not. Teens explore the pleasures of talking sexual trash. People in past generations who were arrested for making obscene phone calls seek their own kind through their computers. There are also sexual predators and desperate people who will stoop to anything to avoid relationships that require faithfulness. These commitment- phobic fools risk all, sell all, and give all to get something they think they want. Sometimes they get what they truly deserve: nothing, save disease, frustration and dysfunctional partners.

All these, and more, can be invited into our homes at the click of a mouse!

---

[138] Firefighters will tell you to stop, drop and roll when you're on fire. When sinful passions are inflamed, the same advice applies: when you're on fire with temptation, stop in your tracks, drop to your knees, and roll the burden on the

Lord in prayer.

Tragically, internet pornography destroys the lives and ministries of people who would never have risked being seen renting an X-rated video or buying a pornographic magazine.

In earlier generations the traveling salesman was stereotypical—a person who could be immoral on the road, where nobody really knew him or could hold him accountable for his actions. The depths of sexual degradation were confined to the "red light districts" of big cities and mail-order magazines and films which were delivered in plain brown wrappers. The antithesis and nemesis of the profligate traveling salesman was the equally stereotypical humble rural pastor whose purity was beyond question, if only through lack of opportunity. Tragically, that innocent country preacher can now be ambushed by his darkest lusts while sitting alone in the privacy of his study with a computer which can take him places beyond the traveling salesman's wildest nightmares.

This is not hypothetical. A convention of a conservative evangelical denomination had to deal with the disastrous spread of this very problem among some of its most promising pastors.

Physical lust is not the only problem. The cyber-pseudo world of imaginary relationships follows the pattern of romance novels, action movies and idolization of athletes, musicians and movie stars. Rather than settle down to our real-life warts-and-all relationships, we imagine ourselves as heroes or heroines, exciting, desirable, powerful, unlimited ("You shall be as gods," said the Serpent). The life of our imaginations becomes more fulfilling than our ho-hum jobs and marriages as we retreat further and further from our commitments to real people. We slip into our fantasies whenever the drabness of reality threatens our illusions about ourselves.

In his short story, "The Secret Life of Walter Mitty," James Thurber gives a humorous portrayal of this pattern. Walter Mitty, a timid man married to an assertive woman, in reality has a very humdrum existence. In the midst of his humiliatingly meaningless routine, Mitty switches to his secret self, the fighter pilot, surgeon and superhero whose exciting adventures and great achievements occur while the meek little man runs trivial errands or waits for his wife. Readers do not laugh outright at Mitty; the response is usually a knowing smile. Since childhood we have all imagined ourselves to be something more, something different. Child's-play can help prepare us for adult responsibilities. Our ability to focus on those responsibilities is jeopardized when we cling to self-aggrandizing fantasies in adulthood.

Indulging in mind games sets us up to act them out. The person who compliments me recognizes my true worth better than my spouse does (we had the toothpaste tube and toilet paper roll argument again last night). The person I helped will never forget what a sacrifice I made (my spouse has no idea how I slave to keep him/her happy). Bringing our fantasy selves into the real world, we imagine that every act of civility or courtesy is romantically charged.

At home, familiarity with a spouse's faults may indeed breed contempt. Outside the home, familiarity with a co-worker may breed over familiarity. We forget that our co-workers are also putting on their public faces and have as many escapist illusions as we do. It is the old "answering the phone in the middle of an argument" persona, that charming self any of us can pretend to be to anyone who does not have to live with us.[139]

"Jesus knows all about me, but He loves me anyway," says a popular bumper sticker. The marriage covenant binds a couple together in similarly comprehensive knowledge and acceptance. Total acceptance by a spouse with total knowledge is the level of unconditional love that God invites us to enjoy. Couples, who can unmask themselves at home, accepting each

---

[139] This has to be the counselor's spouse's worst nightmare. Once, a woman I was counseling met my wife in a supermarket, and told her what a kind and gentle soul I was. My wife correctly replied, "Well, you don't know him that well."

other without illusions, will find the state of their union very strong. Trials and temptations will not easily distract them from their joy in mutual self-revelation and encouragement. As they grow together, building each other up, their one-flesh bond will be enriched by their one-mind approach to the world. Faith in each other is the basis of faithfulness to each other. Both are secured in shared faith in God: obedient faith in God enables a person to be trustworthy and trusting in marriage.

Faithfulness to a partner in the marriage covenant requires a clear-eyed realization that heroism, adventure and fulfillment are found in the depths of commitment rather than in superficial conquest. In a romance novel, nobody but the villain ever has bad breath — not even the horses. In action movies, you seldom see a major character waiting in line. Athletes, musicians and movie stars have real lives which are often tragically swallowed up by their celebrity images. Losing sight of the long-term, even eternal value of a well-lived marriage, people are too easily distracted by less demanding relationships.

Just as unfaithfulness does not always express itself in acts of adultery, adultery is seldom the first sign of an unfaithful attitude. Most people who are facing the threat of separation or divorce tell marriage counselors they had little or no warning that their future was in great peril. Their mates just made the announcement that they were not happy (as if their personal happiness were the most important thing on the planet). The unhappy mates usually say something to the effect that they never really loved them or that it has been a long time since they loved them. What they are really saying is that their own comfort is more important to them than their commitment to their spouses. Sometimes they admit that they are confused about their situation. They are in the hesitation phase of temptation, considering options.

Some typical symptoms suggest that a spouse may be going beyond the hesitation phase and participating in more active unfaithfulness. They become more and more distant emotionally and tend to withdraw physically, as well. They avoid physical touch like the plague, because the slightest touch stirs complicated feelings. The first visible change is in the wardrobe: fancy underwear, new clothes that put them in style for the first time in years. Some men will buy a new sports car, most likely red (in some regions a new pickup truck is more the style). A man who never wore jewelry will purchase a diamond ring for himself. Taste in music reverts to their pagan single days, usually either country music or rock. Then begin long hours at work (more than one bar has been named "The Office" to accommodate this ruse — in a college town loners can drink at "The Library"). They say they need space, time to sort their heads out, less pressure.

When confronted about their behavior or about their relationship with specific opposite-sex acquaintances, they react defensively or angrily. They may move out rather than face the issue, but usually move no further than the far side of the bed or a couch in another room. The next thing they do is affirm that they have a "friend," and see nothing wrong with it. They say it would not bother them if their mate had a "friend," too. Some are in a full-bloom affair, some are emotionally involved and others are considering involvement. Initially, they justify themselves because they are not involved sexually. In one episode of the sit-com "The King of Queens," a couple argued about whether a friend was cheating on his wife through regularly dining out with another woman if there was no act of adultery. They seemed to approach the conclusion that any form of breaking faith (unfaithfulness) is cheating. But cheating is violating the rules of a game; unfaithfulness violates the covenant of marriage.

Viewing unfaithfulness as a game, the cheating spouse falls into more intensely erratic behavior. Wherever and whenever, long phone calls from cell phones keep up communication with the "friend." Cell phone bills skyrocketed (the days before unlimited cell calls) and incoming calls at home (for the few that have them) frequently turn out to be "wrong numbers" or hang-ups. Codes, email and other contacts add to the thrill of the game. If the unfaithful would put just half the time and energy into their marriages that they put into their affairs, their marriages would most likely show significant improvement.

Dividing attention between a spouse and another sexual partner not only violates the covenanted one-flesh union but also creates internal and external conflict.[140] The unconditional love God intends for husband and wife involves their growing knowledge and acceptance of each other. Sexual union is the total physical knowledge and acceptance, which establishes them as one flesh. Sharing the joys, sorrows, hopes and fears (and burnt toast) of life, they become more and more of one mind.

They learn to understand and accept each other as total, albeit finite and flawed human beings. Breaking this pattern through adultery breaks the adulterers themselves.

How does adultery break adulterers? The one who doubts in James 1:6 displays split judgment, hesitating between two opinions. Indecisiveness about faith is at the core of indecisiveness about faithfulness. Will I trust? Will I be trustworthy? An unfaithful spouse often wants both the security of marriage and the fleeting pleasure of sin. The two-souled person of James 1:8 is completely dysfunctional concerning God's provision for true living. The internal conflicts among various lusts not only break out into external conflicts (James 4:1-3); in the adulterer, the two-souled division cuts deeper. I Corinthians 6:16 says that even in prostitution sexual

---

[140] Today it also puts both husband and wife in danger of disease or death.

union creates an incipient one-body bond. The total physical surrender involved in the sex act creates a level of intimacy that God intended for an exclusive lifelong commitment. Joining as one flesh, whether within marriage, outside marriage or before marriage draws the mind and heart towards the partner as God intended would occur only within a faithful marriage. Thus, adulterers are no longer split only in their judgment; they have made themselves emphatically two-souled. The life-defining bond which could have thrived only within marriage has been dispersed abroad.[141]

A society which expects promiscuity trivializes the one-flesh one-mind ideal. God forgives and heals, but few may know how free love can be when it is shared in total commitment to only one mate, or how safe sex can be when it is saved for the covenant union of life-defining lifelong monogamy.[142] Christian counselors must recognize that many, perhaps most marriages fall far short of this ideal. When people are expected to be sexually active as soon as, and as often as possible, their consciences are seared. Even the instability of the two-souled adulterer who has one affair at a time is above the standard accepted by many. Multiplying sexual encounters divides souls, dissolving the ability to comprehend or achieve the more perfect union intended by God. May God help us to proclaim and maintain the biblical standard of one-flesh one-mind marriage and to bring clients to repentance and substantial healing where this standard has been violated.

---

[141] James 1:8 says, "a double-minded man is unstable in all his ways." Two double-minded persons cannot put a stable relationship together — it will be as schizophrenic and unstable as they have become.

[142] Just inside the main entrance of one public elementary school a large sign which says "Safe Sex" draws attention to printed material describing how to use a condom. The same school system introduces topics such as oral sex as early as third grade.

Putting a broken marriage back together requires all the resources a couple can get. Neither of them is an objective observer of the chaos they are experiencing. Both tend to find support from people whose friendly ears encourage them to vent their frustration but do little to correct their problems. The inability to see clearly and to act consistently is precisely why these people need counsel and precisely why many do not seek or follow it.

Christian marriage counseling must rise to the crisis of our culture which manifests itself in the crises of so many marriages. We must educate ourselves not only to earn credible degrees but to become credible guides, men and women who are highly informed about theories, methods and issues and capable of translating our knowledge into practical wisdom. We must qualify ourselves, when necessary, not only for professional certification and licensing but also for clear-headed, warm-hearted consistency and efficiency in meeting real human needs. We must commit ourselves not just to required training experiences and internships, but to a lifetime of coming alongside couples in the valley of the shadow of divorce and giving them hope.

Reconsidering Divorce

People do not enter marriage with the intention of failing. Young people in love have high hopes of a perfect marriage, avoiding all the mistakes others have made. People who marry later in life, perhaps after making their own mistakes, think that they have learned enough to get it right this time. Whatever their beliefs about marriage, people usually approach it with the best of intentions. As I have often said, the road to divorce is often paved with good intentions.

A couple's intentions may be much higher than their realistic expectations. The divorce rate is constantly rising as the culture moves further from God. Cohabiting with minimal commitment is becoming commonplace. Whatever aura of Judeo-Christian tradition remains in the moral notions of our society, the influence of biblical principles over non-believers is rapidly dissipating. Earlier generations debated whether there were any valid reasons for divorce; now there is no consensus about what might be valid reasons for marriage, if there are any. Knowing this, many couples do not vow to enter an "until death do us part" marriage covenant in the sight of God, but make promises to each other about a partnership contract which conforms to prevailing law. The argument for homosexual "marriage" is rooted in the legal advantages of a partnership contract rather than in any real sense of the biblical definition of a divinely sanctioned marriage. Ignorance or rejection of God's purposes for marriage leaves couples to pick their own reasons for marrying. If their self-defined expectations are not satisfied, changing circumstances or new love interests may part them at any time.

Many first-marriage divorces occur within the first five to seven years of marriage, when the promises seem hard to keep and the pleasure of pursuit is contrasted with the confinement of commitment. As one young man said of his eventful dating experience, "I'm in love with love." The freshness of new relationships attracted him away from deeper commitment to anyone. The challenge of adjusting to close encounters of the everyday kind with another human being can be overwhelming. That person squinting at you across the breakfast table bears little resemblance to that vision of perfection that charmed you through your first date. Memories of that enchanted evening are long gone by the second bite of burnt toast. As a third grade teacher told her students, "Cute doesn't count any more." A plaque with that motto would be a good first anniversary gift for a couple who makes it that far.

When a first marriage breaks up, do people learn from their mistakes? If a couple fails at marriage, can each of them expect to get it right next time? Surveys suggest that the second time around is no better than the first, and it just gets worse from there. More people leave second marriages than first marriages, and the divorce rate for third marriages is higher than the rate for second marriages. Figure it out. Without God's intervention this cycle of failure is inevitable. People whose commitments are conditioned by personal expectations will drop their commitments when they do not get what they want or when they decide they want something else. Some have suggested the term "serial monogamy" to describe this phenomenon. It has become socially acceptable to have any number of marriage partners,[143] as long as you are married to them one at a time. "Serial monogamy" is an oxymoron as meaningless as "serial suicide." Monogamy, one-man one-woman union in a covenant relationship entered by vow is a once-for-all commitment with life-defining significance. If you get it right once, you will not do it again.

God says He hates divorce (Malachi 2:16). His standard for marriage is so high that He compares it to the unbreakable bond between Himself and His people. Like marriage, faith in Jesus Christ is a covenant relationship. Jesus Himself is the sacrifice and the guarantor of the covenant. All the promises of God are centered and confirmed in Him. We enter this covenant relationship with Him not by a vow to keep its conditions, but by trusting God's vow that He has fulfilled all of its conditions Himself, in Christ (Hebrews 6:16-20). Everything God offers us in Christ is ours the moment we call upon the Lord for salvation. But God does not immediately transport us into a blissful state of

---

[143] With the Middle East moving rapidly to the West I expect the American and Western Europe idea of marriage to one person to change rapidly to serial monogamy. Already those migrants coming to the U.S. with multiple wives are receiving financial incentives for each wife. Without Biblical understanding people have no absolute standards and moral behavior devolves.

perfection and satisfaction. Our faith needs to be translated into living out God's love in the details of mundane existence.

The covenant relationship has been permanently established, but experience of its benefits and privileges is progressive. Nothing can separate God's people from His love (Romans 8:38-39). Nothing should separate a couple whose marriage is patterned after God's covenant relationship with His people.

When marriage is viewed as a covenant relationship entered by vow, both spouses will be committed to self-sacrifice, kept promises and showing love in the details of life. And quite literally, the Devil is in the details. The cares of this world and the foxes that spoil the vines quickly infest a marriage.[144] A wedding does not zap a couple into an alternate universe where a recorded message tells them, "Nothing can go wrong ... go wrong ... go wrong ..." Couples need to be warned that something will go wrong. Living out love in the details of mundane existence brings daunting challenges. Enjoying the blessings of marriage requires constant vigilance. Growth in oneness comes through facing, enduring and overcoming problems together.

If marriage problems are unavoidable, where are the answers? Right where God put all the answers: in Jesus Christ. Not a little plaster baby Jesus brought out once a year or a glow-in-the-dark plastic Jesus that keeps a child awake at night, but the real walks-with-me-talks-with-me Jesus of the Bible. The whole Bible. As Mrs. Beaver of Narnia says of the Christ-figure Aslan, "He is not a tame lion." The lion whose death paid for sin and who carries His children in resurrection power also uses His claws to tear away a sinner's dragon-flesh. His roar changes times and seasons and He swallows up women, men, boys, girls, kings, emperors, cities and realms. So C.S. Lewis pictures the King to whom we are accountable. He is not a tame God, but the Lord of Creation and Salvation who claims rule over the details of our lives. Just as our salvation did not come through our own good intentions or warm fuzzy feelings, our life in Christ cannot

The little foxes of Song of Solomon 2:15 were seemingly harmless, but their nibbling away at a vineyard's fruitfulness could destroy its purpose and value. Just so, small, seemingly unimportant issues can eat away at a marriage.

be reduced to a bumper sticker or a bracelet. We need to know who this Person is, this God-Man who invaded time and space to bring us eternal riches.

What does this have to do with burnt toast and a squinty-eyed spouse? When Peter and Paul preached and prayed, their goal was that people would get a solid grasp of how knowing Jesus Christ affected all aspects of their lives. Relationships, values, character, even every thought captivated by Him (II Corinthians 10:3-5). Paul noted that some people have zeal without knowledge, trying to do what God wants without paying attention to what God says (Romans 10:2). In Colossians 3:10 he says that believers are renewed in knowledge, that relationship with Jesus Christ changes all other relationships. He prays that believers will know God not only in a general way, but that they will "be filled with the knowledge of his will (Colossians 1:9)." Knowledge of God in Christ, knowledge of the Bible and knowledge of how to live in God's will produce effective faith and love. When Paul says God wants people "to be saved, and to come to the knowledge of the truth (I Timothy 2:4)," he leaves room for the possibility that at least some of the saved need more knowledge.

Peter agrees. He says that faith should be expressed in virtue, knowledge, self-control, perseverance, godliness, kindness and love (I Peter 1:5-7). That would make a good table of contents for a marriage counseling manual. In fact, Peter does say that husbands should relate to their wives with knowledge (II Peter 3:7). We need to grow in knowledge of our spouses, to understand their needs, hopes, fears and deepest thoughts. Just as our knowledge of God grows through intense, comprehensive saturation in His Word, our knowledge of our spouses grows through similar concentration on their expressions of who they really are. Such intimate self-revelation is a privilege and treasure to be cherished by married couples, and none should dare trample on this sacred ground through insensitivity or malice.

When marriage is seen as a lifelong companionship of mutual self-revelation and acceptance, the relationship between husband and wife is secured by ever increasing trust. When marriage is seen as an opportunity for self-satisfaction, disappointment, distress and divorce are logical outcomes. Without a biblical view of marriage, people make individualistic decisions about the personal discomfort of sustaining a commitment to another person. When a person is in a crisis marriage situation or in a marriage which has had irritating problems for years, all that person can think about is getting out of that marriage—the sooner the better. In counseling thousands of couples over the years, I have found that most people who want out of marriage are willing to trust their own feelings about what divorce is and what it does to people. They seem to think Cinderella and Prince Charming could go back to the ball and dance off with new partners (or alone) and everyone could live happily ever after. Many are like the Queen in Alice in Wonderland who believed five unbelievable things every morning before breakfast. Proverbs 18:2 says that someone who values his or her own opinions more than the truth is a fool. "My mind is made up! Don't confuse me with facts!"

The facts indicate that divorce is not a victimless crime. Despite the efforts of some to prescribe a pattern for "good divorce," the fact is that divorce puts asunder people who once thought God or some imaginary higher power brought them together. In fact, many children of divorce are intensely aware that their families have been broken, and never recover from a Humpty-Dumpty syndrome in which they keep trying to put the pieces together again. They feel somehow responsible for the split, and their guilt and frustration form a subtext of subsequent relationships. When parents separate, the shock often leaves children feeling rejected and abandoned.

For latch-key children of single or divorced parents, the sense of abandonment is reinforced by fending for themselves at home while the parent works. Insecurity, fear and loneliness lead to dysfunctional coping strategies such as sexual dependencies and experimentation with drugs and crime. Teachers and police officers are seen as just more incompetent and uncaring adults who probably are as confused about life as children are. A solid marriage demonstrates the possibility of secure connections between human beings. Divorce introduces an indeterminacy principle which potentially destabilizes all human connections, at least in the perception of a child. Children who do not see stability in the relationships of significant adults eventually conclude that they have to raise themselves, accepting the values and advice of peers as being more trustworthy than the patently hypocritical pronouncements of dysfunctional parents. In a world where adults act like children, children will reject the guidance of adults[145].

The psychological distress of children strikes a sympathetic chord among the compassionate; anti-social and criminal behavior gets a reaction from everyone. As these issues have gained public notoriety, they have demanded a response. One development has been an increase in facilities for children's psychiatric care. These facilities are characterized by institutional controlled-environment behavioral modules. While such carefully structured training units may produce immediate short-term therapeutic results, they often have no direct counterparts in real-world experience. Whether classical or innovative, highly controlled behavioristic procedures cannot provide solutions which transfer well into the complex social

---

[145] What every teenager is looking for is someone less confused than they are. Many parents are as confused if not more confused. Society might forgive a mentally ill mother who shoots her teenagers dead for mouthing off, but smoking pot with your teenagers because you would rather join them than correct them shows cowardice.

contexts in which the problems arose. God says that children need moms and dads, and when Mom and Dad are not there, modifying children's behavior will not make them sleep better at night.[146]

The children are not the only ones who suffer. The cycle of so-called serial monogamy is just one tragic option for divorced persons. Fear of commitment may keep them from remarrying, and send them into a degraded life of promiscuity or perversity. Some try to start over from the very beginning, fantasizing themselves as attractive and eligible, and striving to be seen and accepted among younger singles. Those who realize that divorce was a mistake try to minimize the damage, and put prodigious effort into attempts at reconciliation.

For months, one man tried very hard to save his marriage. His wife was seeing another man and had filed for divorce, although she lacked sufficient grounds according to her state's laws. He contested the divorce and a court date was set. It might have taken three years to finalize the divorce. After months of distress to himself and his four children, the man decided to settle with her before the hearing date. She settled for ten thousand dollars and gave him full custody of the children. In this case, the man rejected my exhortation to wait out the court process, allowing himself to be worn down by the day-by-day stress his wife's unfaithfulness created. If he had waited out a three year court struggle, his wife's affair might have succumbed to its inherent instability and burned itself out.

Another man came in lower than the proverbial snake's belly. He told me that he was on his second marriage and was his wife's third husband. She had become involved with a man at work in much the same way as she had met her husband. Her husband said, "I will do anything to save my marriage!" He started attending church and praying regularly, brought her flowers, called her during work breaks and listened to her when

---

[146] Medication might, but that raises an even broader field of debate.

262

she talked. He warned the other man, begged her, threatened her, called her parents and his parents, spent quality time with the children, and contacted the man who performed their wedding— all the time insisting that he was a changed man. After three months he found the girl of his dreams (who had separated from her abusive husband) and moved right in.

His wife, meanwhile, had come to me to say that she had recognized her fault and wanted a chance to get her family back. She started to go to church and prayed for the first time in her life. She dumped her boyfriend, who had already divorced his wife of twenty-some years. She called her husband's first wife, all their friends, his mother, her mother and his pastor. She begged, pleaded with him and got the children involved. But he was "in love," having the best sex of his life, he told her. So she went back to the boyfriend, got engaged within two months, and prepared for the court battle.

When first confronted regarding her adultery, this woman had said, "My decisions are my own." Really? How many people did her affair affect? First, her child from a former marriage who had been adopted by this husband. Then their six-year-old together, her boyfriend's three children and her husband's girlfriend's three children. Three marriages ended, involving six partners and their extended families and friends. Add three judges, six lawyers and at least two counselors and two pastors. The lives and relationships of well over one hundred people were changed forever either directly or indirectly because of one person's insistence upon "her own decision" to move beyond the hesitation of an unfaithful attitude into participation in adulterous acts.

The consequences of divorce are very real. Some of them are irreversible. Spouses who seek reconciliation and restoration face an uphill battle, and many succumb to frustration and failure. Christian marriage counselors soon learn that following biblical principles does not guarantee a happily-ever-after ending to a horror story filled with unbiblical attitudes and actions. But there can be substantial healing when conforming to God's standards. When the holiness of holy matrimony is valued more than the happiness of selfish individuals, the peace of God will accompany any outcome of efforts towards reconciliation.

A man I have seen, whose marriage and divorce were about as messy as any, repented and reestablished a vital relationship with the Lord and accepted his obligation to try to make things right with his wife and children. Through prayer, biblical counsel and a lot of hard work, the family was eventually reunited. Not long after their reconciliation, they were traveling in two vehicles one night; the wife and children leading, the husband some distance behind alone in another car. He lost sight of them for awhile, and then saw the lights of emergency vehicles as he approached a hill. Just over the hilltop, he discovered that a tragic accident had again torn the family away from each other, and he was the lone survivor. He was awestruck at the grace of God which had rejoined them after their earlier separation, and he had the assurance that he would meet his wife and children in the arms of Jesus.

This is what Christian marriage counseling is about. Not a quick fix or a Pollyanna promise of smooth sailing through the storms of life, but a word from God about the real issues of sin, righteousness, judgment and grace. Someone titled his commentary on Romans, *The Gospel for the Whole of Life*. Christian marriage counseling applies the gospel to parts of life for which secular counsel has no authoritative answers. Accepting God's answers to life's questions does not guarantee personal happiness, but it does bring God's presence and power into the difficult situations of life.

Reaching for Direction

For most people in troubled marriages light and hope are hard to come by and even harder to hang onto. In the darkness of disillusionment they push any button that might be a light switch. Drowning in desperation they grasp at any straw that might help them stay afloat. I could multiply examples from my counseling experience to illustrate the eagerness of betrayed spouses to run off in all directions looking for answers.

Life is especially difficult for unfaithful spouses. The Scriptures are clear: the way of sinners is hard (Proverbs 13:15). Not only is their way hard, but they themselves become hardened physically, emotionally and spiritually. Sometimes their physical appearance shows the stress and strain of habitual sinful choices. If some of these people could be shown before-and-after pictures of themselves, they would see the hardening that others see in them. Many faithful spouses have commented that their adulterous mates "look so old."

One woman who looked much older than her years had left her husband and three children to move in with another man in a different state. Her husband was not perfect, but he was a faithful, hardworking man. The man she moved in with was very wealthy, but she soon learned how self-centered and stingy he was. He forced her to work outside the home for the first time in her life and required her to turn her paychecks over to him.

After a year of verbal abuse and broken promises, she happened to see a bumper sticker which read, "Have you hugged your kids today?" She started crying uncontrollably, pulled off the freeway and called her husband. He had been praying for her return the whole time, and so had their children. When she asked if she could come home he was overjoyed. He wired her the money for the trip home. She did not even return to the other man's house for her things.

In this case God acted quite directly to answer the prayer of a covenant-keeping husband. In most counseling cases, reconciliation requires consistent, persistent baby steps in the direction of conformity to God's truth. Usually the ministry of reconciliation involves incredibly hard work. The task is much more like a marathon than a sprint. If your mate is considering getting out of the marriage, then you are put into the difficult position of trying to save the marriage alone.[147] Trying to save a marriage when your spouse rejects you is no easy road. You do not have the luxury of taking the rejection personally and tending to your own wounds. You must stay focused and realize that your mate is temporarily insane,[148] stepping outside God's provision for human well-being. Who but an insane person would give up family, friends, wealth, reputation and relationship with God? The most merciful thing you can do is to fight for the marriage.

Christian marriage counselors deal with very courageous people. When they come for counseling they have already begun to deal with one of their biggest problems: lack of confidence in themselves and in God. We should not depend on our own abilities, but we should trust that following God's truth will make life work. God honors those who honor Him. Our confidence comes from knowing that God strengthens us to do anything He requires (Philippians 4:13).Seeking biblical counsel is a wise and brave step for a person whose life is in disarray.

Some people are so intent on saving their marriages that they work for months doing the right things. They pray, fast, send cards, notes, and letters and do anything else they can think of to show their love and care. Where necessary, they try to make positive changes in themselves to win their spouses back. Counselors need to encourage such people never to do or

---

[147] *How to Save Your Marriage Alone*, by Ed Wheat, MD, is a helpful resource.

[148] Breaking God's laws is the clearest form of insanity.

say anything deceptive or misleading, and warn against doing anything to win their spouse back that they do not plan to keep on doing for the rest of their lives. Getting the spouse back and then reverting to old dysfunctional patterns of behavior would be to get them back on false pretenses.

As long as the unfaithful spouse is in the two-souled limbo between Heaven's truth and Hell's lies, popular wisdom will suggest two options: cut your losses and give up the marriage, or take off the gloves and fight against the adulterer tooth and nail. Like the concept of cheating, the concept of giving up or fighting likens marriage to a game to be won or lost, a competition in which to keep score.

Should you let the unfaithful spouse go, as you would the proverbial butterfly that, once freed, just might come back? Many friends and family members will tell you to let go and get on with your life. For my part, I would be insulted by such miserable counsel. To a great extent, my wife is my very life and as long as we are both on earth I will do everything in my power to protect and nurture her. Letting an already confused mate go will not immediately make him or her more rational. More likely, it will only make the adulterer think that the faithful spouse does not care what happens. When someone is on a bad roll making wrong choices, life does not suddenly go upward — more often it takes a nosedive. Letting go leaves the unfaithful spouse in free fall, and does nothing to heal wounds. Friends and family see you hurting and want the hurt to stop, but giving up a marriage leaves a big empty space in the life you try to get on with.

Others will advise you to forfeit nothing, to go on the offensive and rack up some points of your own. Many well-intentioned people will try to persuade you to create a crisis to prevent the rebellious mate from having a "stolen cake, and eating it, too." Focusing totally on a desired outcome, confrontational speech and manipulative action attempt to match the unfaithful spouse move-for-move. Again, the gamesmanship model is falsely applied and outmaneuvering and outscoring an opponent replaces the one-flesh one-mind process of helping a partner grow in conformity to the truth.

We can trust God to accomplish His purposes as we are faithful in applying His principles. Seeking to take care of what we consider to be our own business, by any means we consider necessary, shows a serious lack of faith. Reasonable alternatives to faith never rise to the glory of God's purposes and usually produce undesirable side effects. God promised Abraham a child, but Sarah was so old that it seemed reasonable to produce a child through her maid. Later, God miraculously brought the promised son through Sarah, but the descendants of Abraham's two sons have been at each other's throats for almost four thousand years. What seems reasonable at the moment may bring lasting negative consequences.

Then where are the resources to restore a marriage when the foundations are destroyed? The disruption of a marriage is, in fact, a crisis of faith. It makes people question all of their assumptions about marriage, their spouses, themselves, life in general and God. It deprives them of what they need most: a clear mind to see things as they really are in order to make wise decisions, a sense of being loved and being able to love wholeheartedly, and the power to act confidently and productively. What replaces these necessary strengths is the weakness of fear. Afraid that their minds have been deluded, their love has been rejected and their efforts have been worse than useless, their fear either paralyzes them or throws them into frenzies of fruitless activity.

How do we minister to these people after we tell them that God's love casts out fear (I John 4:18) and that the Holy Spirit provides the power, love and sanity which they need to go on (II Timothy 1:7)? What can we do when the foundations are destroyed? We can remind them that God is on His throne even when all seems so wrong with their world. No matter how far down the road to destruction a couple has gone, when they come for counseling they have admitted that they have a problem. When both come, they may disagree about what the problem is, and both of them may be wrong. Our problem-solving approach will include gathering all the information we can, but we will also provide tools for getting past the finger-pointing and blame-passing the couple has already done. As the counselor and the couple get an increasingly clear picture of where the marriage has been and where it is now, the issue on the table will be, "What do we do to get where God wants us to be?" From beginning to end, that question determines everything we do.

For example, in cases of apparent or blatant unfaithfulness, the unfaithful will almost invariably fault their spouses rather than admit their own wrongdoing. The typical routine is to constantly cite examples of the mate's shortcomings (bad communicator, bad housekeeper, bad provider, bad sex partner, etc.). The counselor should always take the high road of exploring each complaint as if it were legitimate and use these starting points to teach biblical principles where needed. Taking perceived problems seriously, accepting them exactly as presented, lets clients know that counseling sessions will be characterized by truthfulness and trust, just as their marriage should be. Skirting issues or seeking hidden motives puts people on their guard against manipulation. If the complaint is merely a smokescreen, a serious response often clears the air, and we can move on to more vital issues. If the complaint is sincere, no matter how trivial it seems, a serious attempt to resolve it is the first step towards resolving the whole complex of problems which brought the marriage to a crisis.

Starting with perceived problems, we can demonstrate the effectiveness of a forthright search for solutions. As the problem-solving approach proves its value trust builds and clients begin to open up concerning deeper concerns. We must not jump ahead and preach at them about what we think is wrong with their marriage any more than we should withhold direction in areas where they admit their perplexity. Our approach should be emphatically directive, guiding clients through problem-solving experiences which give them tools for more productive communication at home.

As counselors, we take pride in academic degrees, professional credentials and extensive experience; as Christians, our gifts and expertise are tools for ministry. Paul tells us not to "over think" our qualifications but to think healthily about our responsibility (Romans 12:3). All ministry is to be done in love, without play-acting, without masks (Romans 12:9).

And what is our ministry? Truly Christian marriage counseling is not merely using the Bible to proof text an essentially secular methodology. Truly Christian marriage counseling is the pursuit of God's truth as it applies to marital issues. Our profession may seem to be a sub-genre of therapeutic art and science; our ministry is a particular way of speaking the truth in love so that others can be built up and grow (Ephesians 4:7-16). We are believers whose gifts and expertise give others confidence to call us alongside for encouragement and direction in their times of need. We have a specific ministry of reconciliation within God's provision for reconciling the world to Himself (II Corinthians 5:18-19). We are called to minister without secrecy, deception or distortion of the truth (II Corinthians 4:1-2). We must model the open communication we hope to teach our clients.

In fact, our ministry is an extension of the ministry of Christ Himself. In John 14:16, Jesus, speaking of the Holy Spirit, said that another Comforter would come to continue the work which He had begun. The Greek word translated "comforter" here is translated "advocate" in I John 2:1. This word, transliterated, "paraclete," indicates one called to one's side to plead one's case. A.T. Robertson, preeminent Greek scholar of his generation, wrote, "Jesus [is] our Paraclete, Helper, Advocate with the Father (I John 2:1); the Holy Spirit [is] the Father's Paraclete with us (John 14:16, 26; 15:26; 16:7)."[149] Related words are translated "comfort" and "consolation" in II Corinthians 1:4-7, where the help one receives from God is to be passed along to help others. The same roots are behind the call to exhort one another (Hebrews 10:25) and the charge to Timothy to exhort patiently with accurate teaching (II Timothy 4:2). Being called alongside couples in need of encouragement and direction, we help them with the help that God has given us and challenge them with carefully applied biblical truth.

The foundational truth for all valid ministry is the offer of free access to God through faith in Jesus Christ. Believers can come boldly into God's throne room in prayer. We should be equally open in our communication with one another. One Bible commentator has said of the word "boldly" in Hebrews 4:16, "It means literally 'saying all,' with that confidence which begets thorough honesty, frankness, full and open speech."[150] Thomas Merton says of this Greek word, "Perhaps the most convenient translation is 'free speech:' the word represents in fact the rights and privileges of a citizen. This 'free speech' is at once the duty and honor of speaking one's mind fully and frankly."[151] If we can speak this freely to God, we must speak as openly with each other. Especially within the context of counseling, we must teach, model and expect communication in which there is no guile.

When people are reaching for answers, we need to follow the principle J. Vernon McGee called "putting the cookies

[149] A.T. Robertson, *Word Pictures in the New Testament,* Broadman Press, 1932, Volume V, p. 252.

[150] Adolph Saphir, *The Epistle to the Hebrews,* Christian Alliance, n.d., Volume 1, p. 248.

[151] Thomas Merton, *The New Man,* Farrar, Strauss and Giroux, 1961, p. 72.

on the bottom shelf." Rather than emanating an aura of abstruse professional pomposity, we need to make answers easy to grasp. Starting from a couple's own agenda, careful listening and gentle prodding bring results more effectively than ex cathedra pronouncements about what they should feel or do. Pretending to be neutral while gathering ammunition for a rebuke is as dishonest as trying to control sessions through intimidation or manipulation.

Manipulation can produce short-term change but often returns unpleasantly against the manipulator, as it did in one couple who came for counseling. The man had repeatedly told his wife that if she did not change this or that behavior he would divorce her. During seventeen years of marriage, he had threatened her with divorce sixteen times. The first time had been only six months after their wedding, and she had cried for three days. After the sixteenth time, she went to an attorney and had the divorce papers written up. She put the document into a desk drawer and waited. During a disagreement a few months later, he mentioned divorce again. She told him to go over to the desk and open the drawer. When he saw the papers, she said, "Just sign it, and we're history!" This man manipulated himself into a divorce. Happily, this couple saw the error of their ways and responded well to premarital counseling before remarrying each other. Their divorce showed the disastrous effects of manipulation and pride.

In many less dramatic cases, manipulation begets distrust, anger at being used and retaliatory manipulation. Since power struggles and various forms of deception are at the heart of most marriage problems, it is counterproductive to allow them to intrude into counseling sessions. Clients trust that a counselor has a measure of strength and wisdom, which can help them understand and remedy some of their problems. If strength is used to bully and wisdom stoops to craftiness, the counselor is only repeating and reinforcing techniques dysfunctional couples use to manipulate each other. "Speaking the truth in love" means using strength wisely and letting wisdom show its own power. Forceful confrontation may be necessary from time to time and sessions must be goal-directed, but counseling sessions should model productive communication patterns that the couple can implement at home. People who feel they have been pushed or tricked into changing their behavior soon revert to their old ways.

The more excellent way to encourage and facilitate change is through love, a total and unconditional focus on the good of the other person. This love stirs up good works, which are acts which benefit others no matter what their behavior and attitudes are in return. To sustain such love in the face of insults, curses, indifference, rejection and even hatred requires supernatural power. Without God, it is impossible. According to Acts 20:35, Jesus said, "It is more blessed to give than to receive." God so loved that He gave. We must learn to give if we are to live in conformity to Christ. Self-giving living is essential in building and maintaining sound marriages or in restoring broken ones.

I once told a man that he should do all he could do to save his marriage, because he had obviously been self-centered and inconsiderate throughout the short time he and his wife had been together. His selfishness had overshadowed any shred of love that had held them together. There was no question that the blame for their separation rested squarely on his shoulders, and I confronted him rather strongly. His immediate reaction was not very encouraging, but his long-range response was truly remarkable.

Seven years later, he came in and asked if I remembered him, and told me what I had advised him to do. I routinely give clients similar advice, but for this man it had inspired life-changing hope. He had, in fact, done all he could to save his marriage, and the results showed God's blessing on his planning and hard work. He said he had won his wife back after their separation and subsequent divorce. Now they were planning to remarry, and he wondered if I would provide premarital counseling. I was happy to be part of their reconciliation, and curious about how it had come about.

When the couple came in for counseling, I asked the wife what her husband had done that made the difference. She said it was not a single action but the cumulative effect of seven years of thoughtfulness and persistent pursuit. He had done just about everything imaginable to show his love for her. Cards, short letters, mowing her lawn, sending her flowers at home and at work, even leaving notes on her car for her to find when she returned from dates. Everything imaginable and at least one thing I would never have imagined: he once sent her a dozen frogs with the note, "You will have to kiss a lot of frogs to meet a prince like me!" I have never recommended a box of frogs as a sign of enduring affection, but it worked for them. She recognized it as a gesture of his willingness to go to any length to show how much he valued her love.

The most successful couples learn this active attitude of giving and continue to give throughout their lifetime together. People who cling to illusions about their own supreme importance are most likely to become disillusioned with their marriage partners. The two most common comments from people attempting to leave their marriages are the question, "Doesn't God want me to be happy?" and the statement, "I don't deserve this!" Notice the self-centeredness. In truth, God is not nearly as concerned with our personal definitions of happiness as He is with our obedience to Him. If we received precisely what we deserve, we would all be in Hell right now. By the mercy of God we do not get what we deserve; by the grace of God we get the total acceptance we do not deserve. Showing mercy and grace is the path of reconciliation which saves sinners. It is just as certainly the path of reconciliation which can save marriages.

The more excellent way of unselfish, unconditional love (I Corinthians 13) is not a mystical head-in-the-clouds dream. Many marriage problems are predictable, as potential distractions and disruptions are quite common (I Corinthians 10:13). Clear knowledge of these dangers can prepare couples to deal with them together. Those who have fallen can take courage in knowing that their missteps can be corrected. Preventive and corrective counseling can develop the clear-headed warm-hearted love which empowers couples to live in the joy of God's blessing.

Restorative Discipline

The heart of any ministry of reconciliation is speaking the truth in love. From a strong foundation in shared humanity and an even stronger foundation in shared faith, a Christian counselor seeks to display Christ-like compassion while bringing a couple to an acceptance of the truth about their situation. Divorce always involves sin and the sins of unfaithfulness, abuse and persistent selfishness pollute many marriages, which do not end in divorce. Sin must be dealt with as sin, whatever the sinner believes. Self-judgment, sober assessment of one's offenses against God and other persons, is a necessary step in repairing broken relationships. A sinner who does not respond favorably to correction is subject to the chastening which God gives His children or the condemnation which God reserves for those who reject His grace (I Corinthians 11:31-32). If sin is not dealt with here, it will be dealt with hereafter.

When believers compound their marriage problems by seeking divorce they also increase the complexity of any attempts at a ministry of reconciliation. Different churches equip their members differently. Christian counselors need to know what spiritual resources clients have for resolving their conflicts. What foundation do they have for victory over the sins which have disrupted their marriage? Do they have a clear biblical understanding of what sin is? What do they know about the conflict between their desire to please the Lord and their desire to please themselves? How do they respond to the Bible's warnings and commands? What is their understanding and experience of the Holy Spirit?

If Christians with marriage problems are being disciplined or gently discipled by a local church, their counselor should be aware of the steps which have been taken and coordinate counseling efforts with the church's efforts to reconcile the couple. If churches fulfilled their discipling ministry, there would be less occasion for crisis discipline. Counselors would be delighted to minister to couples whose churches had already brought them to the point where our specific expertise and guidance were all they needed. In reality, we often minister to couples whose churches have taken no active part in the work of correcting and restoring them. We find it necessary to supplement their spiritual resources before we can introduce the specialized resources of our profession. If churches do not follow biblical principles for dealing with sin, how can their members be expected to do any better?

In too many churches, sexual sin and divorce are the only offenses which are disciplined, and the discipline is irreversibly punitive. A man in his twenties had been taught that his divorce meant the loss of his salvation and that he could never be saved again. An older man was a spiritual father and grandfather to many members of a church where he could never hold an office because his wife had abandoned him decades earlier. Some Christians have considered a secret abortion less burdensome than the open shame of raising an illegitimate child in an unforgiving church. We need to be more analytical about discipline and more compassionate toward people.

"Church discipline" is an obsolescent term for two reasons: we refuse to talk about it because we have inadequate ideas of what it means, and we refuse to do it because our narrow definitions distort its purpose. Our definitions of church discipline tend to think of a church as a corporate entity whose purity and reputation must be maintained. Discipline, then, is a matter of restricting or excluding those who jeopardize the church's purity and reputation. This is part of the truth, but viewing church discipline this narrowly reduces it to its negative aspects. Putting offending believers out of sight and out of mind invites controversy, bitterness and, in our culture, the threat of litigation.

Church discipline should not be viewed so narrowly. The goal of church discipline is not only to maintain the purity of the church but also to further the spiritual growth of its members. The Church is the body of Christ, called-out individuals assembled to honor God and to nurture one another. Discipline is, in fact, discipling, using all the assembled gifts of the local church to bring each member into conformity to Christ (Ephesians 4:1-16). In this broader sense it involves a church's total ministry to its members. Where offenses must be dealt with, restrictions or exclusions will be considered temporary remedial steps in a positive ministry of reconciliation. Discipling our brothers and sisters is a matter of reminding them of their position in Christ and challenging them to live up to it.

If a husband and wife are both professing Christians, they should seek reconciliation with each other according to the pattern given in Matthew 18:15-17. A believer who has offended a brother or sister in Christ should be eager to correct any offense as soon as it is pointed out. If a spouse persists in an offense (including but not limited to unfaithfulness or adultery), the offended partner may ask a few other believers to join in confronting the offender. Rejection of such an intervention would make the offense a matter for church discipline, official consideration of the issue and assignment of appropriate consequences by the local church governing body. Rejecting mediation by church officers amounts to self-exclusion from the church's ministry. The church can rightly treat such a person as an outsider, at least in regard to this issue. Whether or not there is some form of official exclusion, the bars against legal conflict between believers are removed. When a person being treated as a believer responds as a heathen would respond, he or she is asking to be treated as a heathen. This may seem a theological technicality, but it is highly significant when a believing spouse is forced into the public court system by an unrepentant adulterer.[152]

When it is necessary for church discipline to exclude a person, he or she may be conscious of being placed outside in the worldly realm of Satan, "for the destruction of the flesh (I Corinthians 5:5)." A professing believer who persists in sin, rejecting the warnings of Scripture and the exhortation of Christian brothers and sisters, is brazenly grieving the Holy Spirit. As long as the sinner is unrepentant, unresponsive to positive spiritual resources,[153] his or her position is no longer in the place of God's blessing. Unrepentant persistence in sin places the professing believer outside the place of communion with Christ and His body. Outside, the consequences of sin and the forces of evil are free to take their toll. "The way of the transgressor is hard (Proverbs 13:15)." One Christian woman told her unbelieving husband, "God will take your money, He'll take your health, and He might even take your life to get you to come

---

[152] I am indebted here to Jay Adams, whose exposition of this issue is very enlightening. See: Jay Adams, *Marriage, Divorce, and Remarriage in the Bible*, Presbyterian and Reformed, 1980, p. 57ff.

[153] Rejecting the means of grace, biblical means of change available among assembled believers.

to Jesus!" That man did lose his business, and found his Lord shortly before he died of cancer. If God will allow such trials to bring an unsaved man to repentance, He will allow them to bring His own children back when they stray.

Sadly, broken fellowship sometimes leads to broken lives. No chastening brings immediate joy (Hebrews 12:8). But there is a distinction between grieving over the pain of the chastening and grieving over the sin which brought it on. In the midst of the judgments described in the book of Revelation, some people renewed their blasphemy against God and continued in their sins (Revelation 16:9). People often sorrow over the consequences of sin without sorrowing over the sin itself. Such worldly sorrow leads only to further deterioration and destruction.

A chaplain was involved with a woman who worked in his office. I knew of the affair and felt responsible to say something about it when I saw him at McDonald's one morning. God let me know that I should witness to the chaplain and warn him of the judgment to come. I really wanted to finish my breakfast and get on with my day, but the Lord would not let me off the hook. I went over to the adulterer and said, "I know you're involved with your secretary. God says you need to repent, and He told me to warn you of the judgment to come." The man cursed at me. That same day, the unfaithful chaplain got into his car and started a trip across the state. He never made it. He ran into an ice storm, his car slid off the road, and he slipped into eternity. He had rejected what may have been God's last call to repentance. If we will not hear the Word of God or the warnings of fellow believers, we can expect to be called to account through difficult, even catastrophic experiences.

When church discipline is effective, godly sorrow brings the sinner to repentance and reconciliation. Recognizing that the consequences of sin include bringing dishonor to the Church as well as to the offender, a process of discipling back into fellowship is necessary. For the individual, the purpose of confession is not only to enjoy God's forgiveness but also to cleanse the sinner. I John 1:9 does not give us license to do as we will and cover it with an "Oops! Sorry!" The issue is fellowship with the God whose light exposes and condemns sin, and fellowship with those who walk in that light (I John 1:5-7). In the Church the goals of discipling/discipline are to clear the local assembly of complicity in sin and to restore the erring one to fellowship.

Reconciliation and restoration of believers whose sin has dishonored the name of Christ is the underside of the gospel. As truck drivers warn each other, "Keep the shiny side up and the greasy side down!" The shiny side of the gospel is the loving communion of believers with the triune God and with one another (John 17:21). The whole book of I John is a commentary on the Lord's commandment to love one another so that the world will recognize that we are His disciples (John 13:34-35). Francis Schaeffer called this "the mark of the Christian,"[154] verification of the Church's witness to the world. When this love, which manifests the love within the Trinity is violated by sin, necessary discipline must be concerned with restoring the love as well as the purity of the Church. This is the underside, the greasy side of the gospel. As truck drivers know, the greasy side is where the work gets done. The shiny side goes nowhere if the greasy side is neglected.

There are not enough good mechanics in the Church. A good mechanic does not just throw away parts that malfunction. He cleans them off, corrects defects and gets them to work the way they are supposed to. There are parallels to this in the

---

[154] "We cannot expect the world to believe that the Father sent the Son, that Jesus' claims are true, and that Christianity is true, unless the world sees some reality of the oneness of true Christians (Francis Schaeffer, *The Mark of the Christian*, Intervarsity Press, 1970, p. 15)."

process of dealing with sin within the Church.[155] Emotions may be intense, but the object is to get the offenders cleaned up, fixed up and working the way they are supposed to work. The godly sorrow which motivates repentance and cleansing includes humble self-examination, repudiation of sin and determination to set things right (II Corinthians 7:10-11). And this is to be the attitude of the church applying the discipline as well as of the repentant sinner. Good mechanics in the Church help dysfunctional members clean up their acts and get back into fellowship and ministry.

In fact, this happened in the Corinthian church, perhaps the most dysfunctional church in the most sinful culture of the New Testament era. After the church had punished a man and he had repented, Paul told them to forgive him, comfort him and confirm their love towards him so that he would not be weighted down with the sorrow of broken fellowship as well as with the sincere sorrow he felt for his sin (II Corinthians 2:6-7). When the church has carried out its ministry of discipline, it can resume the more positive aspects of its ministry of reconciliation. Of course, the offender's response to discipline determines its ultimate result. Those who reject the church's admonition are to be rejected and those who persist in divisions and offenses are to be avoided (Titus 3:10-11; Romans 16:17-18). Those who repent and do their part to restore the church's purity should be restored to the church's love.

A common objection to church discipline has been, "We don't want to hang out our dirty laundry!" Of course not. But think through the real meaning of the saying. Nobody ever hangs out dirty laundry; that would tell the world you lacked the resources or the motivation to clean it. Everybody knows

---

[155] Many people confronted with church discipline resign their membership. The church isn't a club you join for personal comfort and then quit when you are unhappy or discontented. Many pastors are happy when troubled people quit, and quickly take them off the rolls. They are as cowardly as the people who leave under pressure.

we all have dirty laundry. The proper procedure is to wash our laundry so everybody can see how clean our diligent use of our resources can make it. There are no secrets from God: "Be sure your sins will find you out (Numbers 32:23)." Secrets cannot be kept from anyone for long. In the film *Big Jake*, John Wayne's character says, "Don't like secrets, never known one to be kept." Especially dirty secrets. People will know about our sins, and they will know whether our churches deal with them effectively. A church which cannot provide cleansing and restoration for sinners tells the world that it lacks the resources or the motivation to do its laundry.

Resources for Reconciliation

God's plan for marriage is supported by an abundance of resources He makes available to His people. A marriage covenant entered by vow in the presence of God and human witnesses invokes God's blessing through the effective working of the support system which is in place at the time of the wedding. The spiritual and personal resources represented at the wedding can be drawn upon throughout the marriage. For couples who begin well, this support system can carry a marriage through many hazards, and can provide the strength to recover from mishaps and mistakes. For couples who do not have rich spiritual and personal resources, healing and growth can come through building a new foundation for their marriage.

Spiritual Assessment

The spiritual strength of being connected with God and His people is implemented through personal and corporate ministry. Entering marriage with a clear consciousness of God's standards, seeking God's blessing through careful planning, and enduring trials and temptations in a spirit of love, power and a sound mind, a couple's life together can demonstrate God's love to the world. If they drift away from the Lord and from each other, they can be reminded of their first love and encouraged to return to the ways of thinking and behaving which gave them such a joyous beginning.

Christian marriage counselors need to know the spiritual resources of people who come for counseling. If they do not profess to know the God of the Bible in Jesus Christ, they may resist the biblical truth which is the foundation of our ministry. If they say they are believers, their Christianity may be more cultural than personal. Their church affiliation may be a matter of tradition or a real source of meaning and energy for their lives. Their personal religious practices may be perfunctory nostalgia or vital devotion to God.

Effective Christian counseling must begin with an accurate assessment of the spiritual resources available to clients outside the counseling office. It is easy for experienced counselors to fall into the priestly fallacy of thinking they are mediators between clients and God, and have the inside track on spiritual wisdom which clients will find nowhere else. Listening carefully to what clients have to say about their own spirituality removes presumption by revealing varieties of religious experience which must be taken into account in assessing resources for reconciliation.

Salvation

As Christian counselors, we must recognize that our presuppositions affect our methods and that our clients have presuppositions which affect their responses to our counsel. Our assumptions about marriage, morality and ourselves will color our perception of problems and direct our search for solutions. For those who have met the God of the Bible in Jesus Christ, faith adds a dimension which must be considered carefully. In fact, for believers this faith dimension takes priority over all other considerations.

Many Christian counselors have emphasized the power of the Scriptures as applied by the Holy Spirit and minimized the value of assessing and facilitating client responsiveness to the Scriptures. This approach risks being perceived as "preachy," especially when principles are presented with inadequate "nuts and bolts" guidelines for applying them to specific situations. Others practice varieties of generally accepted methods and only occasionally resort to Scripture or prayer. This has the effect of baptizing secular theories as if there were no authoritative word from God about marriage. Our faith permeates everything we think, say and do but we must not proof text our way out of dealing with complex issues. The challenges of life are common to all people, and many secondary counseling tools are effective regardless of our clients' beliefs. Marriages can be preserved and abuses can be minimized on the level of our common humanity; there can be substantial healing of human relationships without a new birth into relationship with God.

Clients who are truly related to God in Jesus Christ can let their faith anchor and define the entire counseling process. If this faith dimension is available, we should tap into it from the start. If it is lacking, we can give clients the reason for our eternal hope as we try to give them reason for temporal hope. In either situation, counseling will focus on defining and resolving practical problems within the marriage. Abuse, unfaithfulness and distrust are the same offenses and leave the same scars in any marriage. No matter what people believe, correcting offenses takes planning and hard work. But it is important to know whether our clients know God, whether they accept His authority over their lives, and whether they are seeking His blessing on their marriage.

How can a counselor assess this faith dimension when working with a couple? Five factors are essential:

Assessment of salvation. Do these people have a real living relationship with God?

Assessment of church background. Do they have an active church affiliation?

Assessment of discipleship. How has their church dealt with their problems?

Assessment of Bible knowledge. How well do they understand what God has said?

Assessment of spiritual growth. Where are they in their personal walk with God?

Evaluating these factors requires sensitivity to the varieties of understanding and experience of the faith within the body of Christ.

If clients profess to be Christians, we can ask them to give their testimonies, to give the reasons for the hope they have in Christ (I Peter 3:15). We need to know whether they really know the Lord or just know about the Lord. There is a vast gulf between generically believing in Jesus and genuinely belonging to Jesus. Accurate assessment of the reality of the faith that clients profess will make a major difference in the way we proceed. Can we draw on Scripture, the Holy Spirit and their fellowship with other believers? Can we expect them to grow spiritually through the course of counseling sessions? We need to know the real object of their faith. Do they trust in their baptism, their participation in the mass or in other religious rituals and practices? We need to know whether they trust Jesus alone for their salvation.

If there are doubts about their salvation, we can ask them the question at the heart of D.J. Kennedy's Evangelism Explosion program: "If you were to die today and stand before God, and He asked you why He should let you into His heaven, what would you say to Him?" If they have hope in anything except the blood of Jesus Christ, their souls are in desperate trouble. Those who think they can enter God's heaven on any other grounds either do not understand the Gospel or have rejected it.

Accepting a generic Judeo-Christian ethic is not equivalent to knowing the God of the Hebrew and Christian Scriptures. In the Hebrew Scriptures, God reveals laws which, if followed, would bring a degree of righteousness to human relationships. A sacrificial system provided for human failure to achieve the degree of righteousness necessary for a relationship with God. The Christian Scriptures reveal that the standard of righteousness required for relationship with God is the very character of God Himself and that all humanity falls infinitely short of this standard (Romans 3:23). The necessary result is ultimate separation from God — a death sentence hangs over each of us (Romans 6:23; John 3:36). Jesus Christ, God in human flesh, took upon Himself our death penalty as prescribed and illustrated in the Hebrew sacrificial system, thus fulfilling all requirements of God's righteousness and establishing a standing in God's presence and a place in God's heaven for all who believe (Romans 3:24-25; 6:23; John 3:36).

We must listen carefully to the terms people use to describe their relationship with God. For some it is an amorphous spiritual experience which is difficult to put into words. Others use phrases taught by various sects or cults. Many name the churches they attend, or declare themselves Catholics, Baptists, Anglicans or Nazarenes, as if they have entrusted their spiritual welfare to second-hand faith, faith in the understanding and experience of others. Whether people use familiar evangelical expressions or not, we need to know if they have met the God of the Bible in Jesus Christ.

The question, "Have you met the God of the Bible in Jesus Christ?" is intended to get beyond the religious jargon to the core issues of the Gospel. "Have you met ...?" Does the person call upon the Lord as someone who can be known and who will answer? Has he or she encountered Him as a person with whom conversation is possible and frequent? "The God of the Bible," not a creature of the imagination but the Creator of all, the one true God who reveals His character and activity in the Hebrew and Christian Scriptures. "Of the Bible" is crucial because true knowledge of God and true relationship with Him come only through believing what He has said about himself. "In Jesus Christ:" the written Word of God directs us to Jesus Christ, the living Word of God, the Word who became flesh and dwelt among us (John 1:14). "Jesus," who could begin with the writings of Moses and all the prophets and expound in all the Scriptures things concerning himself (Luke 24:27). "Jesus," of whom all the biblical prophets testify (Revelation 19:10). "Jesus," whose name identifies Him as the One who came to save His people from their sins (Matthew 1:21). "Christ," the Anointed One, God's appointed ruler of Creation (Psalm 2; Philippians 2:9-11; Revelation 19:6, 16), who yet died for our sins, was buried and rose again the third day just as Scripture had foretold (I Corinthians 15:3-4). "God in Jesus Christ." The God who reveals Himself in the Bible now meets us in His Son, Jesus Christ, who is the Creator and rightful owner of all things, who is the outshining of God's glory and the visible expression of God's character, who holds all Creation in existence by His Word, who purged our sins and who now exercises His ruling authority as the second Person in the triune Godhead (Hebrews 1:1-3).

Those who have personally encountered and are in conversation with this God in this Jesus Christ are biblical Christians, whatever their differences in understanding and experience. Some who quote chapter and verse from the right translation and know all the stanzas to all the right hymns may yet be judged by a Lord who never knew them as His own (Matthew 7:21-23). Raising a hand, walking an aisle and praying a prayer may be a means of coming to true faith, but many who think they are dealing with God only make a deal with a preacher. A young man, when asked if he wanted to invite Jesus into his heart, simply said, "Come in." In later years he laughed at his naïve response, but it had been a real meeting with God.

I learned an unforgettable lesson when a pastor came in for help. He was from a denomination I did not respect, and I wondered whether he was even saved. When he came into my office, he confessed that he was a bad Christian and a bad father. He said, "I don't pray enough, I don't read my Bible enough. Sometimes I pray all night and can't reach heaven. Sometimes I read my Bible and don't hear God speak to me. Sometimes I'll read for days on end, trying to hear God's voice, and it doesn't seem like He's there."

As the pastor went on, I became more and more convicted about my own lack of commitment to Bible reading, prayer and other spiritual exercises. What the pastor sometimes missed was a level of communion with God which I rarely, if ever, attained. I did not even want to know what this self-judged "bad father" sometimes missed in relating to his children. This pastor was not only a true brother in Christ, but a brother whose testimony made me wonder whether I should pay him for the counseling session.

Christians who agree on the faith once-for-all delivered unto the saints differ in how they understand and experience that faith. Even if our counseling ministries are not cross-cultural in a global sense, we must learn to minister to brothers and sisters in Christ who differ from us in non-essentials. When we begin to assess the spiritual resources of Christian clients, we will find differences not only in using what have been called the "means of grace", but in describing what the "means of grace" are.

Church Background

"Whosoever shall call upon the Lord shall be saved (Romans 10:13)." Calling upon the Lord for salvation means inviting Him into our lives, acknowledging not only that His death provides our justification in the sight of God but also that His resurrection power works out our sanctification. There is a consensus among Christians that we are set apart for God's glory and that we are to be conformed to the character of His Son (Romans 8:29). Most Christians agree that this involves a process and that mutual ministry among believers is the means by which we grow into better representatives of Jesus Christ (Ephesians 4:13). The details of the process of sanctification are perceived differently by various movements, denominations and local congregations. Perhaps the major dividing line is our interpretation of such passages as Philippians 2:12-13: "Work out your own salvation with fear and trembling. For it is God which worketh in you both to will and to do of his good pleasure." What is God's work in sanctification? What is the believer's work? What is the work of the pastor, counselor or concerned Christian friend as we endure birth-pangs striving to see Christ manifested in the lives of our struggling brothers and sisters?

We need to know the spiritual resources of the people who come to us for help. Our training is incomplete and our ministry will be hindered if we do not understand the differences in belief and practice among professing Christians. We need to know the distinctions between Catholics, Episcopalians, Lutherans and Nazarenes and the multiplied varieties of Baptists, Methodists and the Presbyterian and Reformed heritages. We should know the history of Pentecostalism and the significance of charismatic phenomena. How vast must our knowledge be? That depends on how wide an impact we want our ministries to have. To minister effectively to the whole Church, we must be knowledgeable about the many churches from which our clients come. If we do not know where they are coming from, our approach to Scripture and to spiritual matters may seem foreign to them. We need to know the differences in understanding, experience and terminology so that we can emphasize agreements about the realities of life in Christ.

We need to do the necessary research to know what we believe and to know what our clients believe. God operates in our lives on the basis of the knowledge we have. He does not zap knowledge down upon us; we have to discipline ourselves to attain it. We can study theology, church history, creeds and denominational profiles. We can keep up with surveys of religious beliefs. We can read as widely and as deeply as possible in our determination to be fully equipped to understand our brothers and sisters in Christ.[156]

We especially need to understand how our clients perceive the counseling situation. Their presuppositions about a believer's relationship to the world will affect their attitudes toward culturally accepted views of marriage, morality and professional counselors. Their presuppositions about a believer's relationship with God will affect their response to the use of Scripture, practical theology and prayer. If the husband and wife are not from the same church background, we need to know how that might contribute to misunderstandings between them. We need to understand the spiritual context in which our clients have lived. If we know how they have learned to relate to the dominant culture, as well as how they have learned to relate to God, we will be better able to translate our insights into words and actions which will be most meaningful to them. Doctrinal positions and church practices are not the only differences among professing Christians. The tension between cultural pressures and spiritual expectations is involved in many marriage problems. We need to know what equipment our clients have been given for handling that tension.

As H. Richard Niebuhr discovered, the differences among professing Christians are not just about doctrine but have been influenced by history, sociology and ethics. In his classic book, *Christ and Culture,*[157] Niebuhr explores how

---

[156] This is not to suggest pursuing the idiosyncrasies of every passing cult: recognizing variant expressions of genuine biblical faith does not require filling our minds with detailed knowledge of counterfeits.

[157] H. Richard Niebuhr, *Christ and Culture,* Harper and Row, 1951.

being related to God affects relationships with the world. The possibilities include:

Christ against culture — a basic separation.

The Christ of culture — an almost syncretistic accommodation.

Christ above culture — a selective synthesis.

Christ and culture in paradox — a delicately balanced duality.

Christ the transformer of culture — a permeation and conversion.

This continuum ranges from hermits and plain folk who try to live outside the dominant culture to restorationists who try to dominate the culture. Most Christians are somewhere in between, recognizing both the need for contextualization of their faith and the risk of enculturation of their faith. As we do our research into the diverse expressions of genuine faith, we can look for indications of how Christian subgroups perceive their relation to the culture around them. As we listen to our clients, we can take note of how their cultural context affects their values and expectations.

Niebuhr pursues this issue further in two thought-provoking books about the interdependency of American Christianity and American culture. In *The Social Sources of Denominationalism*,[158] he considers how history, sociology and ethics, as well as theology, have created denominational differences. In *The Kingdom of God in America*,[159] he suggests that a common consciousness of working towards the Kingdom of God unifies American Christianity and energizes its impact on culture. Historian Roland Bainton is quoted on the jacket of the second of these books: "In *The Social Sources of American Denominationalism* [Niebuhr] points out that cleavages in the social structure impressed themselves upon the structures of church life. In *The Kingdom of God in America* he sets forth the fact that religion has fashioned the social structure."

---

[158] Niebuhr, *The Social Sources of Denominationalism*, World, 1957.

[159] Niebuhr, *The Kingdom of God in America*, Harper, 1959.

This interaction between the Church and the world is one of the major issues in church history and remains an issue in the life of every believer. The missionary going native or the church adapting to cultural norms is dealing with what are considered nonessentials of the faith-life: customs, taboos and forms of expression which do not have clear biblical sanction. Contextualization, speaking the truth into a culture, shades into enculturation, the faith embedded within a culture. We need to know how our clients orient themselves to the Bible and to culture as authorities for dealing with their problems.

Even more fundamental than the believer's relationship with the world is the believer's relationship with God, which is also perceived differently by different groups and individuals. In *Christian Spirituality: Five Views of Sanctification*,[160] editor Donald L. Alexander has compiled representative perspectives of Reformed, Lutheran, Wesleyan, Pentecostal and contemplative writers. Areas of difference among them include: 1) the foundation of sanctification; 2) the meaning of sin; 3) the nature and relationship of the "old self" and the "new self;" 4) the function of the Law; and 5) the role of the Holy Spirit.[161] Differences in these areas clearly will affect a person's response to our counsel.

We really do need to do our homework. If someone protests, "But couples who come for marriage counseling are not thinking about theology; they just want help with their problems." Precisely. They are not thinking about theology. That is precisely why we must think about theology. When people think about theology, they can more or less abstractly compare and contrast ideas in a more or less purely intellectual exercise, confirming or challenging beliefs by which they live. When people are not thinking about theology, they are more or less

---

[160] Donald L. Alexander ed., *Christian Spirituality: Five Views of Sanctification*, Intervarsity, 1988

[161] Alexander, p. 10.

unconsciously living by their beliefs. The theology we do not think about—our presuppositional base line, our engrained training, constitutes the belief system by which we live and provides assumptions about how we relate to God, the world and the people in our lives. As counselors, we must know what beliefs our clients have absorbed, what theology they live by without even thinking about it.

Before describing how church background may more directly affect the counseling process, we must note that few individuals have fully internalized the teachings of any denomination. We all have our idiosyncratic beliefs, some more off-center than others. A man who accepted a rationalistic approach to practical theology reduced love to what he called "a relaxed mental attitude." He claimed to have such a relaxed mental attitude towards his wife. That was not her definition of love. He relaxed himself right out of their marriage. At another extreme was the divorced man whose preoccupation with demons poisoned his relationships with people. He told a friend that it was a sin to stay home from church to care for a sick child, and that unexpected car problems were the work of demons.[162]

Those whose faith is a matter for the head alone have not felt the love of God warming their hearts (Romans 5:5). Those who live in fear of evil spirits have not enjoyed the Spirit of God who brings power, love and a sound mind (II Timothy 1:7). Both extremes, seeking human wisdom or looking for supernatural signs, keep a person from the full benefit of the wisdom and power of God (I Corinthians 1:21-25). Some Christians seem so heavenly minded that they are no earthly good, while others seem so earthly minded that they are no heavenly good. Let it be said, reverently, that cultivating the inner life does not

---

[162] There is such a thing as mental illness and we should recognize it as well. In my experience, bad theology produces bad living and can look a lot like the mentally ill patient. The difference is bad theology can change. Mental illness only managed unless of course God supernaturally intervenes.

294

diminish responsibility to maintain the outer life, including the complexities of human relationships. On the other hand, those who are cumbered about with many outward cares may miss the blessing of sitting at the feet of Jesus (Luke 10:38-42). Neither spiritual laziness nor religious compulsiveness represents the balance of being in the world but not of the world (John 17:11-18).

While being alert to personal differences, we can gain a wealth of information from knowing a person's denominational or local church affiliation. It is not only useful but also necessary to be aware of the distinctive doctrines and practices of the believers with whom our clients identify themselves. The problems brought to marriage counselors include some extremely hot topics among Christians. Approaches to these issues are widely varied.

Some Christian groups have been zealous in condemning a familiar list of sins they seem to consider unpardonable. A church board once asked a pastoral candidate how he would deal with a teenage girl's illegitimate pregnancy. As the prospective pastor was explaining his convictions and how they would affect his counsel, an agitated board member interrupted, "But wouldn't you question her salvation?" Some believers seem just as eager to cast the first anathema at anyone who admits to having serious marital problems.

When Christians come for counseling, we need to know how they have been treated by their church. How have they been discipled? What have they been taught? What has been expected of them? What resources has their church given them for dealing with their problems? How have their church leaders pursued a ministry of reconciling them to God and to each other? As Christian counselors, our mission is to restore brothers and sisters who have been tripped up by their faults (Galatians 6:1). We should consider a client's credible confession of faith an opening for God's presence and power to bless our efforts.

Discipleship and Discipline

Counselors can be partners in healthy discipline and reconciliation, but too often we are left to clean up undisciplined lives and patch up those who have felt the wounds of discipline without the healing hope of reconciliation. Misapplied discipline has given credibility to the cynical statement, "Christians are the only people who shoot their wounded." We have to stop doing that. The primary ministry of Christian marriage counseling is to help couples build or rebuild their marriages. As much as lies in us, we accept their various church backgrounds and the variety of ways their churches have responded to their problems. But as we assess our clients' experiences of church discipline or discipling, we become aware of issues that pastors and other church leaders must address more boldly[163] and systematically.

If the goal of church discipline is restoration to purity and love, what resources are available to accomplish this? We have the Word of God, the Spirit of God and the people of God. When believers follow biblical principles of discipline, the Holy Spirit brings cleansing and healing. Differences among Christian groups include differences in how principles of discipline are perceived and applied. Emphasis on the purity of the Church motivates zealous enforcement of biblical judgments against sin. Emphasis on the work of the indwelling Holy Spirit motivates unceasing intercession on behalf of erring brothers and sisters. Emphasis on bonds of fellowship and love within the body of Christ motivates compassionate exhortation, loving the sinner while hating the sin.

Overemphasis on any of these motivations creates an imbalance in church discipline. Pronouncing judgment coldly and confrontationally is a form of legalism. Praying for the Spirit to work while refusing to be His instrument can be as hypocritical as the Pharisee's self-righteous gratitude that he was not like the publican who cried out for God's mercy. Sympathizing with an unrepentant sinner may deteriorate into

---

[163] In ancient history there is a story of a General who's troops were deserted during battle. He lay down on a narrow pass and said, "You must trample your General if you retreat." This is the kind of boldness I'm speaking of.

condoning his or her rationalization of the sin. Speaking the truth in love is so difficult in dealing with offenses that Jesus outlined a pattern for maintaining both righteousness and peace. True disciples of Jesus will follow His plan for discipline.

How can discipleship and discipline be maintained? First, we must find practical ways to implement Scriptural mandates individually as well as corporately. Ephesians 4:7-16 is not a hierarchical chart delineating the pecking order in the Church. It is a flow chart showing how God supplies nourishment to His people through their ministries to one another. The outcome is an assembly of believers who are individually and corporately equipped to do their servant work, which is to build up the body of Christ. As individuals we are equipped to consider, provoke and exhort one another (Hebrews 10:24-25). As a local church we are empowered to discern and declare heaven's judgment against sin and God's forgiveness of repentant sinners (Matthew 16:18-19; 18:15-20).

The binding and loosing of Matthew 16:18-19 is referred to in Matthew 18:18 in the context of teaching on church discipline. The first stage of discipline is to point out the offense and to offer the offender opportunity for repentance and restoration. Every believer is responsible to minister to other believers in this way, personally challenging them to live up to their position in Christ. If I perceive sin in a brother or sister and do not speak directly to the offender, I know I will speak to someone else about it. This makes me guilty of dishonesty and slander. Leviticus 19:7 rebukes such cowardice: "Thou shalt not hate thy brother in thine heart: thou shalt rebuke thy neighbor, and not suffer sin upon him." If my perception of the offense is wrong, the misunderstanding may be cleared up immediately. If my perception is right, brotherly counsel may help the offender correct the problem without unnecessary involvement of others. If the apparent offender rejects or reacts against my exhortation, I can ask a few impartial fellow believers, perhaps church officers, to join in a further effort at reconciliation. Again, the matter may be resolved quickly if the offender accepts correction, or rejection of this ministry may call for the next level of discipline, formal intervention by the church. Church leadership would evaluate the problem, determine the extent of any offense and hold the offender accountable to take specific steps of confession, repentance and restoration. If the offender rejects the authority of church leaders, he is nullifying their responsibility to watch for his soul. He has stepped outside the church's ministry of reconciliation, and the church must in some way acknowledge this departure. This is the pattern of Matthew 18:15-20.

While this pattern is widely recognized as a model of corporate discipline, it is not always applied to the responsibilities of personal discipleship. Ephesians 4:15-16 and Hebrews 10:24-25 indicate that the true strength of the gathered church is in the personal ministries of individual members to one another. Public ministry is to facilitate private ministry. Just as the mandate to evangelize the world includes both public proclamation and personal witness, the mandate to edify the Church includes both public and personal exhortation. Just as believers must be vigilant in their witness to the world (Colossians 4:5-6; I Peter 3:15), they are to stand by one another to hold each other accountable for growth in conformity to Christ. Accountability to God is not to be delegated to church leaders or to a few carefully chosen peers — it is a matter of concern to the whole Church.

When Paul says that a spiritual person is "judged of no man" (I Corinthians 2:15) he is not discarding all human accountability. Our limitations, faults and sin are no secret, and we can be expected to respond to correction. In the first three chapters of I Corinthians, Paul is contrasting worldly wisdom and power with godly wisdom and power. When he says that a spiritual person is "judged of no man," he means that the world's wisdom cannot comprehend or evaluate the life of faith. If a person considers himself beyond the reach of criticism from even the humblest believer, he is thinking according to worldly wisdom, not according to the wisdom from above which is pure, approachable and willing to yield (James 3:17). Every believer should expect every conversation with any other believer to be edifying, to build both of them up in conformity to Christ (Ephesians 4:29).

How does this relate to marriage counseling? If both husband and wife are professing believers, it is important to know whether they have attempted to follow the biblical process of reconciliation. Have they spoken the truth in love about any offenses between them? Have they tried to stir each other up to higher levels of love and good works? Have they sought the support and advice of fellow believers? Have they discussed their problems with church leaders? Have any measures of church discipline been imposed on either or both of them? If the question of divorce is on the table, have they resorted to secular judges before exhausting the Church's resources for discipleship and discipline?[164] Has their local church exercised its ministry of reconciliation by taking all appropriate steps towards bringing their marriage into conformity with God's plan?

According to Ephesians 4:11-16, a primary responsibility of church leaders is to equip the saints for mutual ministry which nourishes the Church and each of its members. Leaders are entrusted with the care of the souls of those among whom they minister, giving account to God for this ministry (Hebrews 13:17).Throughout church history the care of souls has included corporate concern for the spiritual condition of individuals. If individuals under their care are unresponsive, leaders will grieve. Their joy is in the trust which builds as the

---

[164] As Adams says, "At any time that a believer engages a lawyer to discuss divorce proceedings, he/she is out of line with the Bible and should be told so. The church should step in immediately and, in accordance with I Corinthians 6, should offer its services to help work out the difficulties that led to this action." (Jay Adams, *Marriage, Divorce and Remarriage in the Bible*, Presbyterian and Reformed, 1980, p. 57, note.

people in their care learn that leaders serve with the humble mindset of Christ. When such trust has been earned, people will submit to teaching and guidance, even when it includes occasions for negative application of discipline. Discipling, the ministry of training people to walk in the light of God's Word, can keep many couples from taking the first steps on the road to destruction. Discipline, restricting or excluding those who persist in sin and correcting and restoring the repentant, testifies to the holiness and power of God as well as to His wisdom and love.

Negative application of discipline will include the restriction or exclusion of offenders. During a period of restoration, restrictions may be imposed in proportion to the offense, and to the person's visibility in the ministry of the church. Matthew 18:15-20 sets the standard: the discipline should be no more and no less public than the offense. Fellowship should be restored as privately as possible without whitewashing the sin or covering up its consequences. The persistently unrepentant should be treated as heathen; their choice to stand outside the church's purity leaves them no place in its fellowship.[165] The issue in regard to the church's purity is the contradiction between the person's known sin and his or her known position in the church. Jesus told people not to bring their gifts to God until they were reconciled to people they had offended (Matthew 5:23-24). If the whole local assembly has been offended and the whole community in which it serves is aware of the offense, the offender's continued full acceptance and participation in the church could rightly be compared with hanging out dirty laundry.

---

[165] Social shunning is not appropriate even regarding heathens. The distinction is between those who accept the Gospel with all its implications and those who do not. The heathen are to be evangelized, to be called to unconditional acceptance of Jesus Christ as Savior and Lord. Those who cling to their sins and rebel against Christ's Lordship cannot be treated as saints—they must be evangelized before they can be edified.

The stench of sin and the hardness of the sinner's heart are doubly offensive to God when they are tolerated in the context of worship (Isaiah 1:1-20). Perhaps we have become so enculturated that we are losing our sense of God's holiness and His requirement and provision that we should be holy as He is holy (Leviticus 11:45; I Peter 1:16). In some places not so long ago, even non-Christians knew what sin was, or at least they knew the list of taboos among Christians in their community. In a culture which tolerates everything but solid convictions, it is politically correct for religious leaders to say, "Well, the Bible doesn't really say that, and if it does, it's wrong." Those who hold a high view of the Bible's authority still know that sin is an offense against the character of God (Exodus 20:1-12, first four of the Ten Commandments), and that sin destroys human relationships (Exodus 20:13-17, last six of the Ten Commandments). The Bible gives clear teaching about what offends God and destroys human relationships. God says He wants us to stop it. And He wants believers to stay in the redeemed and sanctified position of "such were some of you" — cleansed, set apart and declared righteous in the name of Jesus (I Corinthians 6:9-11).

If a church expects to maintain peace and holiness (Hebrews 12:14), it must clearly teach and practice biblical discipleship and discipline. Whether in Bible studies, church activities or personal contacts, believers must be encouraged to "consider one another," to develop deep spiritual bonds among themselves so that a word of truth spoken in love might turn a brother or sister away from sin. Beyond this, the church must have a clear plan for implementing biblical discipline. When several members meet resistance in dealing with an offense, church leaders must have an established procedure for hearing and resolving the issue.

Details will vary from church to church, but several elements seem fundamental to healthy church discipline:

Mutual exhortation — in the normal course of ministry, the priesthood of believers includes every believer's authority and responsibility to minister to every other believer, with due regard for differences in gifts and offices.

Discipline plan — the pattern of discipline described in Matthew 18:15-20 must be taught and implemented through all the ministries of the church.

Discipline procedures — local church leadership must develop and implement procedures for dealing with extreme cases which may call for official restriction or exclusion.

Without legalistically adding to what the Bible says or fearfully taking away from the force of its judgments, churches must courageously and compassionately follow the pattern of soul-care which Jesus prescribed.

Marriage counseling should be a specialized ministry of reconciliation. It should be part of a conscientiously applied program of spiritual hygiene which includes the full participation of every member of every church which claims to be following Christ. If personal exhortation and corporate discipline were exercised to the full extent of the biblical mandate for edification, Christian couples would not be so easily entrapped in the same problems that unbelievers fall into.

Bible Knowledge

Differences in church background and in church discipline center in how the Bible is taught and applied. If the Bible's teachings are breathed out by God to show us how to live for Him (II Timothy 3:16), then knowing and doing what the Bible says should be the mission of every church and every individual Christian. Knowledge without action breeds intellectual pride (I Corinthians 8:1-2). Action without knowledge breeds self-righteous legalism (Romans 10:2-4). The Bible is the living, powerful Word of God which cuts through human illusions and exposes our innermost thoughts and intentions, declaring our accountability to an omniscient God (Hebrews 4:12-13). Is it doing that in the lives of the couples who come for marriage counseling? Do they know what the Bible says? Do they believe it? Does it affect their mindsets and lifestyles? Do they acknowledge the Bible's authority and have a good grasp of its essential message? Have they been shown how specific Bible teachings apply to the problems in their marriages?

If a couple's church background is solid, pastors and teachers will have proclaimed and modeled a biblical approach to the Bible. The Pastoral Epistles challenge believers to know what they believe and to live according to their knowledge of the truth. Each letter begins with exposition of doctrine and goes on to describe the implications and applications of what has been taught. In II Timothy, Paul describes the pattern:

Know the message of the Bible (II Timothy 2:15).

Know the purpose of the Bible (II Timothy 3:15-16).

Let the message of the Bible accomplish its purpose (II Timothy 4:15).

This is Paul's charge to Timothy, a young pastor. It is a God-breathed charge to all Christians.

What is expected of all Christians is a ministry of reconciliation, a mission to bring God's truth and love into the lives of the people around us through our speech and action. This ministry of reconciliation requires careful attention to how the Bible's teachings apply to human experience (II Timothy 4:16; Hebrews 10:24-25). We are to be people of warm compassion and firm conviction who minister with patience and sound doctrine (II Timothy 4:2). Public ministry and personal growth are to be built upon loving, truthful communication (Ephesians 4:15-16). Psalm 85, a prayer for forgiveness and restoration, includes a concise description of reconciliation: "Mercy and truth have met together; righteousness and peace have kissed. Truth shall spring out of the earth, and righteousness shall look down from heaven." Proper response to the message and purpose of the Bible brings God's truth into our everyday lives.

To know the message of the Bible, we must be exposed to "reading, exhortation and doctrine (I Timothy 4:16)." Reading, preaching and teaching the Bible have always been characteristic activities of God's people. For the ancient Hebrews, the Law declared the requirements of conformity to God's rule; the Prophets proclaimed judgment and called for repentance when God's rule had been rejected; and the Writings recorded exemplary responses to God's rule. As described in Nehemiah 8, the public reading of the Word of God "from morning until midday" before "those that could understand" was accompanied by careful teaching which "caused the people to understand." Knowing the message of the Bible means hearing the Bible in language we understand, in terms we can apply to our lives. If we are to be doers of the Word as well as hearers, we must hear what the Word tells us to do (James 1:21-25).

What is the message of the Bible? What does it tell us to do? Its message is God's word of reconciliation culminating in a call to come to God in Jesus Christ for salvation. Theologians have analyzed and categorized the elements of this message in various ways. A simplified breakdown might be: **Theology** — teachings about the existence and character of God, the person and work of Christ and the ministry of the Holy Spirit. **Anthropology** — teachings about humanity, sin and salvation. **Ecclesiology** — teachings about the nature and ministry of the Church. **Eschatology** — teachings about God's rule in time and eternity.

Bible knowledge includes knowing what the Bible teaches, knowing its implications for our lives, and responding appropriately.

If our clients have a working knowledge of "all the counsel of God (Acts 20:27)," they will be responsive to biblical counsel. If their Bible knowledge is rudimentary, we will have to provide resources to supplement it, at least in areas relevant to their problems. Churches which neglect clear, accurate and practical Bible teaching leave their members ill-equipped to think biblically. Mainline churches sometimes take such a broad view of doctrine that they minimalize its impact on life. Smaller sects sometimes overemphasize minor issues which they think others have neglected. The balanced Bible knowledge which builds balanced lives comes through clear, accurate and practical teaching of everything the Bible says. To be fully equipped to live for God, we must know that all of the Bible is useful for doctrine, reproof, rebuke and instruction in righteousness (II Timothy 3:16-17; 4:2).

To know the purpose of the Bible, we must be exposed to its sharp edges, its quality of cutting through our illusions to the core of our self-awareness. Doctrine gives us information we need, an understanding of God's truth as the rule for our lives. For Christians, the Law is fulfilled through the grace and truth revealed in Jesus Christ. Reproof, rebuke and correction expose, confront and challenge us. For Christians this aspect of the prophetic mission is continued in the mutual ministry of the members of the body of Christ. Instruction in righteousness gives us the guidance and encouragement to conform to God's truth. For Christians, this is an invitation to respond to the wisdom and power of God revealed in the Gospel with the same obedient faith exemplified by many of God's people in the Writings of the Hebrew Scriptures.

Reproof, rebuke and correction are the disciplinary tools of the ministry of reconciliation. If professing Christian clients do not know the principles and purposes of church discipline, we will need to remind them of God's standard for marriage and point out that living by a lower standard creates a stunted relationship where problems will abound. The Bible's high view of marriage is a foreign concept to the worldly wise — many consider it a bizarre anachronism. But in the wisdom of God revealed in Scripture, a permanent, sacred, monogamous, life-defining heterosexual union of one man and one woman is the foundation upon which all human society is to be built. Failure to maintain this ideal jeopardizes all other human relationships. Reproof, rebuke and correction will point out specific deviations from God's standard and challenge clients to stop doing what is wrong and start doing what is right.

Instruction in righteousness is the positive side of the ministry of reconciliation. For the message of the Bible to accomplish its purpose, we must examine ourselves in the light of our knowledge of its teachings (I Timothy 3:16). In Isaiah 55:10, God says that His Word will accomplish its purposes. The purposes of God described in Isaiah 55 include salvation, forgiveness and restoration for those who turn to God and forsake their sin. This is a concise summary of a ministry of reconciliation — bringing people into a healthy relationship with God and with each other.

As counselors, we need to remind the Church of the twofold nature of this ministry. While II Corinthians 5 is an urgent call to evangelize with eternity in view, its context (and the motif of both I and II Corinthians) is an urgent call to believers to clean up our act here and now, to harbor no divisiveness but to be of one mind as we sort out the issues of life (I Corinthians 1:10). The call to be reconciled to God implies a call to be reconciled to each other. Helping couples to be of one mind within their marriages is a specialized ministry under the larger mandate for believers to be of one mind within the Church.

Couples become more of one mind as they think through the Bible's teachings together. "I'm going to be more loving" is a noble intention, but its feet do not hit the pavement without clear concepts of what love looks like in action. "We're going to straighten out our finances" needs measurable goals and specific steps to reach them. "I'm going to end the affair" may lead to decisive action, but the unfaithful attitude which led to the affair needs to be corrected and trust must be earned and freely given.[166] The Bible addresses these issues, bringing the wisdom and power of God into the details of life.

"I'm going to be more loving." God's love is the standard (I Corinthians 13) and the empowerment (Galatians 5:22-23) for the love He wants us to know and share. The loving relationship which should exist between husband and wife is alluded to throughout the Bible. Ephesians 5:22-23 describes how it works — in the same self-giving, purifying, nourishing and cherishing way that the love of Christ works in His Church. Proverbs 31:10-31 exalts a wife who shows her love through her virtue, diligence, wisdom and kindness. Proverbs 5 teaches that a man's honor in the world and his true enjoyment of life are dependent on his faithfulness to his wife. What is love? It is a consistent and considerate commitment to advance the good of another at whatever cost to one's own rights and desires. Within marriage, love means making it your mission in life to make your mate the most fulfilled human being on the planet.

"We're going to straighten out our finances." The book of Proverbs also provides guidance for straightening out finances. Trusting God to supply what we need to accomplish His purpose, we can stabilize our material welfare by following principles from Proverbs. As I have said elsewhere:

The book of Proverbs begins with a call to see ourselves and our position in the world correctly. "The fear of the Lord," reverence for God and submission to His will, is referred to repeatedly as the basis for wisdom, contentment and avoidance

---

[166] Reconciliation after adulterous unfaithfulness has disrupted a marriage requires careful reconstruction of the connections between husband and wife. Keeping in touch by cell phone throughout the day can reduce anxiety and quiet the whisperings of Satan. Knowing that a spouse can be reached at any time reduces doubts and rebuilds trust. Frequent impromptu conversations enrich any marriage.

of evil. "To hear wisdom," listening to and following instruction and advice, is presented as the basis for living sensibly and successfully.

The apostle Paul tells us that our job as stewards is to be found faithful (I Corinthians 4:2), whether the stewardship is in ministry or in the financial realm. Faithfulness should be our goal, with the understanding that God owns all that we have and all that we are.[167] Straightening out finances begins with straightening out our attitudes about finances and bringing our thoughts and our spending into conformity with biblical principles of good stewardship.

"I'm going to end the affair." Breaking off an affair leaves residual double-mindedness. The two-souled adulterer must submit both body and mind to the renewing wisdom and power of God. This will involve self-examination and self-judgment in the mirror of biblical teachings on marriage, sexuality and faithfulness. How can a marriage violated by adultery be restored to its intended one-flesh status? The first three chapters of Hosea tell of a promiscuously adulterous woman whose husband provided for her even in her sin and eventually took her back as his wife. The betrothal vow of Hosea 2:19-20 is a commitment to lifelong faithfulness, righteousness and love. The reconciliation vow of Hosea 3:3 is a subdued echo of this commitment. It suggests that restoration may have included "many days" of sexual abstinence, perhaps to purify body and mind for a renewal of the oneness which had been lost. No matter how we interpret this and other relevant passages, if our marriage counseling is to be truly Christian it must be biblical. We must know the thoughts and intentions of God as revealed in the Bible and transfer them into the thoughts and intentions of our clients.

---

[167] Dr. Dow Pursley and Gordon Puls, *Finances: Biblical Wisdom/Radical Action* Alethia, 2003, pp. 6, 42 (revised 2008, 2011, 2016). (Now in Spanish.)

Bible knowledge is more than a comfortable acquaintance with the narratives about a few familiar characters. Bible story theology too often consists of superficial moralizing about events which were much more complex than some neatly packaged Sunday school lessons. The real meat of Bible knowledge is in the uncomfortable things the Bible says about us. In the book of Romans, which so clearly and comprehensively proclaims the Gospel, the first step on the road is a step into the abyss of human sinfulness, an inescapable chain of irrefutable accusations. Only after three chapters of unrelieved conviction of sin does the road open up as faith looks to the redemption offered in Jesus Christ, the sanctifying work of the Holy Spirit, and the outworking of God's purpose in human history and within His Church. When we have abhorred ourselves and repented, God lifts us from the dust of death to live for Him. This is the full range of what Bible knowledge should mean in human experience. No matter how dusty our clients are when they come in, they can be washed in the Word and go forth rejoicing.

Spiritual Growth

A couple's profession of salvation, their church background and their Bible knowledge should result in a measure of spiritual growth. Counseling, by definition, is a process of bringing about positive change. We have little to offer those who do not admit their need to grow. We cannot help the adamantly self-righteous. Jesus himself said, "I come not to call the righteous, but sinners to repentance (Mark 2:17)." Charles Spurgeon frequently reminded his hearers that the person who considers himself a hopeless sinner is precisely the person Christ came to save. There is no hope for a self-righteous person who sees no need for repentance. Our ministry is to those who are able to acknowledge that they need to change.

311

Christians are not uniformly Christ-like. Many of us think we are closer to the ideal than some others are, but the Bible warns against conscious comparisons among believers (II Corinthians 10:12; Galatians 6:1-3). Some Christians measure themselves according to the expectations of their denomination or their local church, which may be more cultural than biblical. One man said of a particular local church, "I can't go there; I'm not holy enough." He meant that he could not conform to the congregation's subculture.

Spiritual growth does include affiliation and interaction with other believers. Contrary to the individualism of our culture, Christians are nurtured as we assemble together to share varieties of gifts and ministries. Hebrews 10:24-25 says believers gather to help one another act in love to accomplish the purposes of God. Building up, challenging, correcting and comforting are the ministries of the Word of God (II Timothy 3:16), the Spirit of God (John 16:7-15), the servant of God (II Timothy 4:1-2) and the people of God (Ephesians 4:11-16). The interdependence of mutual ministry binds believers together through the variety of gifts and ministries represented among the members of a local church.

Some churches maintain a folksy tradition which is a good illustration of mutual ministry among believers: the church potluck.[168] Each family brings its house specialty, a dish nobody else makes quite as well — or so the compliments shared at the meal would have it. Usually there is some prearrangement to assure that there will be a balanced meal; if everybody brought meatloaf, there would be no potato salad. A church potluck is a festive occasion, with each attendee at least

---

[168] The term is self-explanatory, "the luck of the pot," whatever people bring. Natives of what is now the northwestern United States periodically celebrated a "potlatch," a cycle of feasting and gift-giving which bound separate local communities in a broader connection of mutual respect and cooperation. When local churches combine services for holidays or other special occasions, they remind members of their vital connection to the whole body of Christ.

sampling a few unfamiliar treats. In conversations after the meal, the cooks enthusiastically exchange recipes, finding new ways to nourish and delight their families.[169]

The spiritual ministry of most churches could learn a few lessons from the concept of a potluck. Each believer brings his or her specialty, a combination of abilities and experiences nobody else duplicates — or so the gifts of the Holy Spirit are designed to minister. Usually there is some degree of organization and planning to assure that there will be balanced ministry; if everybody chose to work in the nursery, there would be no special music. A church service should be a festive occasion, with each member challenged by fresh insights. In conversations after the service, believers can compassionately exchange private exhortation, finding new strength to face the challenges of life.

When facing extreme challenges, Christians become acutely aware of the need for knowledge and wisdom to guide us toward "the new heavens and new earth, in which dwelleth righteousness (II Peter 3:13)." We want God's kingdom to come and His will to be done right here where we are struggling. God has given us a written revelation concerning Himself and His Creation and we diligently seek to understand it correctly so that we can faithfully live out our places in His plan (II Timothy 2:15). God the Holy Spirit offers us comfort, strength and guidance for our innermost selves and our desire is to "grieve not" or "quench not" the Holy Spirit, but to "walk in the Spirit," receiving and following His direction (Ephesians 4:30; I Thessalonians 5:19; Galatians 5:25). God provides the counsel of other believers to aid us in applying Scripture and obeying the Spirit as we assemble together to "exhort one another (Hebrews 10:25)." The truth of Scripture, the indwelling Holy Spirit and

---

[169] Lisa Puls delighted her family by scheduling her wedding during a Sunday morning service at a church in Seneca, South Carolina, on the day of a church potluck. No caterer could have matched the menu of that wedding reception.

the ministry of other believers equip us for our journey through time into eternity with the Lord.

The Bible, the Holy Spirit and fellow believers are not unrelated sources of guidance. The Bible must not be reduced to a grab-bag of rules, riddles and rituals. Nebulous whims and numinous fancies and all manner of exotic experiences must not be ascribed to the Holy Spirit. Theology must not be reduced to me-ology or we-ology to suit the tastes of individuals or groups. God is not the author of confusion; His Word, His Spirit and His people should be in perfect harmony. Aberrations and deficiencies are not the fault of the Bible or of the Holy Spirit. We are the ones out of tune.

Spiritual growth requires productive use of the resources which God has provided. Clients who profess to be Christians can be expected to show a commitment to do what God wants them to do and to become what God wants them to be. Are they gaining knowledge of the Bible to find out what God wants? Are they drawing wisdom and power from the Holy Spirit to become more Christ-like? Are they interacting with other believers in mutual ministries which challenge, correct and comfort them?

Charles Spurgeon said that Christians should be so saturated in Scripture that our very blood becomes "bibline." That requires more than listening to a half-hour sermon once or twice a week. Regular church attendance is one indication of a desire for spiritual growth, but sitting in a pew worrying about your marriage while the pastor preaches his heart out does not connect you with the power of God's Word. Are our clients reading their Bibles regularly? Are they daily seeking a message from God for themselves? Are they reading the Bible consecutively, from beginning to end, seeking all the counsel of God in all the Scriptures? Do they search the Scriptures to judge the truthfulness of what they have been taught and the value of advice they have been given? Are husband and wife reading the

Bible together, sharing responses to its message, letting it unite them as its truth displaces their separate opinions?

If the Bible is to empower us for life, the Holy Spirit must guide us into its truth. The same Holy Spirit who "moved along" those who wrote the God-breathed Scriptures is the Holy Spirit who enlightens us as we read, study and apply the Scriptures. The Holy Spirit was not sent to astonish, entertain or grant wishes. He is here to instruct, convict and comfort according to the Scriptures and to the glory of Jesus Christ. He is not a tame God who caters to our desires and endorses our emotions.

In the movie *Harvey*, Jimmy Stewart plays a man whose closest confidant and advisor is an invisible giant rabbit. He consults the rabbit, Harvey, about major and minor issues and is often heard having one-sided conversations with this friend everyone else considers nonexistent. Although others question his sanity, eventually they concede that his illusion is harmless and it helps him cope with life. The story is told so gently and Stewart plays such a sympathetic character that the theme of patronizing religious tolerance is easily digested. If some people want to talk (pray) to an invisible friend (God), what harm is there in that, as long as they leave other people to believe or disbelieve what they will?

Is that how God fits into our lives? Is He just an imaginary friend? People confide in bartenders, pets, invisible giant rabbits — and God. Is it all the same? Or does the Spirit of God open the eyes of our understanding as we open our Bibles? Does opening our Bibles bring us into conscious contact with the One who opens our lives, exposing our darkest secrets to the light of His Word? Are we really getting through to God when we pray? Does the Holy Spirit move us to pray according to the will of God? Does God answer, showing us which way to turn to walk in the path of His truth?

When our clients talk to us about their problems, we need to know whether they have talked with God and whether their knowledge and experience of the Holy Spirit has had an appreciable effect on the status of their marriage. Have they known His power of conviction and correction? Have they known His love in forgiveness and restoration? Is He giving them sound minds to accept their responsibilities realistically? If the Holy Spirit is the Paraclete who can be called alongside to help, our counseling ministry is only a manifestation of the work He is already doing in clients. If they have not been growing through His ministry, He may use us to help open their eyes to the truth He wants to apply to their lives.

In fact, the established pattern for the Holy Spirit's guidance into the truth of the Bible is to bring believers together to minister to one another. The sin of spiritual pride grows as individuals or groups exaggerate their strengths and overlook their weaknesses and sins. Isolating ourselves or our churches from critics and dissenters, we think we have really arrived when we have merely stopped moving forward. Growth requires the help of friends who speak the truth in love, lighting up our blind spots. Too often, the personal ministries which are the heart of the Church, and its reason for assembling (Ephesians 4:11-16; Hebrews 10:24-25) are neglected in an overemphasis on refining techniques of public ministry. In any case, as believers connect with each other in either corporate or individual exhortation, the Spirit of God applies the Word of God to their needs. The love described in I Corinthians 13 is not an emotion a person can work up in isolation; it is a network of interaction within human relationships. In the Peanuts comic strip, Linus once said, "I love mankind. It's people I can't stand." Love is not a generic warm feeling — it is a pattern of considerate actions and consistent responses which promote the good of others, even at great cost to ourselves.

Are our clients letting other believers be instruments of God's peace who bring lessons of love into their troubled marriage? Are their churches freeing them from the illusions which divide them? Or is each of them seeking divine sanction from believers who will take sides in their misunderstandings and disagreements? Churches have split over divorces and each spouse may be considered the innocent party by some group of professing Christians. Even when church discipline has been implemented, the church on the next corner may offer a second opinion. In true Christian fellowship the people of God are moved by the Spirit of God to apply the Word of God to the sometimes messy details of each other's lives. In superficial church affiliation professing Christians cry on each other's shoulders with ,little or no reference to what the Spirit of God and the Word of God have to say about their problems.

As Christian counselors, we need God-given discernment to see where our clients are in relation to the Bible, the Holy Spirit and the Church. They may know the words and motions without the reality of growing in conformity to Christ. Certainly, living faith is expressed in words, and a person's testimony of life in Christ must be respected. Certainly, living faith is expressed in acts of worship and service, and a person's private devotional practices and public ministries must be commended. But the inner life-giving work of the Word and the Spirit of God should be further evidenced in what couples in counseling say and do about the specific problems within their marriage.

Personal Assessment

Whatever spiritual resources our clients have, we must be aware of other factors, which affect their ability to profit from counseling. Critics have noted that some methods of psychological or psychoanalytical therapy are narrowly culture-bound: they work well only with clients whose social class, educational background and world-view are similar to the therapist's. It has been said that Freud's theory and practice may have been quite well-suited to certain families of a certain socio-economic status in Vienna during a few decades of Freud's lifetime, but are less valid in the global community. Jung traveled the world in search of universal manifestations of his concepts, but the result was the formation of a Gnostic cult whose esoteric insights are reserved for adept initiates. This is not to disparage fragmentary reflections of truth in human attempts to understand what it means to be human. The problem is that generalizations about people do not tell us everything we need to know about the person who comes for counseling.

Common sense suggests that we are more comfortable confiding in or counseling people very much like ourselves. We trust our friends, and most of our friendships are built upon shared interests, shared hopes and fears, and similar lifestyles. The person who comes for counseling comes with a complete set of abilities, limitations, experiences and assumptions which may or may not be readily compatible with the counselor's equally complex personal background. Pointed questions and patient listening penetrate this barrier so that the client's personal resources enter fully into the counseling process.

Capacity of the Couple

When a couple comes in for counseling, we need to realize that the whole situation is uncomfortable for them. They are admitting they need help, which may be a major blow to the pride of people who have been force-fed individualistic doctrines of self-esteem and self-sufficiency since childhood. Besides the humiliation, they may be defensive or defiant as they face the unknown risks of self-revelation. They are stepping onto unfamiliar ground — this is the counselor's turf, and they may be intimidated by not knowing the rules of the game. Putting clients at ease does not mean caving in to their discomfort when bold direction is needed, but it is important to assess and address factors which might interfere with communication and progress.

Professional counseling is a formalized process of communication, which focuses on defining and resolving human problems. The value of our work is not only in the content of our advice, but in our modeling and expectation of purposeful discussion of issues. If clients have little experience or skill in problem solving and conflict resolution, their perception of our motives and methods may be unnecessarily negative. The fact that they come to us with unsolved problems and unresolved conflicts indicates that whatever they have been doing has not worked, but they may cling to their unproductive home-grown scripts rather than let their guard down in the counseling office. The counseling process requires both the ability to express oneself clearly and purposefully and the ability to listen with patience and comprehension. In early sessions with couples, it is important to gather clues about their conversational skills and styles to gain some idea of how far they must be led towards effective discussion of their problems.

What the couple says about themselves and how they say it will give crucial insight into their communications skills. Letting them talk freely during a shared meal or an introductory counseling session reveals not only some of their thoughts but also their styles of expression. It may also give the counselor clues about how they perceive and treat each other in their day-to-day conversations. If they show disrespect to each other in the counseling office, their arguments at home are probably quite destructive. If they show a capacity for give-and-take in conversation, we can commend that and encourage them to build upon it.

A couple's communication patterns develop early in their relationship: If the couple knew each other very long before they were married, they may have had wide-ranging conversations and learned to express their thoughts and feelings relatively well. This would be expected especially if they were childhood friends from stable families. If they met and married under stressful or questionable circumstances their relationship has a weaker foundation, and there may be a time bomb built into it. If it is not the first marriage for either or both of them distrust or open threats will present the question, "What assurance is there that there will not be another affair and divorce?" If anything sinful and destructive figured prominently in how they got together, the flow of communication in their marriage has been poisoned at its source.

A couple's capacity for problem solving and conflict resolution often reflects their family histories. The way each spouse's parents dealt with issues will be the pattern for their behavior until they are taught another model. If they came from homes where stress festered until it broke into verbal and physical violence, every problem in their marriage will be met with anger, or fear of a short-tempered spouse will suppress expressions of concern or discontentment. If feelings were not expressed freely in their childhood homes, they will have difficulty showing affection or sharing hopes and fears. They will follow learned patterns of dealing with emotional situations. Everything they have seen in their parents' marriages will be reflected in their own.

The lessons of childhood constitute the couple's presuppositions about married life, their unconscious assumptions about how marriage works and how they should act as a husband or a wife. Families and subcultures transmit styles of communication and frameworks for relationships which can become traditional or even stereotypical. Following healthy traditions helps hold marriages and societies together; following dysfunctional stereotypes leads to destruction. Counselors can help clients recognize any negative relational patterns they have absorbed and replace them with more positive attitudes and behaviors.

One of the premises of counseling is the belief that constructive effort can bring significant improvement in relationships. A qualifying corollary is that you cannot build something constructive on a destructive foundation. The theological description of repentance is not mere sorrow over sin and its consequences. True repentance includes changing one's mind, forsaking the bad and pursuing the good. If the metaphor of marriage as a journey is valid, some couples need help unpacking counterproductive baggage and taking on supplies more appropriate for where they want to go. Helping them to see what they are doing that does not work is necessary before they will be open to learning what does work.

Several personal capacities are crucial to the ability to change one's mind in a positive direction. Comprehension, the capacity to see the situation as rationally and as objectively as possible, is necessary if the person is to get beyond pessimistic paralysis or defensive posturing. Sequential thinking, the capacity to use logic to map out strategies for change, is necessary to formulate and implement steps towards a better marriage. If the Bible and other helpful books are to be used effectively, reading ability is another important capacity.

We must know our clients' capacities in these areas and adapt our counseling accordingly. If our ministry is to reach beyond highly intelligent scholars (and many of them need it!), we need to know how to adjust to the abilities of our clients and how to help remedy some of their deficiencies. In all of our work, demonstrating what we expect can be a most profitable tool. The ability to communicate calmly, articulately and purposefully about potentially explosive issues can be learned best by example. As issues are defused, clients will see the value of honing their communication skills.

Comprehension is at the heart of wisdom. Perhaps every counseling office should have at least one translation of Proverbs 18:2 prominently displayed: "A fool has no delight in understanding, but in expressing his own heart."[170] In early sessions we can expect a certain amount of emotional venting, but we must guide the couple out of the woe-is-me and curse-you syndrome as quickly as possible. Without denying the strength of their emotions, we can steer them to the "Yes, but what can we do now to make things better?" question. Comprehension means grasping together, seeing connections, getting the whole picture. In distressed marriages, this is exactly what the couple most needs to do and exactly what they are least able to do without help. Highly capable couples may simply refuse to listen to each other; the less articulate may be truly unable to express their differences clearly. The purpose of the assessment process is not to feed the counselor's curiosity but to gather enough pieces of the couple's marriage puzzle to see where to begin putting it together.

In common usage, comprehension is the ability to catch on, to get with the program, to understand communication well enough to act on it. Assessing this capacity in clients, we will find a wide range of differences. Sometimes what seems like stubborn resistance to our counsel is simply an inability to make sense of what we are saying. When clients are less capable of responding to abstract principles, we need to work at a more literal and practical level: "Do you love your wife?" does not evoke as revealing an answer as "Did you take out the garbage last night?" To be sure that communication is effective, we may need to slow down, break our counsel into brief concrete statements, and repeat ourselves until the client can restate what we have said.

Sequential thinking is a vanishing skill in a society of existential immediacy. Living in the razor's-edge present with little sense of past or future, clients may have difficulty

---

[170] Counselors also need to keep Proverbs 18:13 on their minds, if not on their walls: "He that answereth a matter before he heareth it, it is folly and shame unto him."

following our logic. If we want our sessions to leave a more lasting impression than a pop-up ad, we will need to assess our clients' capacities for reflective linear thought. They may experience their marriage problems as phenomena which suddenly appeared and may or may not suddenly disappear; with no clear cause or meaning ("I don't know what possessed me to do that!"). We can help them find patterns in their problems, cause-and-effect sequences which can be altered or eliminated. Unraveling the matrix of destructive attitudes and dysfunctional behaviors in which their problems developed is often painfully necessary.

Reflective thought requires forging links from the present to the past and to the future. How did we get where we are? Where do we go from here? Linear, sequential thinking means choosing to be more than a victimized bystander in one's own life. Tracing choices which have led to failure and making new choices which will lead to better things — this is the liberating secret of success as a human being. Counseling helps people make such course corrections. Change is not just an act of the will; it engages the full capacity of the mind in analyzing the undesired situation and prescribing steps to correct it. In our counseling, we demonstrate sequential thinking as we sort out the pieces of information that clients give us and try to put them together in meaningful ways. As we help them find connections, they will begin to comprehend, to see the bigger picture. Thoughtless actions and responses have brought their marriage to its current crisis. Thoughtful actions and responses can lead them to a better place.

To encourage couples to think, we can ask them to read books or articles relevant to their needs. The success of reading assignments depends on their ability to read, which cannot be assumed. Many adults are functionally illiterate and some very helpful books and articles require well-developed reading skills. The best book is not always the one which most pointedly and thoroughly speaks to an issue, but the one the client can read. Since literature in our field is not published at all readability levels, we must modify our use of what is available and refer especially challenged clients to reading courses and tutors.

We cannot assume that people have even the most basic abilities. I once counseled a successful businessman who owned a chain of restaurants. I gave him and his wife a homework assignment of reading a book I thought would help them. He showed some discomfort over the assignment. When I asked him why he did not want to read the book, he reluctantly admitted that he could not read any book, because he had never learned to read or write. He was great at numbers, and had made a point of conducting his business orally, with subordinates handling written communication. He had made valiant efforts at learning to read, but was unaware of improvements in teaching methods which could overcome his difficulties. I steered him to some helpful resources, and he now reads and writes — and has been reconciled with his wife. His desire to correct the problems in his marriage gave him the courage to deal with a reading disability which he had been hiding all his life.

Assessing a couple's capacity to receive and process information does not mean that our ministry will be less effective for those with severe limitations. It means that we will minister with resources and methods appropriate to their abilities. For the more academically adept, we can speak as we would to colleagues, and assign research in the same scholarly publications we ourselves read. For the less literate, we can remember the educator's dictum: any meaningful concept can be taught at any level in an intellectually honest manner. If what we think has significance in the real world, we can say it plainly in simple words. DVDs, podcasts, and other audio recordings can communicate truth to the hearts of people whose minds would be overwhelmed by a five-hundred-page book.

Knowing a couple's capacities enables us to choose an unobstructed path for them to follow through the counseling process. We can offer them tools appropriate to their abilities and show them how to use them. If our assessments are correct and we make wise use of them, our clients will find our counsel clear, accurate and practical. Counseling is not about us, it is about people who need to find better ways to live with themselves and each other. The goal is to be helpful, not to sell a one-size-fits-all cloak of professional mumbo-jumbo which suits our pride but is ill-tailored to the real needs of real people. Jesus never felt He was lowering Himself to meet the needs of a child, a leper or an adulterer—His mission was to lift people up, and to do that He reached out to them where they were. Our mission is not to minister from a pedestal of personal and professional pride, but to meet people where they are and to share in Christ's work as He lifts them up.

Commitment of the Couple

A couple's capacity for productive communication is of value only if they are committed to using it to rebuild their marriage. Communication and commitment are complementary: open communication invites trusting commitment, proven commitment fosters open communication. If the couple is committed to their covenanted marriage they will be committed to using all available resources to save it. If they do not understand the concept of covenant as applied to marriage, teaching this principle would be the cornerstone of teaching them about commitment.

Are they prepared to commit themselves to the hard work of rebuilding their marriage? Are they emotionally stabilized or has distrust left them irrationally polarized?

Are they psychologically strong enough to work together or might one or both of them need individual counseling first? Are they spiritually sound enough to be of one accord in accepting biblical truth? Are they mature enough to participate responsibly in the counseling process or are they distracted by illusions about themselves and their marriage?

Attitudes evident in early sessions frequently indicate the level of commitment which will characterize future interaction with the counselor and with each other. The man who says, "My wife made me come!" must deal with his resentment before he can deal with his responsibilities. The woman who sobs, "I just don't know what to do!" must set aside her passive pessimism and do the things she knows she can and should do. If there is evidence of clinical psychological disorder in either spouse, referral may be necessary; a mentally unstable person cannot be trusted with another person's emotions.[171] People who are not ready to grow through marriage counseling will sabotage the process in various ways. They will miss appointments or come in late, sit in silence rather than share thoughts and feelings, and burst into anger or tears without warning, sometimes walking out of a session either cursing or crying. Angry spouses will refuse to see truth in anything but their own opinions. Immature people will play mental and verbal games which bypass the seriousness of their problems. The insecure will seek to control; the malicious will seek to destroy.

It is important to pay attention to the couple's motives for coming to counseling. Whether or not they state them clearly, their expectations will be the measure of their commitment to the counseling process. Some may have misperceptions of the role of the counselor and expect a magical "quick fix" or a list of "ten easy steps to a perfect marriage". Some may be suspicious of the counselor's apparent interest in invading their privacy. Some will try to manipulate sessions; others will wait for us to

---

[171] Unlike many Christian counselors and ministers, I never recommend any referral resource which is not distinctly Christian in principle and practice.

give them all the answers. Some couples call a cease fire in the hostilities between them to unite in blocking the counselor's attempts to help them face their problems. Others behave with remarkable civility during counseling sessions and argue all the way home about what was said.

Biblical Christian marriage counseling is committed to seeking out and responding to truth. In a relativistic culture which values comfort more than truth, this is a radical commitment. Expecting clients to commit themselves to the hard work of conforming their marriage to the standard of God's truth contradicts the comfort-seeking advice of friends, self-help advocates, many secular counselors and even some pastors. Avoiding truth to avoid offense is hypocritical and cowardly. Abandoning truth to seek comfort only guarantees further misery. Choosing to endure the discomfort of facing the truth is the only way to lasting peace. Contrary to the wisdom of the world, there is no easy way out of marriage problems.

The reason there is no easy way out is two-fold: getting out of the marriage only compounds problems and getting out of the problems while staying in the marriage requires radical changes in thinking and behavior. First, it must be remembered that God's truth about marriage includes the fact that it is an indissoluble bond, which means that any escape plan falls short of God's ideal and departs from the place of His full blessing. With few exceptions,[172] attempting to put asunder what God has joined together is an act of rebellion which brings God's judgment. Therefore, any sinful human attempt to dissolve the bond of marriage will leave irreparable damage. Secondly, there is no easy way to get out of the problems while staying in the marriage because the problems are symptomatic of wrong thinking which has led to firmly established patterns of

---

[172] Matthew 5:39 and 9:19 make an exception for sexual sin. There is some biblical support for at least temporary separation in cases of persistent adultery or abuse, or abandonment.

wrong behavior. Taking the hard way into a good marriage is ultimately more satisfying than looking for an easy way out of a bad one.

Christian counselors must proclaim, defend and strive towards God's standard for marriage throughout the counseling process. If this means posting the biblical definition of marriage on our office walls, printing handouts and working it into conversations at every opportunity, so be it. Our efforts will be rewarded with the approval of God and our clients will know where we stand—and where they should stand. It will give couples a goal worthy of their effort. As someone has said, "If you don't know where you're going, any road will get you there." Having a noble goal is a strong motivation for taking immediate action. It has also been said, "The road to by-and-by leads to the house of never." If the goal is conformity to God's definition of marriage, we need to keep that goal in sight as we help clients take a straight path to reach it.

Commitment to straighten their course will be strengthened as we help couples see the beauty of the marriage ideal and offer them hope that they can take effective steps to improve their own marriages. Commitment to solving marriage problems is founded upon commitment to marriage itself. Couples need to be reminded that they did not invent the concept of marriage and that they do not have the authority to redefine what marriage is or should be. Nor do they have the right to declare that their own marriages are invalid because they do not meet their personal requirements. Discarding illusions and following God's truth is the only way to escape the frustrating failure of human sinfulness to create righteous relationships.

Commitment to conform to the truth not only establishes the goal of Christian marriage counseling, it also streamlines the process. When a high view of marriage is accepted, secondary personal wishes are put into perspective.

What each spouse is looking for in the other will be less an issue than the responsibility each of them has to their marriage. If we may paraphrase: "Ask not what your marriage can do for you, but ask what you can do for your marriage." Waiting for Mr. or Mrs. Wrong to transform into Mr. or Mrs. Right leads to frustration, despair and destruction. Working to transform oneself and one's marriage leads to incremental success, hope, and a more satisfying life. Incremental success: the hard work of solving marriage problems proceeds by small steps, seldom leaping over tall obstacles in a single bound. The patience to take small steps in hope of covering a great distance is the commitment we are looking for in clients.

Commitment stirs up hope by focusing attention and energy on doing what is possible. When couples recall the months or years of their marriage's deterioration, they have difficulty with resentful memories of marriage-destroying attitudes and behavior. It is understandable that many despair of correcting all the wrong steps and bad choices. We need to remind them that the damage their marriage has suffered was not the result of a deliberate plan to destroy their relationship. Forming a deliberate plan to nurture their relationship provides hope for steady recovery. Missionary explorer David Livingstone had a simple explanation for the accomplishments of his expeditions: "Adventures are a sign of poor planning." He had crisscrossed some of the wildest and most impenetrable parts of Africa by planning carefully and preparing for "adventures," hazards which could be disastrous if not accounted for in plans and preparations.[173]

Experienced marriage counselors know that the failure of a marriage is quite often the result of poor planning. The silver lining of this cloud is that good planning increases the

----

[173] Some missionaries feel a call of God which goes beyond fear and human reason. Renowned explorer Sir Richard Burton balked at going into an area which had been entered by twelve individual missionaries, one of whom returned alive.

possibility of success in marriage. Considerate, consistent adherence to a well-formed marriage plan gives a couple the prospect of growing together in a richer relationship than they have ever known. Those who have been unfaithful in attitude or action should heed the handyman's axiom: "If you take care of what you have, you won't be looking to replace it." The possibility that what they already have could become something absolutely beautiful gives couples the hope needed to fuel their commitment to their marriage.

The transition from despair to hope is rarely instantaneous. At first, a husband and wife may distrust the counselor at least as much as they distrust each other. As they gradually discover that the counselor can be relied upon to be patient, caring and truthful, they will listen more receptively. When a trusted counselor assures them that God has a wonderful plan for their marriage, they will be ready to work out the details of that plan. As they demonstrate their commitment, the counselor can systematically transfer full responsibility for healing and nourishing their marriage onto their own shoulders, where it belongs.

External Support

Marriage is the foundation on which the structures of society are built, but marriage itself is reinforced as the other structures of society fulfill their God-given purposes. Ideally, every individual would be related correctly to God and to other human beings (Exodus 20:1-17; Matthew 22:37-40). Ideally, every marriage would be entered and enjoyed as a permanent, sacred, monogamous, life-defining heterosexual union of one man and one woman (Mark 10:6-9). Such marriages would create and nurture families in a generation-to-generation perpetuation of the ideal. Families, communities and churches would be structured and governed only in the best interests of all their members.

We do not live in such a world. Sin and its consequences have tainted every human being and every human institution. People who seek to conform to God's revealed standards face obstacles and opposition. When biblical mandates were more widely respected, what has been called the Judeo-Christian ethic influenced society more directly. Laws which promoted decency and maintained order supported high views of marriage and family. A society addicted to indecency sinks into disorder. Where God's character and purpose determine morality, what God calls good will be encouraged, and what God calls evil will be restrained. Where human self-interest and desire determine morality, what God calls good will be rejected, and evil will be unrestrained.

Christian marriage counselors carry a heavier load than many realize. We are trying to preserve the foundation of society while others seek to disparage or destroy it. Our society is becoming as indifferent to the need for a sound foundation as one Miami Beach builder was. He cut corners in constructing a multi-million dollar home. His skimping went undetected for years. Then a crack appeared in the floor, spreading across the whole house. The foundation had been poured with no reinforcement. Varying pressures and years of uneven weight-bearing cracked the concrete. The network of steel which would have held the house together had been left out. Strengthening marriages and families in a society which devalues them is like trying to lay a reinforced concrete foundation in a hurricane. The structures of society which should reinforce marriages are being blown about by every wind of opinion.

Just as individuals draw identity and purpose from relationships, couples are shaped and nourished through productive connections with individuals and institutions around them. The extended family can be either a strong influence in reconciling them or an equally potent divisive force. Their community may offer helpful classes and programs to enrich their life together or distract them from each other with a plethora of diverse activities. Affiliation with a sound church can provide a solid foundation upon which they can build or rebuild their marriage; churches which have a form of godliness without the living power of God offer nothing more than religious placebos which have no nutritional or medicinal value (II Timothy 3:5).

Christian counselors need to remember that the people who come for counseling come from the contexts of their families, communities and churches. As we remind couples that a one-flesh one-mind commitment precludes thinking and acting as unconnected individuals, we must remind them that their place in the world precludes thinking and acting as a couple isolated from larger social units. Marriage is the foundational institution of human connectedness, but extended family relationships, community resources and responsibilities, and the mutual ministries of believers within the Church were also instituted by God. Despite aberrations and abuses of the structures of society, their ideal purposes remain.

For Christian counselors, a couple's church affiliation is more than a bit of background information; it is the connecting point where our specialized ministry flows into the main supply line of their spiritual nourishment. If their church background supplies the Bible knowledge and discipline they need for growth, the counselor's task is to encourage them to apply these resources to the recovery of their marriage. A church, which upholds the biblical ideal of marriage through preaching, teaching, discipline, mentoring, and example stabilizes couples, families, and the surrounding community.

The surrounding community may reinforce marriages and families through programs and classes which parallel church ministries. Parenting classes, childcare, financial seminars, adult education, and recreational activities are provided by community centers and schools. Couples can enrich their lives and their marriages by using these resources together. Participation in community activities can also broaden their circle of mutual friends and give them a stronger sense of belonging. Carefully planned involvement can bring them closer to each other, just as a schedule packed with diversions can tear them apart.

Extended families may not be all they were meant to be, but they still provide valuable resources for reinforcing a marriage. Family members whose lives and marriages are relatively stable are often the first to offer help to struggling couples. When conflicts heat up, these are the people a couple calls. Sometimes it involves acting as referees to prevent physical violence. More often, it means acting as mediators whose advice and example are respected by both spouses. People with such close ties to the couple can cool off explosive emotions and help clarify issues. Sad to say, less objective relatives are often the first and strongest proponents of divorce.

Just as the foundational significance of marriage has been threatened through redefinition, compromise and abandonment, the supportive context of the extended family has been distorted. Strong marriages produce strong families; dysfunctional marriages produce dysfunctional families. Our culture's standards for marriages and families fall far short of the glory God intended for these institutions, but we can attempt to strengthen what remains. It is still true that members of their extended families can be the first line of defense for a couple's marriage and the first responders in times of acute distress. Parents, siblings and other adult family members who have compassion for their blood relative may not be objective about the viability of the marriage, but they usually favor the status quo over measures as radical as divorce. In families where divorce has become an acceptable option, the case is precisely reversed — divorced siblings can be the absolutely worst confidants of spouses in turmoil.[174]

Biblically and historically, human government exists to promote the general welfare of human communities. Various forms of government have developed to meet the needs of households, extended families, clans, tribes, ethnic groups, cities, states, and nations. Mutual defense, economic interdependence and shared beliefs and values build a sense of community, of belonging together in common humanness. Being united to preserve the common welfare gives individuals, couples, and families a broader range of connectedness, a social context in which to thrive. According to Romans 13:1-10, membership in a structured community involves a two-sided responsibility: government is to reward good and punish evil; citizens are to love their neighbors in ways described in the last five of the Ten Commandments (the fifth commandment, regarding honoring parents, is fulfilled within the family). The same double-edged duty is an object of prayer in I Timothy 2:1-4 proper uses of authority to maintain security; reverent and redemptive relationships among citizens.

Distortions of the biblical ideal do not render it obsolete. Human society is to be governed in such a way that the benefits of community connectedness are maximized and conflicts are minimized. Since connectedness is created in marriage and extended through family, the structures of society must preserve and build upon these fundamental institutions. We can strengthen what remains. All levels of government still support services which are intended to stabilize and benefit the human community. These community services offer valuable resources for functioning adequately in the society. If there is a remnant of consensus over a Judeo-Christian ethic, it is the ideal

---

[174] Misery loves company. People will do almost anything to justify their own sewer-hovering behavior., including helping others wreck their marriages by reinforcing their sinful behavior.

of community and individual improvement expressed in social service programs. Christian marriage counselors can encourage couples to take advantage of community resources, which will help them achieve God's purposes for their marriages and families.

As helpers called alongside to assist, our task is to encourage people to use all the resources available to them, not to let them become dependent on us for all the answers they need. We can hope that our ministry of reconciliation will have lasting effects, and we can remain available for follow-up, but if we expect a couple to take responsibility for their own marriage, we must work ourselves into their lives and then out again. In early counseling sessions, we can observe their interaction and listen to their self-expression, letting them bring themselves into the counseling process as naturally as possible. The counseling process itself should be structured and purposeful. We are called alongside as helpers whose expertise and experience are useful in clarifying and correcting marriage problems. If we are effective in providing the needed help, our counsel will be integrated into the couple's life together as naturally as possible.

To integrate our counsel into their lives, we can encourage couples to make full use of whatever external support is available to them. This would include the teaching, fellowship, and opportunities for ministry in a local church as means of strengthening them spiritually. It would also include classes, support groups, counseling in specific areas, child-care, and other community programs which would strengthen them personally and socially.[175] Too often, the struggles and stresses of marriage are exacerbated through ignorance or neglect of readily available help.

---

[175] As with all referrals to other resources, it should be made clear that the presuppositions and goals of biblical marriage counseling are distinct from those of secular programs, and discernment is necessary.

Our ministries will be multiplied and intensified as we encourage couples to draw all they can from the resources around them. Their families, churches, and communities offer support, which might have helped them before they came for counseling. It is vital for counselors to know whether clients have already taken advantage of existing support systems. It is equally important to make sure clients connect productively to these resources. The support a couple gets from family, church, and community can reinforce the insights and commitments, which emerge through the counseling process.

Hope for Healing

Any marriage can be brought into closer conformity to the biblical ideal of a covenanted one-flesh one-mind union. Knowing God's standard for marriage establishes a goal which can be reached through planning, hard work, and God's blessing. Making practical plans for handling the various responsibilities of marriage can minimize or eliminate many potential problems. Admitting and correcting mistakes removes shackles of the past which have threatened a couple's future together. Tapping into all of their spiritual, social, and family resources strengthens a couple for the task of building their marriage. Effective counseling helps a couple to help themselves, guiding them through productive communication techniques and problem-solving procedures.

The Heart of the Matter

The purpose of Christian marriage counseling is to help couples focus on The heart of marriage, to build or rebuild their marriage according to God's plan. To accomplish this, they will need:

œ Clear understanding of what the Bible says about marriage
œ Clear plans for constructing a godly marriage.
œ Clear perception of existing or potential marriage problems.
œ Clear assessment of available resources for building a marriage.

The counselor's task is to draw from what the couple already knows in each of these areas, supplement their knowledge as necessary, and help them apply it to their own marriage.

All marriages face similar challenges. This most intimate of human relationships makes us most vulnerable. A mate who knows all about me and loves me anyway is a wonderful gift from God. A mate who uses such intimate knowledge maliciously can be described accurately as devilish. Contentious rivalry and unscrupulous self-promotion create instability in any relationship; the wisdom God gives is pure, peaceful and gentle (James 3:14-17). Couples who honor and nourish a one-flesh one-mind covenant marriage are bound together in love as they share themselves freely and comprehensively. Problems escalate when the sharing is blocked or abused.

The same communication skills and commitment which build a marriage also equip the couple to face their problems. Except in rare cases, marriages are not destroyed by carefully planned campaigns of negative behavior. Even where unfaithfulness and adultery have occurred, both sides of the story are prefaced by the disclaimer, "I don't know how it came to this. It just happened." Except in rare cases, good marriages do not just happen. Good marriages endure the same distractions, disruptions and temptations which take others to the divorce court. How? Through the couple's commitment to open communication about problems, in loving honesty, as problems arise.

A marriage is strengthened when trust is maintained even in the midst of misunderstandings or disagreements. The first conflict which must be resolved is the conflict over how to resolve conflicts. The planning outlines and conversation models we offer a couple build on this simple premise: people who trust each other can work through any misunderstanding or disagreement through consistently considerate communication. We hope to equip our clients to do that. Drawing out their thoughts and feelings, we try to help them see points of agreement as well as offenses. Guiding them through the elements of civil conversation, we try to help them reason with each other more patiently.

The first step to healing, of course, is to admit and define the problems the marriage faces. Two potential conflict zones are inherent in the concept of marriage: there will be misunderstandings over how we perceive and conduct ourselves as individuals, and there will be disagreements over how we perceive and conduct ourselves as a couple. As individuals, we have idiosyncrasies which we cling to as essential to personal identity. Personality, sexuality, self-image and other elements of our innermost selves are so deeply ingrained that we consider them non-negotiable. In marriage, the walls come down, and as we see things in each other which we do not understand, we learn to accept as much in our spouses as we are unwilling to change in ourselves. As a couple, we make decisions which affect both of us. If we disagree over how to manage finances or how to rear children, there will be frequent risks that discussion might turn into argument. Relationships with friends and family can create divisive tension if they are not adjusted to our oneness as a couple. A marriage in which there are divisions over careers, purchases, discipline, recreation and "his friends" and "her friends" is not on the road to two becoming one.

The basic issues which divide couples are the issues which could unite them if handled well. Spouses can be individuals without being selfishly individualistic. Giving each other legitimate respect as distinct personalities is at the heart of all human relationships. How can each spouse retain a comfort zone of individual identity? A word included in traditional wedding vows is seldom used anywhere else: what does it mean to cherish a person? A rather wistful old song said that it is a word used to describe "all the feelings that I have here inside." A dictionary definition gets more practical, and includes such ideas as affection, nurture, thoughtfulness and determined commitment to preserve and protect. A work of art is cherished by someone who appreciates its exquisite uniqueness and takes care to keep it in a place of honor and security. If we cherish our spouses, we will do the same for them.

Our attitude should be: "The exquisite uniqueness of this person who has chosen to share my life is a treasure God has entrusted to me; for the rest of my life, I will devote myself to maintaining the honor and security of this fascinating human being." Spouses who cherish each other will know how to cherish their children in the same way. A father grieving the death of his daughter told a pastor, "God gave us a treasure, and we didn't break her." Cherishing our spouses and our children means not breaking the treasures God has given us, but preserving and nurturing them.

Couples who seek to understand, protect and nourish each other will have fewer serious disagreements and will be able to resolve them more civilly than couples who do not have such deep mutual trust. As they seek to be of one mind, they will adjust to each other's interests and abilities. Wise husbands and wives do not argue about every difference of opinion. They weigh decisions in favor of the spouse who has the best knowledge of an issue or the strongest feelings about it. The submission of the wife to the husband prescribed in Ephesians 5:22 is not blind obedience to a self-willed tyrant, but a voluntary trusting rest in allowing the husband to bear responsibility for the outcome of a difficult decision. When the wisdom of a course of action is unclear and a couple cannot reach perfect agreement, the husband accepts the weight of any negative consequences. The wife's trust is "as unto the Lord," as unto one who cherishes her and seeks to protect and nurture her

There will always be room to grow in understanding of our spouses and there will always be a residue of disagreement over some issues. The average marriage has about seven to ten issues that put uncomfortable wrinkles into the relationship and need to be ironed out. Troubled marriages may have fifteen issues to bring to the ironing board. These are not randomly selected numbers, but the actual number of issues couples can list when asked to do so. The lists are short and simple; paring them down is hard work[176].

People do not argue about everything. They fight about the same things over and over again. If a seemingly new issue comes up, it is quickly identified as a variant of one already in the script for marital debates. Obscure old offenses and milestones of ineptness are dragged to the surface and the disagreement turns into mutual character assassination. If the couple can agree on anything, it is the wearying redundancy of their inability to agree. Some have said that insanity is doing the same thing over and over and expecting different results. This could well describe how some couples handle their disagreements. Their attempts to discuss problems follow familiar lines as logic deteriorates and animosity escalates. Finally, one of them says bitterly, "All right, have it your way!" This rewards the spouse who has been most obnoxious, stubborn, insensitive and verbally abusive. Not a formula for a good marriage.

Unhealthy communication patterns and underdeveloped problem-solving skills are not the worst insanity. Communication patterns can be changed and problem-solving skills can be learned. Real insanity is the willful breaking of God's commandments. When God says to do something or not to do something else and we refuse, that is really insane. God created us, and He created the institution of marriage. What He says about us and about marriage tells us what works and what does not work. God told us to have unity in marriage, and not to do so is disobedience. If there is any truth in the idea that opposites attract, differences which seemed

---

[176] The average couple has 312 fights per year (Internet, Newslite, 1:00 p.m., January 25, 2011). The good news for counselors is that people don't fight about everything, they fight about the same things over and over again. Most couples fight about less than seven issues, very seldom over fifteen issues are

involved in arguments.

romantically attractive during courtship too often become ugly charges and countercharges in divorce court. For believers, unity is a prime directive for any relationship, and most emphatically overrules petty selfishness. Choosing to nurture and preserve the unity God mandates for marriage, a couple will choose healthy communication patterns and work to develop good problem-solving skills.

Counselors can help couples make the transition from endless nit-picking and bickering to productive decision-making. We are neither wonder-working magicians nor indispensable gurus. Myriads of self-help books have confused people about the fact that they need to help themselves. Idolizing an author, speaker or counselor who seems to be less confused than they are has led many sheep to the slaughter — getting all starry-eyed over a quick fix or a guaranteed formula for success, their vision clouds over and they do not see where they are really going, and neglect their own simple responsibilities for the sake of somebody else's grand plan. Clients who expect us to perform miracles will be disillusioned soon enough. Those who depend on us to work out all the answers will be disappointed. Our task is to help them accept responsibility for their own marriage and to help equip them to fulfill their God-given responsibility joyfully and successfully.

While some people will sheepishly follow anyone with a plan, others will resist guidance and cling to their dysfunctional habits. A piano teacher once had a difficult time with a student who wanted to do things his own way rather than conforming to accepted musical conventions. After the aspiring virtuoso had charged through an exercise, clumsily man-handling the rhythm, she tried to correct him: "Those were supposed to be quarter notes." The young genius said quite matter-of-factly, "Well, that's how I play quarter notes." An unaccompanied soloist can play notes quite freely, although at some risk of offending more knowledgeable hearers. The duet of marriage requires playing the song in tune with each other, giving each note its true value. The musical metaphor has at least one more lesson: except in discordant experimental music, it is customary for those who want to make beautiful music together to make sure they are on the same page.

Back in the counseling office, our task as guest conductors is to help couples find a way to be on the same page in their relationship, and go on from there to live together according to God's plan. God's high standard for marriage must be lived out as written, with each element given its true value. When people know what God says a marriage can and should be, it is the height of presumption to go in another direction and say, "Well, that's how I do marriage."

The brave people who seek Christian marriage counseling may feel as trodden down as a bruised reed or as burned out as smoking flax, but they can find victory in conforming to God's purposes (Matthew 12:20). There is no gimmickry in Christian marriage counseling. Christ-like character lived out in Christ-like behavior brings power, love, and a sound mind into all relationships. For believers, recognizing our position in Christ and being led by the Holy Spirit make it possible to fulfill the high standards the Bible establishes for every aspect of life—including marriage.

For any marriage, substantial healing comes when both spouses set aside selfish posturing and realistically face their responsibilities together. Various mental therapies have been called "talking cures" because much of their purported value lies in getting clients to talk about themselves in ways which lead to enlightenment and healing. Much of the talking is one-on-one in the therapist's office. Marriage counseling directed towards reconciliation focuses on couples, rather than isolated individuals; the goal goes beyond restoring one wounded person at a time. A husband and wife come to counseling as two personalities having difficulty maintaining the one-flesh one-mind relationship that God prescribes for married couples. In most cases, there has been abundant talking about their problems, but almost all of it has been counterproductive, if not downright vicious. They are not going to be helped by further venting to a counselor: they need guidance and practice in effective communication — not a talking cure, but a cure of their way of talking to each other.

Getting Acquainted

If marriage is thought of as a journey, marriage counselors are trip planners, driving instructors, mechanics, paramedics and police officers. To help people on their way, we need to know where they are, where they are headed, what resources and skills they need, and what hindrances and misconceptions need to be dealt with. We need to listen and observe very carefully to avoid making premature judgments or giving poorly timed advice. When people recognize the appropriateness of wise counsel, "a word spoken in due season" can work wonders; unwelcome advice stirs anger and resentment. An old pastor called his counseling ministry the "come let us reason together department," and saved his preaching for the pulpit. We need to get acquainted with clients well enough to know what makes them tick as well as what ticks them off.

The counseling process necessitates a structured professional relationship which may be uncomfortable for most clients. Counselors are trained to be attentive and purposeful in conversation, and may gain insights into a couple's situation before either spouse is ready to accept advice from a relative stranger. Therefore, it is essential to build trust as soon as possible. Establishing trust proceeds on two levels: as a professional, the counselor's expertise, objectivity and ethics must be above reproach; as a person, the counselor's compassion and good will must be apparent from the start. Beginning well on both levels is crucial to ultimate success. As in any human relationship, early impressions set the tone.

When doing premarital counseling, I find it helpful to take the couple out for lunch so that we can get acquainted in a familiar social context. I observe their patterns of relating to each other and their general social skills. I am particularly interested in whether the young man is courteous and respectful to his chosen bride. I watch to see whether he opens doors for her while getting into and out of the car, and at the restaurant. Will he seat her where she can enjoy the view and has a clear sight of activities? Does he sit where he can see only her and the wall behind her? Does he stand until she is seated? Does he help adjust her chair? When she speaks, does he stop eating, put his utensil down, and make eye contact with her? Does he or she have any unsavory habits that need to be addressed? Do they laugh too much or too loudly, pick their teeth or blow their noses at the table, or have other irritating mannerisms? Do they feed with greediness, lean on the table, eat too much in a bite, talk with food in the mouth, or soak their bread in their soup? Do they show a cheerful countenance and follow generally accepted rules of etiquette? Do they use reproachful language when speaking about someone or speak injurious words in jest or in earnest? Is their conversation tedious, trite, and meaningless? In a culture where "anything goes," common good manners may be quite uncommon, but they are never outdated. Going out for lunch lets me see the couple interacting in part of their natural habitat.

After sharing a meal with premarital counselees, I tell then what I have observed and begin working with them to map out how to go forward from where they are. Of course, there will be more thorough analytical assessment, but basic table manners afford a comparatively non-threatening place to start. A meal in a restaurant, simple as it may seem, can give indications of the quality of a relationship. Whatever the cultural norms may be, a couple who cannot share a meal politely is ill-equipped to share a life. Shared meals will be at the heart of their relationship throughout their marriage, and they had best learn to make the sharing as nourishing as the meals. I sometimes go so far as to give couples copies of etiquette guidelines, such as George Washington's *Rules of Civility*, or something more recent. I believe it is integral to the counseling process to coach them towards civility. I insist on polite interaction during counseling sessions and assign exercises which can help couples converse more constructively at home.

Mealtimes often give a true measure of relationships. As a fast-food commercial put it, "You gotta eat!" Eating together provides opportunities for talking to each other about everything from the weather to deep convictions and emotions. Friendship is a lifelong conversation, and mealtimes are primary occasions for people to come together long enough to converse. Sociologists tell us that shared meals are crucial to a family's sense of togetherness and direction. The traditional Sunday dinner after church has strengthened the bonds within Christian families for generations. Anthropologists tell us that sharing ritual meals has been a vital means of tribal and religious bonding in almost all cultures. Holidays, reunions, and all sorts of special occasions are celebrated with shared meals. Bible scholars point out that the peace offering described in Leviticus 7 included a shared ritual meal symbolizing fellowship with God and with one another, and suggestive of when Israel's leaders "saw God and did eat and drink" on Mount Sinai (Genesis 24:11). The apostle Paul reminds us that the Lord's Supper is a shared ritual meal which must be partaken of worthily, recognizing union with the Lord and His Body.

Meals are necessary for physical survival; good manners are essential to the survival of civilized social interaction. At the highest levels of society and business, civility and courtesy are the keys to acceptance and success. The son of England's Lord Foot told me of a lesson he learned about the importance of good manners, and the graciousness of well-mannered people. When he was eight years old, his father was the Governor of Jamaica and Governor General of the United Nations, and the Queen came for dinner. For two weeks before she came, little Oliver and his brother were given daily eight-hour lessons in protocol, by Princess Dianna's father. One rule was heavily stressed: you must eat everything you put on your plate. On the great occasion, the eight-year-old sat there in his white linen suit with his white formal napkin, and there on his fine china plate on the white tablecloth, he put too much roast beef. He put the napkin on his lap, slipped the roast beef into the napkin, wrapped it up, and stuffed it into his pocket. Later, when the children were being excused from the table, he heard someone call, "Oliver, come here." It was the Queen. He took two steps towards her, bowed quite correctly, and said, "Yes, Your Majesty." She said, "No, I mean right here." When he walked up to her, she leaned over and said quietly, "I saw what you did. That will be our little secret. Now you run out and play." The incident left a lifelong impression.

Lord Foot's son went on to relate the experience of an oil company vice president. This man was the up-and-coming young executive in his company — everyone knew he would one day be president. He went to Scotland with the company's president to close a multi-million dollar deal. While there, they were invited to have dinner with the Queen. This was a great honor, but the young man did not rise to the occasion. At the dinner, his manners were so atrocious that the company president decided to fire him. This was not a power lunch where power ties and power haircuts might carry weight: the presence of royalty requires highly developed social graces. The president knew that a man who would embarrass him in front of the Queen lacked the poise and finesse needed to negotiate with the real power brokers of the business world.[177]

Good manners are not just for the Queen and the CEO. Couples who treat each other like royalty possess the civility and courtesy to negotiate even their sharpest differences. Most couples have had at least minimal experience with "company manners," the elevated level of politeness extended to very important persons. In fact, most couples at one time treated each other as very important persons. Dating is usually a time for making a good first impression, putting your best foot forward, and being on your best behavior. Even the most uncouth know how to flatter to get what they want. As counselors, we need to refresh our clients' memories regarding basic human politeness and simple social graces. We need to insist that everything said or done in the counseling process is said or done decently and in order. We need to make sure that young couples know good manners, and that all of the people with whom we work treat each other with dignity and respect. Effective counseling and successful marriages require a certain degree of civility.

When I take a couple to lunch, I am not gathering ammunition for an etiquette lesson or taking pride in my own urbane manners. While it is true that courtesy is most clearly expressed in refined behavior, cultural, regional and local

---

[177] A top corporate lawyer with a paint company took a team to Japan to negotiate a deal. The Japanese executives communicated through an interpreter throughout several days of talks. When it came time to close the deal, the Japanese revealed that they all spoke English fluently, and had heard and understood all the discourteous comments the Americans had exchanged among themselves. The deal fell through.

customs vary. A couple can be quite mannerly without knowing which fork to use for a bucket of chicken wings.[178] I do look for generally accepted social graces, but the point is not to be judgmental. What I really want to see is whether the couple interacts with respect and dignity. Some couples take each other for granted so inconsiderately that it is quite evident that their familiarity has, indeed, bred contempt. If a young man is more polite to a waitress than he is to his bride-to-be, he is headed in a dangerous direction. I want to see how the couple behaves in public — how they interact privately is usually less courteous.

Of course, the couple is also observing my behavior. My own manners and mannerisms give them an idea of who I am and how I will conduct myself in counseling sessions. The restaurant provides a neutral setting for getting acquainted, and they can focus on their impressions of me as a person while sharing the common human experience of eating together. Stepping into a counselor's office intimidates people who are reluctant to have a third party evaluate their relationship. People who would be uncomfortable or defensive on the counselor's turf are more at ease in more familiar surroundings. Especially in our initial contact, I want my clients to be themselves, and I want them to feel comfortable interacting with me.

Good table manners only begin to make comfortable interaction possible. My own contributions to mealtime conversation establish communication patterns, which are fundamental to both the procedure and the product of my ministry. Polite conversation is simply considerate conversation, conversation free of sarcasm, rudeness and crudeness. The most effective tool I can give anyone is the capacity for considerate conversation about even the most volatile or delicate issues. When I take a couple out for lunch, I hope to model the upbeat and constructive conversational style which characterizes

---

[178] None. I try to choose places where the meals are served on real plates, with silverware.

effective communication. Whether in my counseling office or in their homes, I want couples to learn the pleasure and productiveness of courteous conversation.

Analyzing table manners and conversational patterns is not manipulative — it is the essence of being a civilized human being. Many perceived offenses are unintentional. "I didn't know you felt that way," "I didn't mean it," and "Why didn't you say so?" are semi-apologetic admissions that carelessness, rather than malice, creates most problems in relationships. "I wasn't thinking" is a truthful, yet unacceptable explanation for foolish behavior and speech. A truly courteous person thinks through the consequences of speech and behavior, and avoids unnecessary offense.

Professional ethics dictate that the objectivity of the counseling relationship must not be compromised by any other relationships between counselors and clients. Informal meetings with clients, such as get-acquainted meals, are not counseling sessions, but they are purposeful. My aim is not to get people to like me or to disarm them by "shooting the breeze" about anything and everything. Sharing a meal and a conversation sets patterns for productive interaction. Getting acquainted with their counselor in a neutral setting establishes ground rules for courtesy and communication, and lays a rudimentary foundation for trust. Paying attention to good manners diminishes counterproductive behavior. Paying attention to considerate conversation diminishes counterproductive speech. Since bad behavior and rude speech are at the heart of most marriage problems, this is a logical place to begin the counseling process.

Setting the Course

From the start, every aspect of the counseling situation should be designed to facilitate accurate observation and effective interaction. A relatively small counseling room with several comfortable chairs gives clients options as soon as they walk in. I take note of where they sit, how they sit, and their general demeanor. They might move chairs closer together or further apart, or to face more towards or away from each other or the counselor. Various conversation pieces kept in the office may evoke meaningful reactions. I do not exaggerate the importance of every tiny detail, but I do take note of clues to the couple's attitudes.

As in premarital counseling, the initial goal with already-married couples who come for counsel is to get acquainted as naturally and as positively as possible. Even in the midst of their considerable distress, I want to pick up on whatever optimism is left in their marriage. Their frustration with each other may have been fueled by the pessimism and bad advice they heard from people around them. I do not want to guess at what they think or feel; I want to let them speak for themselves. Tears, for example, may express relief at finally getting help rather than sadness, shame, or fear. I ask short questions, and am pleased when they give long answers.

Christian marriage counselors are most decidedly directive in approach, but we must avoid saying things which might send people in the wrong direction. I have heard counselors make potentially destructive comments:

"You'll never make it!" Joanne and I were told that several times in our first decade of marriage, but God has been miraculously gracious in preserving our marriage—at times simply through my stubborn determination to prove the pessimists wrong.

"Studies show that people like you will not stay married." Nobody is exactly like these two people; the studies were done with other people, at other places, at other times—not in this room at this minute with this couple and this counselor.

"You should never have gotten married!" Well, they did, and as in all Christian ministries, the past should never hinder our reaching for God's best for the future. God is, if point of fact, more sovereign than our choices.

"You have nothing in common." What about the shared life, the common interests and mutual attraction of their first days together, their shared experiences, shared friends and family, and their children? And they were in fact married on the same day!

"You have absolutely no reason to stay together." They have their marriage covenant, the command and promise of God, and His warning against separating what He has joined together.

"Neither of you is marriage material." That one would take us beyond zero population growth to zero population. Absolutely nobody is marriage material if that means being mature enough and selfless enough to bring only unmitigated good to the marriage — "I found the perfect woman, but she was looking for the perfect man." Every marriage is flawed by the imperfections and sins of both spouses. In successful marriages, God uses spouses to help each other grow as each of them unpacks emotional baggage and tosses out egotistical illusions.[179]

In the first session with a troubled married couple, I let them tell me about their marriage, rather than whipping out a handy-dandy list of solutions for their handy-not-so-dandy list of problems. I begin by asking each of them to speak for a few minutes about their goals for counseling. Couples have many motivations for coming to counseling. Some approach it as a perfunctory step to justify putting an end to their marriage

---

[179] Luke 17:32 warns us to "remember Lot's wife" as an example of fatal attachment to material comfort. We should also remember Job's wife, whose trust in God collapsed under the pressure of material discomfort. A relationship with God and with each other should not depend on the perks. Job himself became an example for the rest of recorded history of a godly response to adversity.

("Tried counseling. It didn't work."). They see their marriage as terminally ill and want it put out of its misery, painlessly euthanized by a pastor or other authority figure. They may see it as already dead, and want it to have a decent funeral. Others still have some hope but no clue as to how to go about fixing their marriage. Some people come out of respect for the wishes of their mate, a pastor, or a friend, or because they feel that God wants them to. Some come only to continue the wife- or husband-bashing they have been doing at home. Whatever their reasons, I find it valuable to hear from their own mouths what they expect from counseling.

What couples expect from counseling is sometimes something they could have done for themselves if they had been able to calm down and think through their situation. Many counseling theories tell us that clients have all the resources for change within themselves. Anyone who has been involved in marriage counseling for many years knows that people need significant direction in using their resources. Letting couples talk about themselves provides initial clues concerning their ability to define their problems and concerning their willingness to make the necessary effort to resolve them. Frankly, if a couple's expectations are totally unrealistic and their commitment is superficial or nonexistent, counseling might be an exercise in futility, wasting the counselor's time and the couple's money. If they recognize their need to accept help in defining issues, assessing resources and planning improvement, the counselor can proceed wholeheartedly.

At the end of the first thirty minutes of the first session, I ask each spouse to tell how they met and what attracted them to each other. This does not miraculously rekindle their first love, but it does let them say and hear some good things about each other and their relationship. It also gives me insight into where they have been and how far they are from where they started. How long and how enthusiastically they talk about their meeting can be very revealing. Information they provide can help measure the strength of their relationship. Meeting in a cheap singles bar is not the same as having been childhood sweethearts whose families sat next to each other in church.

After discussing the couple's meeting, I interview each of them alone. This ensures a safe environment for revealing issues of physical or sexual abuse of either the spouse or of the children, or any potentially explosive conflicts. Such secrets are not held long when they can be released safely. If there is abuse, the abusive spouse can be brought in and confronted; if abuse continues (pushing, hitting, or otherwise causing physical endangerment), I report it to the police or make a citizen's arrest. In cases of child abuse, police must be called immediately, and they should arrest the offender right in the office. This is sterner stuff than our hearts and our ministry of reconciliation might prescribe, but the epidemic of abuse requires strong medicine.[180] Most marriage problems do not require immediate legal action. In fact, couples who come for counseling usually have enough stability to want to resolve their problems as amicably as possible. They have enough hope to think that counseling might help.

To help save and strengthen a couple's marriage, we need to know how they perceive their problems. In mathematics, there is a truism that "redundant equations have extraneous roots." Roughly translated for counseling purposes, it means that if problems are not presented clearly and accurately,

---

[180] Satan loves to exploit physical abuse. One man told me, "All I did was shove her." That was true, technically. That was all he did. But when he shoved his wife, she tripped over some carpeting, hit her head on a coffee table, and went into a coma. She had been in the coma for nine months when I visited her husband in jail.

answers will be meaningless. We need to work hard to get each couple to agree on basic descriptions of their problems, encouraging them to avoid packing repetitious accusations into circular arguments which somehow keep taking them down the same dead end street. To move forward, the couple needs clear, accurate consensus concerning what is wrong and a determination to quit blaming each other and do what they need to do to correct their problems. No more "I have a problem with my spouse" from two voices, but a newly unified "We have problems in our marriage, but we will work together to overcome them."

What are their problems? Details will vary, but problems in relationships can often be placed in one of three familiar categories:

œ Misunderstandings, which can be minimized through more open communication.

œ Disagreements, which can be ameliorated through objective negotiation.

œ Distrust, which can be remedied only through persistent, consistent rebuilding of trust over time.

If I do not understand a person, I can work to be better informed about his or her needs, interests and motives. If I do not agree with a person, I can negotiate a truce, conceding what matters most to him or her, being granted what matters most to me, and respecting the remaining differences. If I do not trust a person, I need time to be convinced that he or she is trustworthy. I can live with a person I do not understand completely, and I can live with a person with whom I do not agree in every detail. I do not like to be around anybody I do not trust. Misunderstandings and disagreements can be dealt with or lived with by people who trust each other; where trust has been broken, the warm give-and-take of the relationship is displaced by cold demands and refusals. This is a defining characteristic of unfaithfulness.

The "he always"/"she never" complaints of distressed couples bring counselors into the middle of communication breakdowns which may have descended into deep distrust. Our task includes imposing restraints on negative expressions and guiding couples towards more open, objective, and effective communication. Within counseling sessions, we must insist on truthfulness and patience and try to establish the mutual trust needed for productive discussion of misunderstandings and disagreements. We can outline procedures which couples can use at home to resolve current differences and to deal with issues that may arise in the future.

In marriage, trust is grounded in the original covenant. The words "pledge thee my troth" have disappeared from many wedding rites, and long ago became too archaic for many couples to understand. A "pledge" was a guarantee of truthfulness, often including transfer of a physical object symbolizing commitment to keep a promise. "Troth" is loyalty, faithfulness, trust, trustworthiness, truthfulness and commitment. Biblical marriage brings together a man and a woman who totally entrust themselves to each other. Couples who share this ideal know that misunderstandings and disagreements which threaten to divide them should be occasions for seeking constructive, creative, and ultimately unifying solutions, based on their mutual trust.

Trust is broken through being inconsiderate or inconsistent. Concern for a spouse includes being considerate of his or her interests, limitations and idiosyncrasies. Confidence in a spouse includes knowing that he or she will be consistent in affection and responsibility. A considerate spouse will apologize for offenses and try to be more pleasant and helpful. A consistent spouse will be loving and reliable at all times, no matter what difficulties arise. These are defining characteristics of faithfulness, the considerate consistency which builds or rebuilds marriages.

Christian counselors must let couples know that our counseling goals and methods are based upon a biblical view of marriage, and that our intention is to help them conform to that standard. If they accept a lower view of marriage, they may resist our attempts to guide them. They may even consider divorce a less rigorous option than the hard work of rebuilding their marriage. Our minimal expectation must be that they will at least trust each other and us to be truthful and patient in trying to resolve their problems. Letting clients know the foundation and goal of our counseling ministry is only fair. It eliminates misunderstandings, establishes if we are in basic agreement, and lays the groundwork for building effective trust.

Modeling and Mentoring

The heart of marriage counseling is equipping couples to work out their differences and become of one mind as they face life's challenges together. The ministry of reconciliation entrusted to the Church is carried on through the multiple "one another" responsibilities of believers — we are to lighten the load for those overwhelmed by their burdens, but ultimately each of us is responsible to live a life of faithful obedience to God (Galatians 6:1-5; I Corinthians 4:2-5). Proverbs 15:22 provides the motivation for seeking counsel: "Plans go wrong with too few counselors; many counselors bring success (Living Bible)." Christian marriage counselors are called alongside to help couples use all available resources to make better plans for their marriages, and to make their plans work. The motivation for counselors is suggested in Proverbs 20:5: "Counsel in the heart of man is like deep water; but a man of understanding will draw it out." The insights of a counselor and the deepest thoughts of clients must be brought together to make wise plans for improvement.

Godly wisdom does not always come in non-negotiable pronouncements from on high:

The wisdom that comes from heaven is first of all pure and full of quiet gentleness. Then it is peace-loving and courteous. It allows discussion and is willing to yield to others; it is full of mercy and good deeds. It is wholehearted and straightforward and sincere. And those who are peacemakers will plant seeds of peace and reap a harvest of goodness, James 3:17-18, Living Bible.

This is the kind of wisdom a Christian marriage counselor must model; couples must be mentored towards displaying this kind of wisdom in planning and problem-solving. Christ-like character and godly wisdom set the standard for Christian counseling as well as for biblical marriage.

Godly wisdom is pure, clean and reverent even when dealing with the messy, dirty details of a marriage in disarray. The Christian marriage counselor will not seek out all the sordid details, but will glean enough accurate information to have a clear picture of the problems a couple faces. There will be no obscenity or coarseness, and no tasteless trivializing of serious issues. All counseling procedures and referrals will be consistent with the high biblical view of marriage.[181]

Godly wisdom is characterized by quiet gentleness. It is not bombastic or unkind, even when dealing with rebellious, contentious people. A Christian marriage counselor must be unshockable, unshakeable and calm. Arrogant self-righteousness and angry legalism were chief sins of the Pharisees. Jesus never compromised God's righteousness, but almost always spoke tenderly even to grievous sinners. His most

---

[181] Dr. Wheat's work towards reconciling couples sexually was revolutionary on two fronts. Conservative Christians had not dealt with sexual issues so frankly, and the secular media made jokes about "fundies in their undies." On the other hand, humanistic marriage clinics were advocating and providing "sexual surrogates," male and female prostitutes who would supposedly "warm up" spouses so that they could enjoy each other more fully. Sexual purity is compromised by ill-informed secrecy and destroyed by sinful promiscuity.

forceful accusations were against those who interfered with true worship and true compassion. Gentleness is not weakness; Peter's denial of Christ was strongly rebuked by a gentle look from his Lord.

Godly wisdom is peace-loving and courteous. God's grace is not incompatible with common social graces. Peace with God brings inner peace and peaceful relationships with others, even in the midst of trials (Romans 5:1-5). The gospel is God's word of reconciliation, which is the core message of our ministry of reconciliation (II Corinthians 5:18-21). The patience of a person who is at peace with God is displayed in courtesy towards others. Social graces are simply learned behaviors, which have proven useful in preserving harmony in human relationships. Christian counselors should model gracious behavior, which couples can learn to imitate in relating to each other.

Godly wisdom allows discussion and is willing to yield. This is far from the selfish attitude which says, "Okay, I'll listen to your idiotic opinion, but don't expect me to change my mind." A major facet of the biblical concept of repentance is changing one's mind. Transformation into Christ-like character is triggered by renewal of the mind (Romans 12:2). Non-negotiable demands short-circuit profitable communication. True discussion gives a fair hearing to opposing views and seeks consensus on essential points.

Willingness to yield when faced with convincing facts is evidence of true reasonableness. Willingness to yield when faced with pain caused to another is evidence of true love.

Godly wisdom is full of mercy and good deeds. There is a subtle distinction here. Mercy acts to benefit the undeserving as well as the weak, and treats others kindly regardless of their character and actions. The focus of mercy is primarily on the needs of others. Good deeds ("good fruit", KJV) express good character — they are natural products of godly wisdom. Believers are "created in Christ Jesus unto good works (Ephesians 2:10)," and demonstrate their faith by helping others. Mercy disregards the character of those it serves; good deeds display the character of those who do them. Being considerate and helpful shows conformity to Christ.

Godly wisdom is wholehearted, straightforward and sincere. There is no deception, no manipulation, and no hypocrisy. In the early history of the Church, there was controversy over how the value of the means of grace (preaching, baptism, serving the Lord's Supper, pastoral care) was affected by the character of the person who administered them. In heart-to-heart counseling, there can be no question that the credibility of the counsel is inextricably bound to the integrity of the counselor. As I have often emphasized, it is foolishly dishonest to try to export what you do not possess. Biblical standards of integrity and openness apply to our counseling practices as well as to our personal lives.

Godly wisdom sows seeds of peace and reaps a harvest of goodness. A ministry of reconciliation heals relationships without compromising either truth or love. Speaking the truth in love brings the peace which only righteousness engenders. Being right with God makes it possible to make things really right with other people. Conversely, seeds of peace bring a harvest of goodness as peace with God frees people to act righteously toward others. Christian marriage counseling does not beat clients over the head with scathing accusations, nor does it sidestep confrontation of sin to avoid discomfort.

James describes godly wisdom as the alternative to the kind of so-called wisdom of the world:

For jealousy and selfishness are not God's kind of wisdom. Such things are earthly, unspiritual, inspired by the devil. For wherever there is jealousy or selfish ambition, there will be disorder and every kind of evil. James 3:15-16, (*Living Bible*).

He had just warned his readers about the dangers of uncontrolled tongues: "If anyone can control his tongue, it proves he has perfect control over himself (James 3:2, LB)." After expounding on the damage that poisonous speech can do, he contrasts selfish worldly wisdom with unselfish godly wisdom. He then goes on to explain that relational conflicts come from selfish individualism: "What is causing the quarrels and fights among you? Isn't it because there is a whole army of evil desires within you (James 4:1, LB)?" Worldly wisdom looks out for selfish interests at whatever cost to relationships. Godly wisdom seeks rich relationships at whatever cost to selfish interests.

It is crucial that Christian marriage counselors model godly wisdom. Speaking the truth in love requires attention to the process as well as to the content of counseling. As Paul says, "Although being a 'know-it-all' makes us feel important, what is really needed to build the church is love (I Corinthians 8:1, LB)." Godly wisdom goes beyond knowing the truth to knowing how to live the truth, and how to explain the truth with such compassion that it will be received and applied by others. If the truth itself offends a person, we must not compromise for the sake of temporary comfort—only the truth can bring lasting peace. If anything about the way we communicate the truth is offensive, we must set aside our pride and find ways to speak it more lovingly.[182]

Besides modeling godly wisdom, we must mentor couples in communication skills, which are consistent with godly wisdom. This will mean reviewing what it means to conform

to the character of Jesus Christ as well as specific training in

---

[182] A lesson I am still learning. In my early career, I was extremely dogmatic and confrontational regarding doctrinal and practical issues relating to counseling. Dr. Wheat was patient and reasonable in attempting to reconcile some of our few differences. Jay Adams and James Dobson were used by God to help me adjust my views, and to build a more balanced ministry. My treatment of those with whom I disagreed was often inexcusably inconsiderate. The years have not diminished my youthful zeal, but I hope that I have gained some knowledge about how to "speak the truth in love."

patterns of purposeful conversation. It is not enough to analyze marriage problems and prescribe solutions; we must exemplify and teach patterns of thought and speech which conform to the biblical standard of Christ-like love. The basic difference between godly wisdom and worldly wisdom is the contrast between faith and fear. The position of faith bases relationships on trust—trusting God frees us to trust each other. The position of fear bases relationships on distrust—looking out for self means distrusting others. Communication grounded in trust is upbeat, positive and productive. Communication grounded in distrust is suspicious, negative and self-protective. As James explains, problems in relationships stem from patterns of thought and speech which are characterized by fear rather than by faith. Shifting from a position of fear to a position of faith will revolutionize communication between spouses and head them towards a healthier marriage. Mentoring couples in working out the practical implications of this shift is at The heart of marriage counseling.

Communication Patterns

Counseling sessions should establish communication patterns which will help couples solve their own problems. Information about their backgrounds, resources and expectations provides a rough idea of where they have come from and where they hope to go in their marriage. Their own descriptions of the ups and downs of married life not only reveal their thoughts about their situation, but also reveal their capacity for purposeful conversation. Can they organize information so that its relevance to decision-making and problem solving is clearly evident? Are they able to prioritize approaches to specific issues, sorting out what is most significant and what steps must be taken first? Are they committed to the hard work of reaching consensus and moving forward? What they lack in these areas defines much of the counselor's task. They must learn to converse purposefully about major issues which arise in their marriage.

Paul spoke of being "all things to all men, that by all means we might win some (I Corinthians 9:22)." Our ministry of reconciliation requires flexibility, but we must realize that no matter how we adapt our approach, we will win some, not all of those who call us alongside to help. Jesus spoke very directly and personally to the woman at the well and to Nicodemus, using their curiosity about Him to lead them into the truth about themselves. The story of the prodigal son was more indirect, leaving room for personal application even among hostile hearers. Without holding back or sugar-coating unpleasant facts, we can adjust to our clients' readiness to hear and apply the truth.

When Nathan confronted David about his sin with Bathsheba, he began indirectly, telling a story about a rich man who confiscated a poor man's cherished lamb (II Samuel 12:1-25). David could relate to the story on many levels. As a shepherd, he knew the emotional attachment which grew between a shepherd and the sheep he called by name. As a man who had risen from relatively humble beginnings, he knew the hardship which might come to someone whose only treasure was stolen. As a member of an agrarian community, he would feel indignation at unfair treatment of a neighbor. His zeal for righteousness and his aversion to injustice would motivate him to use his kingly authority to set things right. As a man after God's own heart, the noblest qualities of David's character would condemn a rich man for stealing a poor man's sheep. When David had pronounced his judgment, Nathan simply had to say, "Thou art the man." David immediately felt the full weight of his sin in taking, not a poor man's lamb, but a loyal soldier's wife.

This incident has momentous implications for Christian counselors. We need to know people thoroughly before we can help them. Why do they think and act as they do? What is important to them? What values have they learned from their backgrounds? How have their families affected their approach to life? What are they passionate about? As many have said, people do not care what you know until they know you care. We must care enough about people as people to find out how they perceive themselves, their marriages, and the world. Nathan drew a heartfelt response from David because he knew what was in David's heart. The best counsel is not bits of advice dictated to a person from the outside, but positive suggestions which resonate to the core of a person's being. In seeking to pierce the armor and prick the conscience, the only reliably effective tool is the Word of God which discerns the thoughts and intents of the heart (Hebrews 4:12). As the Holy Spirit gives us discernment to apply God's truth to our clients' innermost needs, our ministry of reconciliation reaches far beyond the pragmatic patch jobs of merely human counsel.

Many couples find this depth of communication unfamiliar and uncomfortable. In the shallowness of pop culture, people rarely bring their innermost thoughts into the light, and almost never question the assumptions by which they live. The Bible's talk about renewing minds, changing minds, having the mind of Christ, and having a mind set on things above — all this is foreign to most people, even professing Christians. Yet this is the depth we have to reach to begin to understand what it might mean for a married couple to be of one mind as intimately as they are one flesh.

How do people reveal what is in their minds? Through words. Non-verbal communication can be ambiguous and misleading without some verbal explanation of intentions. We form opinions about each other by assuming that what people say reflects who they are, that conversations reveal character. We are drawn to people who make us comfortable in conversation, and we are repelled by people whose speech is caustic.

Husbands and wives are especially sensitive to the words they speak to each other. Just as dating couples hang on each other's every word (especially the three little words — "I love you"), married couples are deeply affected by what they say to each other, and how they say it. Careless, inconsiderate speech can cause lasting wounds. Kind, encouraging words bring healing.

Both actions and words can have unintended effects. It is vitally important to consider the potential benefit or harm any words or actions might generate. Within marriage, two important questions should be considered before speaking or acting: "Is what I am about to do or say going to help or hurt my mate?" "Is what I am about to do or say going to build or tear down my partner or our marriage?" In some marriages, over familiarity becomes contempt, and spouses act and speak in ways they would never think of mistreating a stranger. Thoughtless words sometimes evoke reactions which stop communication altogether.

In early counseling sessions, the counselor must model and insist upon good communication patterns. Listening attentively, responding gently, and keeping focused on the issue at hand — this is the minimal foundation of effective conversation. Taking the other person seriously means not interrupting, not monopolizing the conversation, and expressing thoughts and emotions objectively and succinctly. Understanding comes only when conversation is approached as an opportunity to solve a problem or reach an agreement, rather than a chance to win an argument or conquer the other person. Couples must understand the ground rules early in the counseling process. The counselor will offer insights and advice when appropriate and necessary, but the primary goal of counseling is for the couple to learn and practice effective communication patterns.

Each counseling session should have a distinct pattern of beginning, middle and end. Sessions should begin with a review of what is already known, including what was said in previous sessions, what plans and assignments have been made, and what the couple has done to implement what has been learned. The middle of the session should be a purposeful exchange of information, thoughts and feelings directed towards making further improvements in the marriage. At the end, the counselor should summarize the session and challenge the couple with specific things to do with the insights they have gained. Reviewing commitments, encouraging the couple with reminders of their progress thus far, and giving them homework suited to their situation, the counselor "closes the deal" on their purposeful conversation. Whether or not the clients are believers, I ask their permission to pray with them before they leave: "It is my custom to pray with everyone I work with. If that doesn't offend you, I would like to pray for you now." The prayer is short and to the point, invoking God's help, asking for wisdom for them and myself, praying that they will have a safe trip home and a growing oneness until our next session.[183]

The homework I assign always includes practice in communicating with each other. For many couples, counseling sessions are their first experience with really purposeful conversation about their marriage. Some spend so little time together that they hardly ever talk about anything that really matters to either of them. Every couple needs at least twenty minutes each day to sit down and share the day's experiences. During this "couple time" they should just relax and enjoy being together. If there are issues which must be addressed, husband and wife should discuss them at least to the point of agreeing that problems will be handled reasonably and that anger will not be allowed to grow into bitterness between them.

---

[183] I am always aware that there might not be a next session. Death has unexpectedly intervened in a number of cases. D.L. Moody's sense of the urgency of the ministry of reconciliation was powered by his regret at once telling an audience to go home and consider the claims of Christ until their next meeting—the Chicago fire claimed many of their lives that week.

I find it helpful to remind couples that just being in the same room with words coming out of their mouths is not necessarily conversation, and that conversation can take various forms. Many couples discover that misunderstandings between them are often rooted in misinterpretation of offhand remarks they have made to each other. Sarcasm, even when intended as humor, leaves cuts and scars. If one spouse speaks lightly about something which matters a great deal to the other, there will be lasting damage to their relationship. Therefore, it is always of primary importance to mentor couples toward more thoughtful communication.

Counseling sessions provide a context in which to explore patterns of communication. By example and by direct instruction, the counselor can train a couple to discuss their problems more effectively. Several simple elements of effective conversation can be modeled by the counselor and taught to the clients:

Physical proximity. Being in the same room is the minimum requirement for effective communication. Shouting from one room to another can sound like anger, and the conversation may be impeded by incomplete hearing. There is no adequate substitute for being physically close enough to communicate through vocal tone, facial expressions, and body language as well as through words.

Eye Contact. This shows that the listener is giving full and undivided attention. It affirms the speaker's value to the listener and communicates that the listener's heart is open and ready to respond. Looking into a person's right eye shows respect and focuses listening. Avoiding eye contact is associated with evasiveness and distrust.

Physical Contact. This indicates safety, encouragement, and united spirit. A touch on the shoulder communicates sincerity and understanding. I recommend that all conversations between spouses or family members begin with a touch, a squeeze, or a hug. Holding hands in prayer is a must when embarking on difficult, delicate topics of conversation.

The counseling room should be set up so that the counselor can observe how well the couple is doing in these areas, and gently introduce improvements.

The art of clear conversation is a vital ingredient in any relationship. It is important to hear and be heard effectively. Effective conversation is a skill to be learned and practiced. To begin with, the various types of conversation must be recognized:[184]

Casual Greeting. The most rudimentary verbal exchange, communicating almost nothing of real substance. Courtesy and civility require at least some form of acknowledging the presence of another person, even a total stranger, who comes within a socially determined distance. Simple greetings, generic comments or questions about the weather or other neutral topics — this level of conversation consists in the small talk of people who are brought near each other briefly.

Informal Chat. Simple information passing and gathering, usually on a nuts-and-bolts level. Co-workers conversing on breaks, "bread-and-butter" phone calls to friends and relatives — this level of conversation expresses comfort in the presence of familiar people, but is not charged with emotion or directed to specific goals.

Power Talk. Forceful communication of commands. Demanding, controlling through choice of words, content and non-verbal cues. There may be threatening eye contact or withholding of eye contact. This level of conversation is really not an exchange, but a one-sided listing of non-negotiable demands. The legitimate use of this type of communication is in necessary

---

[184] Much of my approach to communication skills is described in my book *How to Get There from Here: Effective Communication Using the Conversation Map.* The Conversation Map exercises guide couples through a problem-solving procedure, taking couples from issue stage through resolution, based on research into the techniques of highly successful communicators.

use of authority to motivate or correct subordinates. The image which comes to mind is of a military commander or a no-nonsense boss.

Communication of Intention. A straightforward delivery of thoughts, feelings, and plans. Among friends, this type of conversation may include mutual counsel and encouragement. At this level, the degree of self-revelation indicates willingness to confide in people who can be trusted.

Serious Talk. The deepest level of communication, with full disclosure and full commitment to resolve issues. Problem solving, exploring the depths of a relationship, making commitments — the focus is on personal connectedness. This type of conversation is vital to a healthy marriage.

Couples should be alert to the different types of conversation in order to be sure they are working at the same level when they talk with each other.

Many communication breakdowns occur when couples come into conversations at mismatched levels. A "Hi, how are you doing?" spoken as a casual greeting does not resonate well with the serious response, "The doctor says it's malignant." If there is a reason for postponing a serious talk, it should be given, and the couple should agree to talk later. Couples should enjoy regular informal chats, letting each other know the little events of each day — too many people underrate the value of "small talk" as the glue that holds relationships together. An executive who is accustomed to giving power talks at work may have a hard time adapting his or her style to the give-and-take of conversations at home. Scheduling couple time and family conferences does not impose an artificial structure on relationships; it is a necessary measure to ensure that participants are prepared for the appropriate level of conversation.

Communication patterns during counseling sessions should be monitored closely, and clients should be encouraged to use the elements and types of conversation wisely. At all times, the counselor must fulfill his or her responsibility as an effective communicator, keeping the couple as comfortable as possible while digging up and examining the roots of their problems. Coaching the couple through guided conversation with tools such as the Conversation Map gives them experience in analyzing and controlling their communication patterns. The effects of what they say to each other are heavily dependent on how they say it. Similarly, the quality of conversations during counseling sessions is measured in terms of the process as well as the content of communication.

From Here to There

Marriage problems have many causes and multiple complications. When God's standards have been rejected or neglected, it is no wonder that so many marriages quickly self-destruct. When husbands and wives seek their own individual comfort rather than developing Christ-like unselfishness, it is no . wonder that so many go their separate ways so soon after their weddings. When couples do not discuss and plan their lives together, it is no wonder that their marriages fall apart. Without planning, hard work and God's blessing the wonder is that some marriages last as long as they do.

When a couple comes for counseling, they know that something is wrong with their marriage, but do not know where to begin to fix it. If they have tried to define the problem, they have separate definitions and thus no hope for agreeing on a remedy. Many couples have already had so many fruitless arguments that communication between them has completely broken down. They often blame each other, and even in the counseling office some are barely able to tone down the accusations and name-calling they spew at each other at home. I make it clear that such disrespect will not be tolerated in counseling sessions, and that I am not there to take sides with one spouse or the other but to help find a way to be reconciled to each other, and to God.

"Can two walk together, except they be agreed (Amos 3:3)?" The oneness God prescribes for marriage is the most comprehensive level of agreement between two human beings. The free exchange of thoughts and emotions within marriage brings out numerous differences of opinion which could escalate into harmful conflict. To defuse these time bombs, couples need communication skills which enable them to iron out their differences without burning each other. Their covenant commitment to walk together for the rest of their lives demands a commitment to reach agreement on basic life issues as completely and as considerately as possible.

Being considerate of one another makes more complete agreement possible. Shouting matches have no winners — the volume of one's voice is inversely proportional to the credibility of what is said. Verbal posturing, emotional venting and personal attacks are counterproductive. Current issues should not be encumbered with residue from past arguments. Sticking to the point is essential. Listening, questioning, pausing thoughtfully — effective communication includes respectful silence as well as courteous conversation. Without considerate civility, talking about serious concerns deteriorates into destructive blame-shifting.

For Christians, the real issue in any life or marriage is the question, "What do we do to get where God wants us to be?" All of us can say with Paul, "I haven't learned all I should even yet, but I keep working toward the day when I will finally be all that Christ saved me for and wants me to be (Philippians 3:12, Living Bible)." The counseling process revolves around the question of conformity to the character of Christ and obedience to the revealed will of God. To use the imagery of James 1:21-25, the biblical marriage manifesto is the mirror we place before a couple to see how well their marriage reflects God's ideal. The object is not to discourage them, but to stir their hearts to do what God enables them to do to bring His blessing into their marriage. Hebrews 10:24 tells believers to "provoke" one another to love and good works.[185]

Knowing what to do to get from where a couple is to where God wants them to be requires wise counsel and purposeful conversation. Everything the Bible says about marriage shows them where God wants them to be. Everything which comes to light through the assessment process pinpoints where they are. The differences are sometimes overwhelming: it may even seem that there is a great gulf fixed between their morass of problems and the mountaintop of God's blessing. Getting to the place of blessing together requires finding and taking necessary steps in the right direction. Setting the biblical marriage manifesto before them as the goal displaces the inadequate selfish goals which divided them. There is, in fact, a great gulf between holy matrimony which unites a couple in obedient faith and unholy matrimony in which spouses selfishly do what is right in their own eyes.

Having chosen to move themselves and their marriage in the direction of God's ideal, a couple will need to correct communication patterns which have contributed to their distress. Initially, the counselor's role in conversing with a couple will be to direct them towards more profitable communication patterns. Before directly training them in specific conversational skills and procedures, the counselor may interrupt their comments for any of four reasons:

Clarification — polite interruption to ask simple questions, making sure that what has been said is understood as intended.

Checking flow — making sure that feelings are under control and keeping the conversation on target.

---

[185] This can be painful. The word translated "provoke" in Hebrews 10:24 also describes the sharp contention between Paul and Barnabas in Acts 15:39.

Regrouping thoughts — pausing to give the speaker and listener time to think through what has been said.

Prayer — conversations dealing with serious issues should begin and end in prayer, and prayer can be called for at any time it seems necessary.

The counselor may interrupt more frequently in early sessions as the couple gets used to the ground rules.[186] Pausing to think before speaking is the one thing lacking in almost every marital dispute.

Moving on to more direct instruction, conversations can be pared down to their most useful and least inflammatory elements. Some years ago I asked some of my graduate students to find out what makes great communicators great communicators. We worked from a list of business, political and religious leaders who were well known for effective communication. The results of this research suggested that these were people who did not waste words or unnecessarily offend their hearers. Gleaning lessons from their success, we made up a short list of specific skills which almost anyone can learn. My Conversation Map exercise is the result — an arrangement of effective communication skills designed to facilitate conflict resolution.

Basically, effective communication says what needs to be said without going off on tangents or becoming bombastic. Troubled married couples need to learn how to have serious talks. Conflict resolution requires more purposeful input than casual greetings or informal chats, and more interaction than power talks or simple communication of intention. The necessary elements of a serious talk fall into a logical pattern which most likely is quite different from how distressed people converse. Reminding couples of the characteristics of courteous

---

[186] These four "stop signs" are integral to the success of the Conversation Map I use to guide couples in developing productive communication patterns.

speech and training them in healthy communication patterns is essential to my counseling ministry.

Structured conversations make the best use of the skills learned from good communicators. Self-control in expressing concerns clearly and without unnecessary offense requires thinking before speaking. Learning to remain calm and reasonable even when discussing highly sensitive issues can save a marriage. Truly two-way communication requires active and considerate listening skills. Learning to be receptive and responsive even when confronted with troubling information can keep a conversation from becoming a heated argument. Besides modeling these skills, the counselor can give couples a context for learning and using them. Counseling sessions can become coaching sessions during which the counselor guides the couple as they converse with each other about their marriage. Mentoring people to be considerate speakers and listeners is among the counselor's most valuable ministries.

On the speaker's side, presentation of an issue should follow a logical pattern for opening discussion:

Positive Affirmation—a personal word to the listener, affirming his or her worth, mentioning several positive things about him or her. This reminds both the speaker and the listener that however difficult the issue is, their relationship is highly valued.

Topic of Concern—one positive sentence which states the issue succinctly. It should be clear that the speaker has every hope that the two of them will work out a solution which will satisfy both of them.

My Contribution—thoughts, feelings, observations and interpretations regarding the issue, including acceptance of responsibility for my part in solving the problem.

My Hope—positive statements about hope for the resolution of the issue and the benefits to self, listener, and their relationship.

Strict adherence to this pattern eliminates everything extraneous or offensive. The issue stands out clearly as the topic of conversation, and the good will and good intentions of both speaker and hearer are brought to the fore.

On the listener's side, effective communication skills displace inattentive impatience:

Active Listening—giving the speaker serious regard. Eye contact, physical touch, and careful thought. Seeking to understand what is being said is more productive than thinking about how to rebut it.

Careful Reflection—checking for alignment, restating what the speaker says to be sure it has been understood. Regardless of emotions, trying to form an accurate concept of the speaker's perception of the issue.

Tender Questions—asking open-ended questions to draw out more information which can be useful in solving the problem as presented.

Sweet Responses—giving words of pleasant affirmation. The listener returns the speaker's affirmation of their importance to each other, and expresses appreciation that the issue will be addressed in a way which will improve their relationship.

Following this pattern carefully will open up the conversation, as both the speaker and the listener commit themselves to sober, non-threatening consideration of the issue.

During counseling sessions, couples can be mentored in communication patterns which make good use of these skills. The counselor can guide a conversation by calling for specific types of expression: "Give her a positive affirmation." "Ask him a tender question about what he just said." Perhaps more importantly, at least at the beginning, the counselor can point out comments and questions which are not positive and productive. As a couple learns to confine conversation to types of communication in this short list, emotions will be reined in, and constructive discussion can begin. Thinking before speaking is a learned skill, and self-control while speaking does not come easy, as James 3 tells us.

Providing a structure for a serious talk puts effective communication into a pattern which facilitates problem solving. I devised the Conversation Map to graphically remind couples to follow the rules of purposeful conversation. Besides limiting comments to the list of positive elements of conversation, the map exercise makes speaker and listener take turns according to a logical structure which leads to the highest consensus possible. The steps toward conflict resolution are depicted as stepping stones on a mat placed between the speaker and the listener as they sit facing each other, close enough for a couple to hold hands throughout the conversation. Stop sign symbols at the corners of the mat represent the four legitimate reasons for interruptions. As the conversation progresses, the speaker and listener each put one foot on the stepping stone which signifies the type of communication called for at various stages. Either one may step on a stop sign for an appropriate reason. The speaker's role is taken by the person who introduces an issue of concern; the listener participates as a learner, seeking to understand the speaker's thoughts and feelings.

With or without a physical map, purposeful conversation becomes easier as it is conducted according to the logical structure of effective communication. These steps should be followed carefully:

Prayer — seated facing each other, holding hands, the speaker leads, or both may pray in turn. Prayer should be for the success of the process and the oneness of the relationship.

Positive Affirmation and Active Listening — the speaker assures the listener of his or her appreciation and good will in introducing the issue; the listener receives the message attentively.

Topic of Concern — the speaker states the issue in one clear sentence which suggests optimism that the conversation will have a positive outcome.

My Contribution — the speaker expresses his or her thoughts, feelings, and conclusions regarding the issue.

My Hope — the speaker concludes with positive comments about the prospect of resolving the issue and enriching their relationship through this conversation.

Active Listening and Careful Reflection — the speaker now listens as the listener tries to paraphrase the presentation of the issue. Clarification will continue until the speaker is satisfied that the listener understands.

Tender Questions — the listener gently asks for further information to make sure there is a solid base of understanding from which to discuss the issue.

Sweet Responses — the listener expresses love and optimism.

This pattern allows the couple to enter the problem solving process as calmly as possible, and gives each of them assurance that their differences can be discussed without personal attacks or threats to their relationship. Reaching consensus on how to describe a specific problem is essential to conflict resolution.

After mapping out a problem, the couple can take steps to solve it. Agreeing on a one-sentence definition of an issue, the couple covenants with each other to work at resolving it. Each then writes a list of potential solutions, in the order of their importance and workability. Comparing lists, they may find that they already agree on some possible courses of action. Discussion and compromise then develop a plan to implement one or more of the solutions. Making any necessary allowances for circumstances which may interfere with success, the couple commits themselves to trying to make the plan work. There should always be the option of moving to Plan B or C as needed. Summarizing and praying about the agreement should close the discussion. A date should be set for evaluating progress and making adjustments.

Structuring conversation to facilitate conflict resolution is the counselor's task in the office; it becomes the couple's responsibility at home. Effective communication patterns should characterize every counseling session, and should be passed along to clients through direct instruction and practice. It is not a gross exaggeration to say that if a couple knew how to talk with each other at home they would not be talking with a marriage counselor. My major goal in counseling is to work myself out from my job, changing my role from referee to coach to a respected teammate. The only third party in a healthy marriage is God Himself.

Speaking in Love

Counseling sessions provide a format for dealing with specific issues which arise in marriages. Structuring conversations to keep them productively focused helps couples learn communication patterns which can take some of the heat out of their disagreements.

The Conversation Map and other techniques lower the emotional temperature of serious discussions. Modeling and mentoring teach couples to speak to each other civilly. The goal is to guide them towards being more rational and less emotional about problems in their marriage.

Where is the romance in being more rational and less emotional about marriage problems? Decreasing expression of negative emotions leaves more room to express positive emotion. The heart of marriage is the love between husband and wife, and love which involves the whole personality is heavily charged with emotion. If fear of being left or forsaken enters the relationship, negative emotions will disrupt communication. If faith and faithfulness protect the marriage covenant, positive emotions will prevail. In seeking to approach issues reasonably, it is not necessary to become rationalistic. Love is most definitely not a relaxed mental attitude in the stoical sense of resigned emotional detachment. Being reasonable does not preclude feeling and communicating the warm emotions of real love.

"It's not what you say; it's how you say it." Speaking the truth in love helps believers grow up (Ephesians 4:15). Ephesians 4:1-3 lists some elements of the kind of love that communicates effectively:

Lowliness — humility, awareness of one's limitations and weakness, an attitude of openness to correction.

Meekness — gentleness, mildness, respect for another's feelings and opinions.

Longsuffering — patience, constancy, perseverance, willingness to pursue long-term goals in a relationship.

Forbearing — sustaining, holding up, accepting and supplementing the limitations of another.

Keeping unity — guarding and tending to deeply rooted basic agreement.

Bond of peace — being bundled together in security and tranquility.

It is not enough to speak the truth; the truth must be spoken in love. Counselors should note well the adage, "People don't care what you know until they know you care."

"Actions speak louder than words." Real heart-to-heart communication goes far beyond merely speaking and hearing. Speaking in love means speaking in a loving manner, but it also involves speaking in the context of a loving relationship. Love is the fixed position which gives the speaking credibility. Speaking in love is not mere exchange of words, but open, honest, sincere communication within a context of consistent loving actions — a context of faithfulness. Love must be shown in behavior which proves the truthfulness of loving words.

How does humility act? Repeatedly apologizing for offensive behavior suggests that the apologies are as self-serving as the behavior. "Don't tell me you're sorry — convince me you won't do that again." Humility takes into account how actions will affect other people. Even exercising one's perceived rights is no excuse for unnecessary offense to one who perceives things differently. Humility avoids misunderstandings by considering the other person's perceptions and responses as having at least the same value as one's own.

Meekness actively seeks to accommodate the other person's feelings and opinions. In marriage, that means working to eliminate unpleasant surprises and confrontations. Attentive listening and quiet speaking characterize meekness, but it goes beyond verbal communication. Doing the little things which make life pleasant for others shows loving understanding of their needs.

Longsuffering goes into action even when the other person's attitude and action do not show love. Constancy through strife and perseverance through trials give evidence that the core bonds of love are intact. Better, worse, richer, poorer, in sickness or health — longsuffering patiently endures. People have named dogs "Fido" because of their characteristic faithfulness; the unconditional loyalty of the old family dog is more representative of longsuffering than a puppy's love which is fed by regular treats.

Forbearing one another is definitely at the heart of successful marriages. Lack of forbearance is an element in almost all failed marriages. Living together gives couples the privilege of knowing each other's faults, foibles and flaws. The marriage covenant gives them the responsibility to help each other overcome these limitations, sustaining each other, holding each other up, rather than dragging each other down. Far too often, counselors deal with couples who have abused privileged knowledge, picking on each other's weaknesses, pushing each other's buttons until their marriages self-destruct.

Keeping unity requires vigilance in protecting and maintaining the marriage covenant. Having vowed to be one flesh and become one mind, the couple must guard that commitment by constantly reinforcing their basic unity. Any interests or issues which threaten to divide them must be dealt with in the light of their marriage vows. Going off in different directions begins small and ends disastrously.

The bond of peace brings security and tranquility into a marriage. There may be emergencies, but there will be no panic — husband and wife are together for the long haul and their love for each other will not be at risk at every unexpected turn in the road.

"Speaking the truth in love" — love is the context and the manner in which the husband and wife relate to each other. It is also the language in which they communicate.

They should speak in love as fluently as anyone speaks in English, Spanish or Swahili.[187] Like any other language, love has a system of meaningful symbols, which go together to create effective communication. Humility, meekness, longsuffering, forbearance, unity and peace are prerequisites for learning the language of love. As Gary Chapman aptly points out, people communicate (or attempt to communicate) love in a multitude of dialects. To communicate love within marriage, husbands and wives must learn each other's love vocabularies, including the rare idioms, the ways of expressing or receiving love, which others may not think of or understand.

Husbands are to live with their wives "according to knowledge (I Peter 3:7)." This certainly means with intelligence and wisdom regarding marital roles, but also implies deep understanding of gender differences and the spouse's unique personality. It means that throughout marriage a couple will seek to learn more and more about each other in order to

---

[187] Gary Chapman has popularized the concept of "love languages," various ways of communicating love (see Gary Chapman, *The Five Love Languages*, Northfield Publishing, 2004.

be more effective in building each other up.[188] The learning never ends, because every human being is a work in progress, continually changing. A six-year-old girl who considers a rag doll her best friend becomes a sixteen-year-old who considers it an embarrassing piece of junk, and then a woman of a certain age who considers it an heirloom. Boys tend to be less reflective about their toys — what they play with just gets bigger and more expensive. The point is that learning what really matters to our spouses is a never-ending quest. The life-long conversation at the heart of this most intimate of friendships must be carried on in an ever-growing vocabulary of love.

"How do I love thee?" If instead of saying, "I love you," you asked your spouse, "Do I love you?" what kind of answer would you expect? Most of us think we show our love all the time, and could list things we have said or done which our spouses certainly must recognize as evidence of our enduring affection. How do you know your spouse loves you? Again, most of us could list actions or words we treasure as signs of love. But when husbands and wives compare such lists, they find discrepancies. He thought he was showing love when he bought her a box of candy when she had the flu. She thought it was a loving gesture when she washed his lucky shirt before the big game.

World travelers are warned that a gesture which means one thing in one culture may mean something dangerously different somewhere else.[189] Dwelling with each other according to knowledge means learning each other's signals. Verbal communication has limits — couples must learn to read situations, body language, and other clues to each other's

---

[188] As I have often said, when my own marriage was at its worst, I had to take a crash course in "Joanne 101" to get my act together. I seem to have passed the mid-term, but I still have a lot to learn.

[189] Someone even did research on "The Spontaneous Gesture," trying to find out whether *any* symbolic movement transcended cultural associations.

emotions. Sometimes it is very much like being in a foreign culture. It is not a matter of "What do women want?" or "What do men want?" but of "what would please and encourage this specific woman or man right now?" Some gestures of love may be universally appreciated, but many are learned. Everybody has had some experience with the awkwardness of giving or receiving "the wrong gift." Whether it is an actual object or a well-intended action, there is no way to erase or forget the facial expression—it is very much like the look of someone whose cat has just offered a dead mouse as a token of loyalty and affection. Some gestures require timing and finesse—some are just wrong.

It is important to realize that spouses may have learned different ways to express and receive love. Chapman says there are five love languages: words of affirmation, quality time, receiving gifts, acts of service, and physical touch.[190] I believe that each of these is vital to speaking in love. Appropriate and timely attention to each of these ways of communicating love will enrich any relationship. Within marriage, there can be open discussion of how to speak each other's "love languages," and there is a lifetime together to become fluent at speaking in love.

Dwelling together according to knowledge, couples learn what works and what does not. Over the years, sensitivity to each other's moods and needs grows as husband and wife observe each other's responses. Speaking in love mellows into an atmosphere of understanding which makes even sitting together in silence deeply satisfying. This is not something a counselor or a handbook can teach. The uniqueness of each human being and the variety of our backgrounds make it impossible to guess or prescribe how to express the love which grows as two people carry on the lifelong conversation of marriage.

---

[190] Chapman, *The Five Love Languages*, Northfield, 2004, passim.

Reconciliation

Jesus is the answer. In Jesus Christ, God invites people into a covenant of companionship with Himself. Before Creation, God the Son carried self-existent life and light within Himself; He came to earth in human flesh to bring life and light to those who respond to Him in obedient faith (John 1:1-14). The only place of true blessing is in knowing the God of the Bible in Jesus Christ, and living according to His plan. Created in the image of the triune God, humans are designed to live as personalities in relationships, not as autonomous individuals with no binding commitment to God or to one another. A marriage manifesto which emphasizes covenant commitment to God and to each other may seem revolutionary in a culture which exalts autonomous individualism, but it is the unchanging biblical standard.

In the beginning of Creation, humanity was created male and female, so that a covenant of companionship (marriage) could be entered as the foundation of all human society (Genesis 2:18-25). According to the narrative, Eve was called alongside to help Adam. God walked with Adam and Eve in the Garden, offering His companionship as they responded in obedient faith. Their sin violated their relationship with God; their shifting of blame violated their relationship with each other (Genesis 3). The penalty of their sin would be death—separation from each other through mortality and separation from God for eternity. The promise that a descendant of the woman would defeat the evil one indicates that One would be called alongside whose help would be infinitely powerful against sin and its consequences. Companionship with God and with each other could be restored only through satisfaction of God's judgment against sin through the substitution of a mediator capable of enduring and conquering death on behalf of sinners.

Isaiah 53 is the classic prophetic exposition of substitutionary atonement. The prophet laments that God's plan of salvation is so contrary to worldly wisdom that many will treat it as foolishness. A Person precious to God but disregarded by arrogant humanity will be misunderstood and mistreated, rejected out of hand by the very people whose sorrows and grief He came to bear. Most people will not realize that His troubles are not a punishment for any fault in Him, but a willing acceptance of the curse of God against their own sin. This Person will be weighed down and abused because of the sins of His people, even to the point of suffering an ignominious death at the hands of those whose sins He takes upon Himself. This will all be according to God's eternal plan, and this mediator will return to life, satisfied with the blessing He has won for a new race of redeemed sinners, who will then be counted righteous in God's sight because of His sacrifice and intercession. Christians recognize this passage as a strong statement of the gospel revealed and accomplished in Jesus Christ.

The covenant in which God's blessing and companionship are restored transcends the weakness and sinfulness of human inability to achieve the righteousness required for a relationship with God – the perfect righteousness of God Himself. Jeremiah repeatedly chastises God's people for violating the covenant which God offered them. The only solution to their hopeless sinfulness is God's offer of a new covenant, in which God's law is no longer merely an external yardstick, but its revelation of the character of God is worked into the character of His people through internal knowledge and experience of the presence of God – God will forgive their hopeless sinfulness and relate to them in terms of His own righteousness (Jeremiah 31:31-34). Christians recognize this description of the new covenant as a concise summary of the place of blessing entered through faith in Jesus Christ.

What does all this have to do with building or rebuilding marriages? Everything. Counseling from the position of faith presupposes the biblical truth that a covenant relationship with God is the foundation of the covenant relationship between husband and wife. The prophet Hosea illustrated and explained how this works. Hosea's marriage to an adulterous wife was on-again-off-again because of her unfaithfulness, but ultimately Hosea's faithful commitment reconciled them to each other. This illustrative marriage paralleled the relationship between a faithful God and His unfaithful people. When God declares that he will ultimately reconcile His people to Himself, He uses the format of a Hebrew marriage covenant. The Jewish Publication Society's treatment of this declaration is quite revealing. They translate Hosea 2:21-22:

> And I will espouse you forever:
> I will espouse you with righteousness and justice,
> And with goodness and mercy
> And I will espouse you with faithfulness;
> Then you shall be devoted to the Lord.

A footnote explains the place of righteousness, justice, goodness, mercy and faithfulness in this renewal of the marriage covenant: "As the bride-price which the bridegroom will pay, He will confer these qualities on her so that she will never offend again."[191] The Bridegroom's character elevates the Bride's character, and thus sustains the marriage. Whatever position is taken regarding fulfillment of this prophecy to national Israel, it is clear that God Himself provides whatever is needed for both parties to meet the requirements of His new covenant with His people. The covenant of companionship which God offers His people does not depend on the worthiness of the people, but on the righteousness and faithfulness of

---

[191] *Tanach: The Holy Scriptures*, Jewish Publication Society, 1985, p. 984.

God.[192] Christians recognize this as the fullness of God's grace revealed in the Gospel of Jesus Christ.

This is made explicit in I Corinthians 1:30, which teaches that believers are "in Christ Jesus, who is made unto us wisdom, and righteousness, and sanctification, and redemption." All the provisions of the covenant of companionship between God and His people are underwritten by the infinite perfection of God the Son, Jesus Christ. Just as Hosea underwrote the welfare of his straying wife, God welcomes wanderers home according to His own riches in Christ Jesus. Believers who have received God's grace are compelled to share it with others. Those who have met the God of the Bible in Jesus Christ become His ambassadors to the world (II Corinthians 5:20).

In Numbers 6:24-26, the place of blessing for God's people is described as a place of God's personal presence: "The Lord bless thee, and keep thee. The Lord make his face to shine upon thee. The Lord lift up his countenance upon thee, and give thee peace." Christians recognize the parallels with the place of blessing in fellowship with God in Jesus Christ: "For God, who commanded the light to shine out of darkness hath shined in our hearts to give the light of the knowledge of the glory of God in the face of Jesus Christ (II Corinthians 4:6)."

Again, the new covenant transcends the old, making God's presence effective internally as well as externally: "But we all, with open face beholding as in a glass the glory of the Lord, are changed into the same glory, even as by the Spirit of the Lord (I Corinthians 3:18)." This is not abstruse, impractical doctrine, but eminently practical theology. Those who have met the God of the Bible face to face in Jesus Christ will be ever more closely conformed to His character. A relationship with God in Jesus Christ will transform relationships with everyone else. The light which Jesus Christ brought into the world is now entrusted

---

[192] This is at least suggestive of the sacrificial faithfulness of a spouse whose character reflects the character of God, regardless of his or her mate's reaction.

to His people, whose ministry of reconciliation includes walking in the light and taking the light to others.

Jesus is the answer not in some abstract or ethereal sense, but in the practical difference that knowing Him makes in human character and behavior. Philippians 2:14-16 makes this clear. Believers are to "do all things without murmurings and disputing" — the carping, argumentative communication patterns of self-centered sinfulness must be set aside, and we must speak the truth in love. Believers are to be "blameless and harmless," forsaking the underhanded and abusive behavior of conniving worldlings. "Sons of God, without rebuke" — believers show their companionship with God by displaying His character and obeying His Word. "In the midst of a crooked and perverse nation" — others may do what is right in their own eyes, but believers will not reject God's standards. Believers are to "shine as lights in the world," not letting Satan extinguish their blazing zeal for God's glory, even in the midst of lovers of darkness.

What does this have to do with building or rebuilding marriages? By now it should be clear that presupposing that there really is a God and that His character determines what is right and wrong makes all the difference in the world to a Christian marriage counselor. No piecemeal approach to exploring sexuality or consolidating debt can ever get to the heart of a marriage, where the real issues are rooted. In Mark 7:21-23 Jesus warns that external distractions and temptations do not ruin a person unless they find a responsive chord within the person's inner character. Adultery, fornication, and lasciviousness are among the evil things inside which break out into destructive violations of the marriage covenant. In God's eyes, the heart of marriage is in the radical hearts of husbands and wives. Counselors are called alongside for encouragement, speaking to the heart, getting at the real rottenness in a poisoned relationship.

The heart of Christian marriage counseling is the heart of all Christian ministry: radical proclamation and application of the Gospel of salvation by grace through faith in Jesus Christ. What we do and what we say extend God's ministry of reconciliation to those who call us alongside to help:

All these new things are from God who brought us back to himself through what Jesus did. And God has given us the privilege of urging everyone to come into his favor and be reconciled to him.

For God was in Christ, restoring the world to himself, no longer counting men's sins against them but blotting them out. This is the wonderful message he has given us to tell others,

We are Christ's ambassadors. God is using us to speak to you: we beg you, as though Christ himself were here pleading with you, receive the love he offers you — be reconciled to God.

For God took the sinless Christ and poured into him our sins. Then, in exchange, he poured God's goodness into us. II Corinthians 5:18-21, Living Bible

About the Authors

 Gordon Puls is a graduate of Michigan State and of Grand Rapids School of the Bible and Music. His advanced studies in gifted education were motivated by the needs of his own children. In fact, if you ask Gordon about his life, he will talk about his family. As a child, when asked what he wanted to be when he grew up, he replied, "A man, a husband, and a father." He is still growing up, but those have been his primary roles.

Gordon's other roles have varied. He has taught at every level from elementary school through college, and has ministered at every level from nursery through nursing home. He has also been a furniture worker, time study analyst, school bus driver, encyclopedia salesman, and security guard. He has written occasional articles for Christian and family-oriented periodicals.

Gordon met his wife, Joyce, when they both became involved in street ministry with Dow Pursley and other friends. Married since 1971, Gordon and Joyce now reside in Lantana, Florida. Joyce is a graduate of Calvin College, and has taught fourth grade for many years. Gordon plays trumpet, and Joyce plays flute with the praise team at New Hope Community Church. They consider their home their primary place of ministry, and have had the privilege of sharing life with the most fascinating people they have known: their children, Michele, Amy, Lisa, and TJ.

Their grandchildren are delightfully enriching a new generation.

Gordon is now with the Lord.

 Dr. Pursley worked with Ed Wheat, M.D. at the Wheat Clinic in Springdale AR, for 18 years. Dr. Dow Pursley is now a retired professor and clinical director of programs at the Love-Life Marriage and Family Center at Baptist Bible Graduate School. He specialized in marriage counseling and taught on the spiritual, emotional, and physical aspects of marriage from a biblical viewpoint.

Dr. Pursley attended the Cornerstone University in Grand Rapids, Michigan; graduated with a B.A. in Theology from Central Baptist College in Conway, Arkansas; M.S. in Community Service Counseling from the University of Central Arkansas; and Ed.D. in Counselor Education from the University of Arkansas in Fayetteville, Arkansas. Joanne was a Presidential Scholar at the University of Arkansas, worked as Vice President of the Arkansas Fitness Center and currently as a Flight Attendant for Delta Airlines.

Dr. Pursley and his wife Joanne have been married for more than 50 years and have three children: Melissa, Sarah, and Jacob (all actively serving in missions in the 10/40 window) and nine grandchildren as well as two great-grandchildren.

Index

394

Made in the USA
Coppell, TX
04 August 2021